Psychoanalytic Supervision

Psychoanalytic Supervision

Bhaskar Sripada, M.D.

IPBOOKS.net
International Psychoanalytic Books

International Psychoanalytic Books (IPBooks)
New York • http://www.IPBooks.net

Psychoanalytic Supervision

Published by IPBooks, Queens, NY
Online at: www.IPBooks.net

Manuscript Editor: Phyllis Stern, LightWords Editorial Services
Cover designer: Kathy Kovacic, Blackthorn Studio
Typesetting and book formatter: Noel S. Morado

ISBN 978-1-956864-85-4

Dedicated to Cliff Wilkerson,
my teacher and friend.

Contents

CONTENTS

Preface

In this book, I recount twenty-nine psychoanalytic supervisory sessions, documenting the journey with Ching Kong, my supervisee.[1] Through comprehensive narratives of each session, reflections, observations, and my personal insights, I invite you, the reader, to engage with our supervisory relationship and, by extension, the broader psychoanalytic process. During this time, Ching was engaged in the psychoanalytic treatment of Chi, an eight-year-old girl struggling with anxiety due to being teased for falling behind in math class, and being labeled as "stupid" by her peers. She also faced difficulties in making friends, while her mother, frustrated by these challenges, resorted to physical punishment to push her to improve in math.

Merton Gill, Leo Rangell, and Arnold Goldberg, pioneers of psychoanalysis, played a crucial role in shaping my analytic identity. For seven to ten years, I met or corresponded with them, and their significant teachings had a lasting impact on me. Gill developed a new constructivist, active observer-based definition of transference focused on a relational perspective. Rangell emphasized the unitary perspective of classical psychoanalysis and the Oedipus Complex. Goldberg clarified the role

---

1 Ching Kong is a pseudonym chosen by the candidate I supervise. He has explicitly consented to use material from our supervisory and therapeutic sessions in this book. Additionally, Ching received permission from Chi's mother to utilize her pseudonym and details of their therapeutic interactions. When I first began supervising him, he had adopted the Western name, Leo Sparrow. In this book, I refer to him as Leo until the end of Chapter 3; thereafter, for clarity and consistency, I call him Ching.

of negotiations in self-psychology, empathy, and consideration for the analyst to test his anticipation of the patient.

With their unique psychoanalytic theories, Gill, Rangell, and Goldberg found their differences irreconcilable. However, by incorporating Freud's ideas on the unconscious, transference, and resistance, along with their insights, I developed Essential Psychoanalysis. This approach, a versatile form of psychoanalysis, allows the therapist to be an active participant-observer. It integrates concepts about the brain's predictive functions and a pluralistic framework tailored to individual cases. Essential Psychoanalysis aligns with various perspectives, including Instinct, Ego, Object-Relational, Self, Intersubjective, Developmental, and Neuropsychoanalytic approaches. It values the freedom of both the patient and the analyst, emphasizing psychoanalysis principles and prioritizing the analyst's discretion in deciding technical matters.

In this book, I aim to demonstrate Essential Psychoanalysis's integrative and flexible application, incorporating psychoanalysis's fundamental principles into supervision and guiding a supervisee's learning and clinical practice. I believe the reader must understand Essential Psychoanalysis and the context of my integrative work, as it will provide valuable insight into my approach and the field of psychoanalysis.

Foundations of psychoanalysis and its techniques

Describing psychoanalysis's foundational principles, Freud (1914)[2] stated, "The theory of psychoanalysis is an attempt to account for two striking and unexpected facts of observation which emerge whenever

---

2 Freud, S. (1914). Remembering, repeating and working-through (Further recommendations on the technique of psycho-analysis II). *Standard Edition* 12:145–156.

an attempt is made to trace the symptoms of a neurotic back to their sources in his past life: The facts of transference and of resistance. Any line of investigation which recognizes these two facts and takes them as the starting point of its work may call itself psychoanalysis, even though it arrives at results other than my own." (p. 16). Freud (1925)[3] described psychoanalysis as the science of unconscious mental processes.

Understanding the relationship between Freud's intrinsic criteria (unconscious, transference, and resistance) and extrinsic criteria (a minimum of three to six psychoanalytic sessions per week and use of the couch) is critical. Most analysts appreciate that seeing patients more often increases the opportunities for interpreting associated unconscious, transference, and resistance processes. The frequency of engagement in psychoanalysis is not just a topic of considerable debate but a crucial factor that can significantly impact the effectiveness of the treatment. It is widely acknowledged that increased frequency can accelerate learning and strengthen retention, as consistent practice tends to reinforce neural pathways and habits. This principle is evident in activities such as mastering musical instruments or sports, where regular practice is crucial for advancement. More frequent exposure to material in academic pursuits often leads to better comprehension and recall.

However, relying on external criteria as a prerequisite for psychoanalysis, such as frequent treatment sessions and using the couch for the analytic process, could be a categorical error (Ryle, 1949)[4]. The error is comparable to equating devotion, an internal process, with a rosary bead necklace, confusing a wedding band for marriage, or trying to interpret a dream solely by its manifest contents. Frequent sessions are beneficial, but core principles such as unconscious processes, transference,

---

3 Freud, S. (1925). An autobiographical study. *Standard Edition* 20:1–74.

4 Ryle, G. (1949). *The Concept of Mind*. Chicago: University of Chicago Press.

resistance, and related concepts should always be central to psychoanalysis and not overshadowed by external factors. The American Psychoanalytic Association and the International Psychoanalytic Association have created guidelines that set standards for training and psychoanalytic education analysis. These standards include various external factors and represent psychoanalysts' accumulated knowledge and wisdom, which benefits the profession. Thus, analysts and supervisors must be mindful of the differences between intrinsic fundamental principles of psychoanalysis and techniques of psychoanalysis.

Freud later acknowledged that his techniques suited his personality and encouraged other analysts to adopt methods based on their personalities, the patient's pathology, and the analytic task. Freud (1913, p. 111)[5] clarified, "This technique is the only one suited to my individuality; I do not venture to deny that a physician quite differently constituted might find himself driven to adopt a different attitude to his patients and to the task before him."

Science should not rely solely on techniques suited to Freud's personality; instead, these methods must be grounded in basic principles and adjusted for each analyst's perspective and attitude and the challenges they face with their patients. In their clinical practice, analysts must be free to select the most suitable technique for each patient rather than enforce a uniform approach.

Freud (1913)[6] remarked, "In what follows I shall endeavor to collect together for the use of the practicing analyst some rules for the beginning of the treatment. I think I am well-advised, however, to call these rules *recommendations,* and not claim any unconditional acceptance for them

---

5 Freud, S. (1913). On beginning the treatment (Further recommendations on the technique of psycho-analysis I). *Standard Edition* 12:121–144..

6 Freud, S. (1913). On beginning the treatment (Further recommendations on the technique of psycho-analysis I) *Standard Edition* 12:121–144.

[italics mine]. The extraordinary diversity of the psychical constellations concerned, the plasticity of all mental processes and the wealth of determining factors oppose *any* [italics mine] mechanization of the technique." (p. 123)

Freud clearly emphasized the importance of flexibility in psychoanalytic practice. He offered guidelines as "recommendations" rather than strict rules, recognizing that the complexity and variability of psychological states and mental processes' dynamic nature make rigid standardization impossible. Freud cautioned against mechanizing psychoanalytic techniques, as the diversity of psychological factors and the uniqueness of each case argue against a formulaic approach. Therefore, extrinsic factors must be navigated with adherence to the fundamental principles of psychoanalysis.

Freud emphasized that the psychoanalytic technique was not rigid and should be adjusted based on the patient's pathology. Freud (1910, p. 145)[7] stated that "analytic technique must be modified in certain ways according to the nature of the disease and the dominant instinctual trends in the patient."

While the principles of psychoanalysis regarding the importance of unconscious, transference, and resistance processes remain constant, the psychoanalytic technique is always subject to modifications based on the patient's wishes, pathology, and the analyst's tasks at hand.

Freud's seminal contributions to psychoanalysis, such as the unconscious, transference, and resistance, are widely acknowledged as the intrinsic criteria or principles of psychoanalysis. These foundational elements are the core of psychoanalysis and depth psychology. In contrast, Freud proposed external criteria, including rules on the frequency of

---

7 Freud, S. (1910). The future prospects of psycho-analytic therapy. *Standard Edition* 11:139–152.

sessions and the use of the psychoanalytic couch, referring to them as "rules" and "recommendations."

Classical psychoanalytic methods laid down strict guidelines, such as holding sessions four to five times a week and using the couch, which were considered vital for effective treatment. Nevertheless, Freud himself frequently strayed from these protocols, demonstrating that psychoanalysis can be both adaptable and practical while retaining its core principles—unconscious processes, transference, and resistance. This illustrates Freud's impact beyond rigid techniques and shows that the true essence of psychoanalysis lies in its foundational tenets, permitting treatments to be customized to meet each patient's unique requirements.

Freud's (1893)[8] accidentally encountering a young girl named Katharina became a significant factor in developing his Seduction Theory. Katharina confided about an inappropriate advance by her uncle, who was later identified as her father. Katharina's disclosure of an attempted incestuous seduction by her uncle (later revealed to be her father), where she woke up with him in her bed and reported suddenly "feeling his body," was a pivotal moment. Despite her not verbally confirming this, Freud inferred that her reference was to his erect penis from her facial expression. This event, which caused Katharina distressing symptoms like nausea, panic, and visions of her assailant, was crucial in shaping Freud's theory that childhood sexual trauma is often the root of adult psychological disorders.

Freud (1909)[9] published the Analysis of a Phobia in a Five-Year-Old Boy, which describes Little Hans, who is afraid of horses, in love with his mother, and fearful of his father. He was intensely preoccupied with

---

8 Freud, S. (1893). Katharina, Case Histories from Studies on Hysteria. *Standard Edition* 2:125–134.

9 Freud, S. (1909). Analysis of a phobia in a five-year-old boy. *Standard Edition* 10:11–50..

his "widdler" (penis) and the anatomical differences between the sexes. In formulating the dynamics of the infantile Oedipal sexual life of a child, Freud described Little Hans's conscious and unconscious feelings toward his parents. He understood the little boy's phobia as an instance of displacement, *viz.*, the unconscious transference of feelings from his father to fears of a horse. Little Hans's father analyzed Hans with the help of a correspondence with Freud. Freud saw Little Hans only once, yet Freud did not hesitate to call his effort an "analysis."

Freud's (1911)[10] case study of Judge Daniel Paul Schreber is a significant contribution to psychoanalysis. Schreber was a highly respected judge who, in the middle of his life, fell ill with repeated psychotic episodes and spent much time in different psychiatric institutions. His condition began with hypochondria and insomnia but deteriorated into pathological delusion. Schreber wrote a vivid account of his nervous illness, which included a desire to become a woman, delusions about his doctor, and a belief in a special relationship with God. Freud never met him but analyzed Schreber's case to develop his theory on paranoia, proposing that delusions in paranoia, such as jealousy, erotomania, persecution, and grandeur, were distortions of unconscious homosexual wishes and fantasies.

In these three cases – a one-time meeting with Katherina, indirect interactions through the father in the analysis of Little Hans, and no direct contact with Judge Schreber – the concept of four or five weekly sessions or the use of a psychoanalytic couch becomes irrelevant. However, these examples underscore Freud's freedom, adaptability, and openness to diverse methods in his psychoanalytic contributions. This adaptability is a

---

10 Freud, S. (1911). Psycho-analytic notes on an autobiographical account of a case of paranoia (dementia paranoides). *Standard Edition* 12:1–82.

crucial aspect of his work that remains relevant in modern psychoanalytic practice.

Essential Psychoanalysis

Using the term Essential Psychoanalysis, I (Sripada, 2015)[11] reiterated Freud's foundational definition of psychoanalysis thus: Any line of treatment, theory, or science that recognizes the facts of unconscious, transference, or resistance and takes them as the starting point of its work, regardless of its results, is psychoanalysis.

1. Essential Psychoanalysis prioritizes the foundational principles of the unconscious, transference, and resistance over technical and other considerations.

2. These principles may be developed according to various approaches, including Instinct-based Psychoanalysis, Ego Psychology, Object Relations Theory, Interpersonal Psychology, Self-Psychology, Intersubjective Psychoanalysis, Developmental Psychoanalysis, and Neuropsychoanalysis. Each of these schools has advanced a version of psychanalysis, but it is beyond the scope of this book to further describe. Because the terms unconscious, transference, and resistance will vary in meaning across different psychoanalytic modalities, this book does not attempt to define these terms for each specific approach. Instead, each psychoanalytic practitioner must clarify how they use these terms within their theory, practice, or research context.

---

11 Sripada, B. (2015). Essential psychoanalysis: toward a re-appraisal of the relationship between psychoanalysis and dynamic psychotherapy. *Psychodynamic Psychiatry* 43: 396–422.

3. In the appendix, I will explain key psychoanalytic terms that practitioners might find helpful.

4. Essential Psychoanalysis allows for flexible adoption of session frequency, couch usage, and in-person or virtual sessions based on the specific circumstances of each case.

5. Essential Psychoanalysis assumes that its foundations are dimensional rather than categorical. Therefore, the foundations of psychoanalysis are the dimensions of unconscious-preconscious-conscious systems, transference-countertransference, and resistance-facilitation processes.

6. Essential Psychoanalysis also considers both patient and analyst active participant observers, each influencing the analysis. Accounting for this contribution is an integral part of the analytic process.

7. Additionally, integrating contemporary neuroscience insights, it incorporates prediction and prediction error (the difference between anticipation and sensory input, experienced as the degree of surprise) into treatment.

Rangell and a unitary approach

I must also briefly describe a unitary approach favored by others. Rangell (2006)[12] proposed a comprehensive anxiety theory that integrates Freud's toxic and signal anxiety concepts, highlighting castration anxiety's importance in psychoanalysis. He argued that psychoanalysis is optimally designed as a unified system to elucidate a range of phenomena

---

12 Rangell, L. (2006). An analysis of the course of psychoanalysis: the case for a unitary theory. *Psychoanalytic Psychology* 23:217–238.

observed in symptoms, dreams, personality, psychopathology, and the nuanced psychological experiences of daily life, all rooted in a consistent intrapsychic framework. Rangell championed a unified theory that evolved over the last century, incorporating valuable contributions from various psychoanalytic traditions. Rangell observed that the rise of theoretical pluralism, including approaches like the Kleinian object-relational perspective, Kohut's self-psychology, and intersubjectivity theories, has contributed to the fragmentation of the unified and cohesive framework in psychoanalysis.

For instance, adopting Rangell's unified method means the analyst will probably rely on the toxic theory of anxiety, the signal theory of anxiety, and castration anxiety. It is unlikely that the analyst will apply Bowlby's attachment concepts from *Attachment and Loss* (1973)[13] or Mahler's theory of rapprochement anxiety from *The Psychological Birth of the Human Infant* (1972[14], 1975[15]), which relates to the infant's separation-individuation process. This practice of limiting explanations to within-theory concepts is not exclusive to Rangell or the ego psychological perspective. Self-psychologists, relational psychologists, and intersubjective psychologists also typically adhere to their specialized terminologies and avoid describing castration anxiety.

---

13 Bowlby, J. (1973). Anxious attachment and the 'phobias' of childhood. In *Attachment and Loss: Volume II: Separation, Anxiety and Anger* New York: Basic Books, pp. 258–291.

14 Mahler, M.S. (1972). Rapprochement subphase of the separation-individuation process. *Psychoanalytic Quarterly* 41:487–506.

15 Mahler, M.S., Pine, F., & Bergman, A. (1975). *The Psychological Birth of The Human Infant: Symbiosis and Individuation*. New York: Basic Books.

A Pluralistic active participant-observer approach

Essential Psychoanalysis builds upon the core concepts of the unconscious, transference, and resistance processes, as initially proposed by Freud, yet reinterpreted through modern psychoanalytic theories and practices. Although the roots of psychoanalysis are firmly established, the evolution it has undergone since its early days is noteworthy. There are marked differences between Freud's original conceptual framework and the contemporary interpretation of psychoanalytic principles. These variances bear significance both in clinical practice and theoretical understanding. This book provides a comprehensive clinical examination of the distinctions discussed. In this section, I emphasize the differences in perspective on the concept of termination between Freud's theories and those detailed in Essential Psychoanalysis.

In his seminal essay *Analysis Terminable and Interminable* (1937)[16], Freud delves into the intricate challenges of psychoanalytic treatment, sparking a thought-provoking exploration of whether psychoanalysis can ever be fully completed. This essay, a cornerstone of psychoanalytic literature, not only acknowledges the significant therapeutic progress that can be achieved but also unveils certain factors that may prolong or prevent the full resolution of treatment, adding layers of complexity to the subject.

Freud identifies both biological and psychological obstacles in achieving a definitive end to psychoanalysis. For instance, he references biological elements like women's "penis envy" and men's passive tendencies toward other men as rooted in universal developmental conflicts. These aspects, Freud suggests, may limit the potential of

---

16 Freud, S. (1937). Analysis Terminable and Interminable. *International Journal of Psychoanalysis* 18:373–405.

psychoanalysis to resolve deep-seated issues. In addition, unconscious defense mechanisms, which are often deeply ingrained, resist change and complicate the therapeutic process. Freud suggests that while setting a termination date may help uncover some unconscious material, it may also leave other parts of the psyche walled off from therapeutic efforts, thus impeding full resolution.

Freud explores the analyst's countertransference, which contributes to difficulties in completing the analytic process during termination. For example, he highlights the risk of analysts failing to apply insights about their own unconscious defenses, misusing their power, or losing their capacity for objective investigation, all of which could interfere with the termination. To mitigate this, Freud emphasizes the importance of regular reanalysis for analysts to maintain self-awareness and prevent personal issues from influencing treatment.

Modern psychoanalysis, including the framework of Essential Psychoanalysis, has evolved significantly beyond some of Freud's earlier patriarchal and gendered concepts, such as "penis envy." This evolution, which builds on Freud's work, prioritizes empowering patients to create meaningful narratives. The shift recognizes that each individual articulates psychological conflicts uniquely, depending on their context and subjective experience. Analysts are increasingly mindful of avoiding the unconscious assumption of privilege or power inherent in traditional roles, particularly by refraining from imposing rigid theoretical frameworks, such as outdated gender theories. This empowerment in the therapeutic setting fosters a collaborative environment where the patient actively participates in shaping the dialogue, ensuring that it aligns with their perspectives.

For instance, when a girl expresses a wish to be a boy, or a man exhibits anxieties around other men, these themes are relevant if they emerge naturally within the patient's free associations. However, they should be explored in a context-sensitive, experience-near manner, free from unnecessary or imposing theoretical jargon. Freud's patriarchal language often reflects the power dynamics between analyst and patient, but his principle—that the material within free associations should be thoroughly explored—remains valuable.

In contemporary practice, the once-dominant ideals of objectivity and the "blank screen" have largely been abandoned. These concepts positioned the analyst as a neutral and detached observer, but they are now seen as misleading and reinforcing the power dynamics that favor the analyst. Instead, modern psychoanalysis acknowledges the analyst's inherent subjectivity and the inevitability of their personal history, emotions, and unconscious reactions (including countertransference) shaping the therapeutic relationship. This recognition promotes greater transparency and helps to limit the analyst's power within the process, fostering a more collaborative and egalitarian dynamic in which both the patient's and the analyst's experiences contribute meaningfully to the therapeutic journey. This shift allows for a richer, more authentic dialogue in the therapeutic space.

The concept of countertransference has also been redefined in contemporary psychoanalysis. Initially viewed as an obstacle, it is now recognized as a valuable therapeutic tool when adequately managed. The analyst's emotional responses to the patient can offer important insights into the patient's unconscious world. However, psychoanalysis today also acknowledges that specific countertransference reactions may stem from the analyst's own unresolved personal issues, which must be addressed to maintain therapeutic integrity.

Essential Psychoanalysis takes a more open-ended approach to theory, integrating various perspectives to best fit individual patient care. The basic psychoanalytic concepts of the unconscious, transference, and resistance are widely accepted by all depth-psychological schools, with some modifications. Additionally, there is a less explored area in theory and practice where analysts may unconsciously use techniques from different schools beyond their primary orientation without formal recognition. While certain psychoanalytic traditions emphasize caring, concern, compassion, containment, tolerance, empathy, and tactfulness, these qualities are increasingly valued across the field for supporting emotional regulation and patient care. These attributes foster a therapeutic environment essential for recovery, even if not always emphasized in theory. Analysts may inadvertently use cognitive-behavioral techniques, just as cognitive-behavioral therapists may incorporate dynamic techniques without realizing it. This overlap occurs naturally as practitioners prioritize effective interventions over strict adherence to a particular theoretical framework, drawing from various approaches to meet the patient's needs.

An analyst's perspective strictly adhering to a particular school of thought often contrasts with the patient's. Analysts tend to categorize patient information within the top-down framework of their chosen theory. In contrast, Essential Psychoanalysis uses a bottom-up approach, prioritizing gathering clinical data with active patient involvement. While analysts may have a preferred theoretical model, they remain open to alternative approaches if resistance arises. After considering various interpretations, the analyst flexibly selects the one that best fits the situation and may easily experiment with an approach from a different school of thought, remaining adaptable to patient feedback for further refinement.

Much like a thirsty person seeking relief—open to various options like Coke, Pepsi, milk, or water—without being tied to a particular brand, the patient in therapy prioritizes improvement over loyalty to a specific psychoanalytic theory. Essential Psychoanalysis similarly values patient outcomes over theoretical consistency, integrating whichever approaches best benefit the patient. This departure from rigid frameworks makes it more adaptable and patient-centered, addressing the patient's unique needs without the constraints of a singular theoretical lens. Therefore, while the distinctions between psychoanalysis and dynamic psychotherapy hold significant importance for some analysts, Essential Psychoanalysis focuses primarily on the dynamic processes within the therapeutic relationship and does not dwell on such theoretical distinctions. Its emphasis remains on the foundational principles of psychoanalysis, leaving techniques to the analyst's discretion, allowing for a more flexible and adaptive therapeutic approach.

This pluralistic approach presents challenges, increasing the analyst's burden of navigating and synthesizing multiple theories effectively. While some may view this approach as irregular or heretical, Essential Psychoanalysis sees it as an adaptive collaboration with the patient and a potential strength. Unlike other frameworks, Essential Psychoanalysis adopts a bottom-up approach. Beyond core principles like the unconscious and transference, it is not anchored to any single theory. Nevertheless, balancing multiple theories can be demanding and may seem unconventional to those adhering to a single approach.

The book comprehensively examines the psychoanalytic process observed over twenty-nine supervision sessions. It focuses on the early stages of child therapy, offering valuable insights into how the therapeutic relationship and techniques evolve during this critical phase rather than presenting a complete case history. Instead, it offers a detailed description of the initial stages of the analytic process, ensuring readers gain a nuanced understanding.

Analytic process

Auchincloss and Samberg (2012)[17] define the analytic process as "the progressive unfolding over time of a psychoanalytic treatment during which conscious and unconscious aspects of a patient's mind are revealed, elaborated, and explicated" (p. 16). This unfolding allows for a deeper exploration of the patient's psyche. Interpretations of this process vary. Some regard transference as a reenactment of past relationships, while others see it as a co-construction, an interaction between therapist and patient. Hoffmann (2019)[18] provided an overview of differing views on the analytic process, stating that the analytic process "occurs (1) within the patient and is understood by the analyst via the patient's words; (2) within the patient as revealed to the analyst both by the patient's words and actions as well as by the analyst's understanding of his or her own subjective experience in response to the analysand; and (3) as a result of the real interaction between patient and analyst, not merely the vicissitudes of the patient's transferences. All these conceptualizations maintain that the AP can only be observed in the flow of what occurs between analysand and analyst over a period of time."

Psychoanalytic supervision is intricately linked with psychoanalytic therapy, sharing common debates essential for understanding the analytic process in both contexts. This process involves a complex interaction among the dynamic unconscious (comprising unconscious, preconscious, and conscious levels), transference (including transference and countertransference), and resistance (alongside facilitation).

---

17 Auchincloss, E.L., & Samberg, E. (2012). *Psychoanalytic Terms and Concepts.* New Haven, CT & London, UK: Yale University Press.

18 Hoffman, L. (2019). Analytic process from the perspective of conflict and interpersonal/relational theory: A potential linguistic indicator. *Contemporary Psychoanalysis* 55:349–372.

The psychoanalytic method provides profound insight into psychological events. It involves analyzing symptoms, conflicts, and dreams and fostering compromises. It also includes recognizing dynamics within the therapeutic relationship, the patient's self-perception, and the interaction between the patient's and analyst's selves. This method explains momentary slips of the tongue and parapraxis, captures the key elements of a clinical vignette, and comprehends the rhythm of a therapy session. It is crucial for transformation and change, whether in a single session or an entire analysis. Provided the analyst describes their introspective process, the psychoanalytic process can elucidate the genesis of interpretation. Supervisory oversight offers a unique vantage point for the co-evolution of a candidate's analytical conclusions. It shows how these ideas emerge and develop within the supervisory relationship, thereby deepening our understanding of the process behind their interpretative reasoning.

The understanding of the psychoanalytic process has evolved considerably from traditional foundations to contemporary approaches like Essential Psychoanalysis. In the traditional model, the analyst was viewed as a neutral, abstinent, and objective observer—a blank screen onto which the patient projected their transference, minimizing the analyst's role. Contemporary psychoanalytic schools, including Essential Psychoanalysis, view the analyst as an active participant observer, acknowledging that transference is co-created and shaped by the analyst. This shift highlights the interactive and dynamic nature of the therapeutic relationship; the analyst is no longer seen as neutral but as an active contributor to evolving transference and countertransference.

Despite this shift, many contemporary analysts still approach co-created transference with a broad understanding, often maintaining a neutral posture in practice. Case examples and clinical vignettes may highlight the analyst's contributions to transference dynamics, but they frequently remain brief and technical without fully delving into the complexity of the ongoing interaction. More thorough examples of active participant observership are needed, showcasing the co-creation of transference and how the analyst's role shapes the psychoanalytic process over time. By documenting the origins of their interpretations and tracing sources of insight—ranging from the patient's actions to the analyst's experiences—we can better grasp the co-created nature of transference and the analyst's involvement.

This comprehensive understanding is crucial for advancing insight into the analytic process, which is further refined through peer criticism. Nonetheless, the analyst shares only relevant and helpful information with the patient, maintaining focus on the therapeutic outcome.

Both patients and analysts might agree on the surface details of interactions yet interpret events differently. For instance, while the analyst may believe they are offering care or concern, the patient might perceive their actions as threatening. Analysts must realize that the patient's subjective perception of their behavior triggers emotional responses. Bridging this gap underscores the significance of addressing transference reactions.

An analyst's experiences during analysis often mirror the patients', providing a broad countertransference laboratory to hypothesize about the patient's emotional state, conflicts, personality, or sense of Self. Drawing from their own emotions and unconscious responses, analysts connect with the patient, aligning with theories of unconscious communication, mutual attunement, empathy, and entanglement, highlighting the unseen link between analyst and patient.

Analysts use several methods to hypothesize about a patient's emotional world. One empathic approach involves vicarious introspection that allows the analyst to intuit the patient's inner life directly. Another method involves recognizing an experiential overlap between the analyst's experience and that of the patient, relying on analogical inferences where the analyst perceives a pattern in the patient's Self resembling their Self. These methods collectively represent the analyst's broad countertransference, helping to access and understand the patient's inner experiences. Analysts should clarify these interpretive sources to the patient, collaboratively ensuring that such insights align with the patient's reality.

Ching's reactions and emotions in understanding Chi during treatment are shared throughout the supervision narrative. Reflecting personal responses encourages readers to explore their reflections, fostering transparency in line with the philosophy of the active observer.

Essential Psychoanalysis shifts focus from analyst authority to the value of interpretations, which must resonate with the patient. Unlike traditional approaches that empower the analyst, this method depends on patient agreement and the relevance of insights. Emerging from genuine dialogue, empathy, and compassion, interpretations encourage patients to evaluate their worth, delivered in familiar language at thoughtful timing, respecting their independence.

A complete psychoanalytic case study from start to finish is unfeasible due to its extensive length. Therefore, this book zeroes in on the intricate aspects of psychoanalytic supervision and the early phases of therapy presented by Ching. Initially inexperienced with treating children, Ching rapidly progressed in understanding case dynamics, establishing a working alliance, and conducting psychoanalytic psychotherapy with an eight-year-old girl experiencing anxiety.

In the narrative, paragraphs with Ching's quotes are indented, distinguishing between his statements, my observations, and commentary, ensuring clarity and ease for the reader.

Board Certified in Adult and Child and Adolescent Analysis, I bring a unique cross-cultural perspective to this supervision. Having lived in India for twenty-four years before emigrating to the United States and with four decades of psychoanalytic practice, I offer a rich understanding of international psychoanalytic training difficulties. The genesis of this book was Ching's assignment as my supervisee. With no prior experience treating children, our dialogues alleviated his anxieties, explored his current knowledge, reviewed parent engagement, facilitated office creation, and eased his entry into patient care. Cultural barriers and varying expectations introduced novel circumstances, captivating my interest and inspiring this book.

Acknowledgments

Chi, a cherished child, is the center of this story. Her mother's and her own aspirations clashed, resulting in the need for psychoanalysis. Raising a child poses many challenges for any family. Chi represents not just one girl from China but the universal potential and hope for all children. Her future is like a blank canvas. Through Chi's tale, we grasp the collective duty of all in fostering the next generation.

I deeply thank Ching Kong for his critical contribution to this book. He generously welcomed Chi into his office with kindness. Initially, she responded positively but later became hostile, leaving Ching puzzled until he understood why. This change was significant in their therapeutic process, unveiling insights into transference dynamics.

Ching primarily led Chi's treatment while I supervised, offering guidance without imposing my methods. Supervisors should mentor rather than control, promoting autonomy in their supervisees.

Cliff started as my supervisor and later became a friend. Initially, psychoanalysts prided themselves on interpreting patients' conditions confidently from an omniscient viewpoint, often overlooking their biases. They claimed objective insights into patients' personalities, providing definitive interpretations while minimizing their own influence. This approach created a distance, hiding the analyst's perspective behind a facade.

About ten years ago, Cliff and I reconnected. Now a novelist, Cliff realized that abandoning an omniscient voice leads to deeper human understanding. In his creative writing, he moved towards an active voice and first-person narrative, capturing subtleties missed by a god-like omniscient perspective. Cliff's journey showed me that an omniscient narrative fails to convey life's complexities, whether depicting a WWII soldier or a ballerina's career. He believed psychoanalysts could benefit from more relatable writing. Using an active voice and first-person storytelling can better illustrate therapist-patient dynamics.

So, in this book, I have strived to speak clearly and in my own voice.

Neal Spira and I have shared a deep-rooted dedication to serving our community for many years. Our collaboration began when we took on advisory roles at a local center, which included a specialized day school designed for children grappling with intense psychological disorders, providing them with the necessary care that standard outpatient services and regular schooling could not. It was through this experience that we both came to understand that a child's progress is the true measure of success, rather than adherence to any particular theoretical framework. This focus on the patient's well-being has been a guiding principle in my analytical practice, emphasizing unconscious-transference, the foundations of psychoanalytic work over the technical differences between psychotherapy and psychoanalysis. In the process of authoring my recent book, I found myself captivated by the notion of "entanglement" and its potential to shed light on the nuances of Ching's interactions with Chi. Despite my initial reservations about introducing a novel concept, Neal persuaded me that 'entanglement' could enrich the narrative, offering a fuller, more nuanced understanding of the treatment process.

Paul Hollinger emphasized vigilance against physical punishment and advocated enlightened parenting. Societal norms around discipline shaped Chi's upbringing and posed therapeutic challenges.

I am grateful to Peter Czarnowski for his interest and Art Neilsen for helping frame discussions about Essential Psychoanalysis constructively.

Together, they helped me clarify my central message. Ultimately, this book integrates supervisory processes with the ideas of Essential Psychoanalysis. In Essential Psychoanalysis, the transference-countertransference matrix may seem overwhelmingly complex because there is no privileged, objective, or omniscient perspective. However, the patient's acceptance or rejection of the analyst's interpretations leads to provisional resolutions, including progressive exchanges between the patient and the analyst. These interactions foster mutual recognition, potentially resulting in a shared understanding, a tentative agreement, or an appreciation of differing viewpoints.

This process enhances connection and mutual empathy, which can be helpful for both parties. Essential Psychoanalysis recognizes that some indeterminacy remains while specific negotiations can be clarified within the therapeutic setting. Furthermore, the negotiated understandings between patient and analyst are provisional and open to future revision. Despite the uncertainty, mutual recognition in therapy allows for tentative solutions. Bridging psychoanalytic divides this way becomes a practical tool for improving patient care.

I thank Dr. Arnold D. Richards, Editor-in-Chief, and the staff at InternationalPsychoanalysis.net for publishing this book and providing me with encouragement and guidance throughout its publication.

Bhaskar Sripada, M.D.
Trondheim, Norway

Psychoanalytic Supervision

Supervision, a transformative process in preserving and advancing psychoanalytic practice, serves as a bridge between generations of analysts. A candidate's education typically involves personal analysis with a training analyst, academic instruction in psychoanalytic theory, and supervised clinical practice. These functions—personal analysis, academic teaching, and supervision—though interconnected, are distinct. Under a supervisor's mentorship, candidates learn to integrate theory with clinical practice and develop their "analytic identity." The supervisor plays a crucial role in guiding the trainee's growth, enabling them to apply psychoanalytic methods to cases effectively.

This book offers a detailed exploration of the supervisory process and personal observations from early treatment phases, summarizing key aspects of supervision in psychoanalysis and psychotherapy. Psychoanalytic terms and concepts, far from being abstract, are practical tools in clinical settings, empowering both psychoanalytic communication and patient care. The methods used to understand psychoanalytic cases also apply to psychoanalytic supervision, providing a solid foundation for effective practice.

Identifying the concrete situation in which a concept applies is necessary in supervision. This is not a magical process. When accompanied by appropriate clinical context, psychoanalytic ideas and constructs provide optimal opportunities for the reader to appreciate the workings of that theory's construct. This narrative, which maintains the first-person perspectives of both the candidate and supervisor (although from my viewpoint), can be brought to life by the reader through empathy, recreating a scene that is meaningful to them. It does not mean the reader will agree with me, but the context provides adequate material to engender meaningful acceptance or rejection. Because it is concrete in its narrative, it facilitates such an outcome.

This account captures the dialogue between the supervisee and the supervisor and the progression of their relationship. It allows readers to witness the exchanges of words and actions between the patient (or the patient's parents) and the candidate analyst. Through these interconnected descriptions, readers can directly observe whether there are significant emotions, conflicts, divisions, identifications, and similarities or differences in transference-countertransference between the patient, the analyst, and the supervisor. These patterns might initially be subtle, but supervision and clinical descriptions can bring the clinical material and supervisory process to life, transforming theoretical abstractions into tangible experiences.

Therefore, by weaving together process notes, reflective commentaries, and thoughts, I aim to bring to life the vibrant core of supervision, the moments of anxiety, uncertainty, breakthroughs, and the deep connections between supervisee and supervisor that shape the path toward clinical knowledge. In clinical supervision literature, the intricacies of the supervisor-supervisee relationship are often shrouded in theoretical frameworks or abstract conceptions that fail to capture the spontaneity of real-world interactions. This book attempts to peel back those layers, offering a raw and unfiltered glimpse into the supervisory process through supervisory process notes. A candidate must first identify and understand a real-life situation through the lens of depth psychology. Only then can the analyst appropriately generalize this understanding to other cases. This book facilitates this process by providing the raw material of supervision and my supervisory musings, usually soon after the supervisory session, fostering a sense of engagement and connection with the material.

Generalizing insights from supervision helps derive principles applicable to broader contexts, but overgeneralization risks overlooking unique case details. Trainees may struggle to apply abstract concepts without concrete examples, leading to misunderstandings. Hence, supervision must provide specific clinical contexts to ground theoretical ideas effectively.

This book aims to demystify the supervisor-supervisee dynamic, presenting it through concrete narratives and first-person perspectives. By showcasing real exchanges between patients, analysts, and supervisors, the account captures the emotional and intellectual evolution of the supervisee. Through process notes and reflections, the text brings the nuances of supervision to life, illustrating how candidates develop clinical knowledge and apply psychoanalytic concepts to real-world cases.

Supervision versus Psychotherapy

Ekstein and Wallerstein (1972)[19] argued that supervision should not be equated with psychotherapy. While supervision aims to educate the candidate about treatment theory and practice, psychotherapy focuses on addressing and resolving a patient's internal conflicts. Thus, incorporating interpretation into supervision may neglect the fundamental differences in objectives between these two processes.

---

19 Ekstein, R., & Wallerstein, R.S. (1972). *The Teaching and Learning of Psychotherapy.* New York: Int. Univ. Press.

Taking the contrasting perspective, Gorman (1996)[20] argues that supervision is crucial for interpreting the transferences and countertransferences that emerge within the supervision process and are relevant to the case being supervised. According to Gorman, no training analysis or other therapeutic or educational approaches can replace this analytical aspect of supervision. He uses a clinical example to illustrate the value of interpreting a supervisee's resistance, showing how such work can positively impact diagnostic, therapeutic, and supervisory processes.

Transference and Supervision

Wagner (1957)[21] identified three foci in supervision: patient-centered, therapist-centered, and process-centered. In patient-centered supervision, the focus is on teaching technique. Therapist-centered supervision concentrates on the therapist's reactions, blind spots, and countertransference. Process-centered supervision highlights the analogy between the patient and the supervised analyst, emphasizing their shared role as help seekers. However, such an emphasis may transform a supervisory session into a therapeutic-like session, with the candidate-analyst assuming the patient's role and the supervising analyst acting as the treating analyst. DeBell (1963)[22] notes a primary controversy regarding whether supervision should include therapeutic efforts. He warns that when supervision becomes akin to therapy, the supervisor

---

20 Gorman, H.E. (1996). Interpretation of transference in psychoanalytic supervision. *Free Associations* 6:379–402.

21 Wagner, F. (1957). Supervision of psychotherapy. *American Journal of Psychotherapy*, 11:759–768.

22 DeBell, D.E. (1963). A critical digest of the literature on psychoanalytic supervision. *Journal of the American Psychoanalytic Association*, 11: 546–575.

may force the candidate into the patient's role, resulting in reluctant or rebellious passivity.

Fleming and Benedek (1983)[23] believe that a candidate's motivation to learn originates in a "positive transference to his teacher in the supervisory process," similar to the patient's transference. However, Glover (1952)[24] points out that the trainee's identification with the supervisor may limit the candidate's development and creativity, potentially causing a lasting fixation on the supervising teacher and their theories. Peltz (1972)[25] notes that transferences to supervisors occur, increasing the danger of collusion between the candidate and supervisor.

Despite the potential pitfalls, supervision is widely recognized as an essential teaching tool. A detailed exploration of its nuances is beyond the scope of this discussion.

Countertransference and Supervision

Freud (1910) initially recognized countertransference in the analyst. Reich (1951[26], 1960[27]) later detailed a narrow definition of countertransference related to the analyst's unconscious needs and conflicts. Heinmann

23 Fleming, J., & Benedek, T. (1983). *Psychoanalytic Supervision: A Method of Clinical Teaching*. New York & London: Grune & Stratton.

24 Glover, E. (1952). Research methods in psychoanalysis. *International Journal of Psychoanalysis*, 33:403–409.

25 Peltz, W. (1972). Transference and psychoanalytic case supervision. Comments on a blind spot in clinical research. *Psychoanalytic Quarterly*, 41: 384–401.

26 Reich, A. (1951). On Countertransference. *International Journal of Psychoanalysis*, 32:25–31.

27 Reich, A. (1960). On Countertransference. *International Journal of Psychoanalysis*, 41:389–395.

(1950)[28] broadened the definition to include the analyst's total response to the patient, noting that countertransference can be valuable for understanding the patient's transference.

Recognizing the candidate's countertransference is a high priority in supervision. Blitzten and Fleming (1953) stated that supervision aims to help a candidate recognize unresolved conflicts that interfere with effective analysis. Fleming and Benedek (1983) noted that these "unresolved complexes" are easily observed by the supervisor and reflect "flaws in the analytic instrument." They argue that resolving these flaws belongs in the candidate's own analysis or self-analysis. DeBell (1963) adds that some candidate reactions may mirror the patient's, necessitating more analysis.

Models of Supervision

Independent and parallel models can help understand the psychotherapy supervision process. Many supervisory processes derived from psychoanalytic training are also applicable in psychotherapy supervision.

Independent Model

The independent model views the patient and therapist as primarily engaged in a therapeutic relationship, while the candidate-supervisee and supervisor engage in a learning-teaching relationship. The supervisee, who may have transferences to the supervisor, is seen as a student

---

28 Heinmann, P. (1950). On Countertransference. *International Journal of Psychoanalysis,* 31:81–84.

of psychotherapy, independent of the patient's transference to the candidate-analyst. Supervision is considered an educational enterprise, separate from psychotherapy treatment. Critical learning factors such as motivation, readiness, reinforcement, conditioning, cognition, and imitation are essential for effective supervision.

Dewald (1987)[29] subscribes to the view of the supervisor as an educator, balancing cognitive didactic instruction with demonstrating the supervisor's thinking process. Ekstein and Wallerstein (1958)[30] and Lewin and Ross (1960)[31] also consider the main task of supervision to be the direct teaching of psychoanalytic technique. However, this model, while useful in imposing distinctions between therapy and teaching, does not always allow for the exploration of the complex and overlapping interrelations between these two domains, which can sometimes make this distinction impossible.

Parallel Model

Searles (1955)[32] describes a "reflection process" in which the therapist forms an unconscious link between the patient and the supervisor. He contends that aspects of the patient's unconscious communications not understood by the analyst are nonverbally communicated to the supervisor, as the candidate unconsciously attempts to demonstrate less

29 Dewald, P.A. (1987). *Learning process in Psychoanalytic Supervision: Complexities and Challenges*. Madison, CT: International Universities Press.

30 Ekstein, R., & Wallerstein, R. (1958). *The Teaching and Learning of Psychotherapy*. New York: Basic Books.

31 Lewin, B.D., & Ross, H. (1960). *Psychoanalytic Education in the United States*. New York: Norton.

32 Searles, H. (1955). The informational value of the supervisor's emotional experiences. *Psychiatry* 18(2):135–146.

understood behaviors during supervision sessions. While Searles sees this process as systemic, involving patient, candidate, and supervisor, it remains a one-way process in supervision.

In contrast, Doehrman (1976)[33] argues that the supervisor's behavior toward the therapist frequently influences how the therapist interacts with patients. Her study showed that each therapist "played supervisor with his or her patient," reenacting or reacting to the supervisor's own core neurotic problems.

Windholz (1970)[34] notes that a patient's transference may extend to the supervisor, citing an example of split transference, where one aspect is directed toward the analyst and another toward the supervisor. Occasionally, supervisors may use their emotional reactions as cues to understand a case, but errors may be introduced in this unconscious communication chain.

Sarnat and colleagues (2018)[35] define the parallel process as "a supervisee's unconscious reenactment of therapy session material within the supervisory dyad." Thus, a parallel process represents a "bottom-up" reenactment in the supervision of an unconscious dynamic originating in therapy.

In the parallel model, the patient and candidate-analyst engage in an analytic relationship, while the candidate-supervisee and supervisor engage in a parallel supervisory relationship. This relationship is additive to the learning-teaching relationship. Due to the parallelism, the candidate may be identified with the patient, and the supervisor may

---

33 Doehrman, M.J.G. (1976). Parallel processes in supervision and psychotherapy. *Bulletin of the Menninger Clinic,* 40(1): 2–104.

34 Windholz, E. (1970). The theory of supervision in psychoanalytic education. *International Journal of Psychoanalysis,* 51:393406.

35 Sarnat, J., Hopsicker, R., Montojo, P., Plumb, E., & Goodyear, R. (2018). In H. Zetzer (Chair), Back to the future: Investigating parallel process in psychodynamic supervision. Symposium at the Meetings of the American Psychological Association, San Francisco, CA.

assume the analyst's role. The model assumes that the therapist's reactions to the supervisor reflect the patient's transference to the therapist, and the supervisor's reactions to the candidate may reflect the candidate's countertransference toward the patient.

Although terms like identification, working through, insight, ego growth, transference, and countertransference apply to both psychoanalysis and supervision, fully working through these processes in supervision is not always possible or appropriate due to its learning-teaching mission.

Kernberg (2010)[36]emphasized that the phenomenon of parallel process vividly illustrates the activation of unconscious dynamics within the supervisory process. Here, the supervisee's unconscious countertransference reactions are enacted during supervision. These reactions are then "discharged" through a role reversal, where the supervisee unconsciously identifies with the patient's experience while projecting their own countertransference response onto the supervisor.

From a structural point of view, the id encompasses impulses, affects, and wishful phantasies of love, hate, and their combinations; the ego consists of relatively rational, reality-oriented mental processes; and the superego embodies moral demands, ideals, prohibitions, and feelings of guilt, including needs for punishment or reparation.

Racker (1957) provided a structural theory-based understanding of the dynamics between the patient and the analyst, emphasizing the tensions and conflicts within the analyst's own id, ego, and superego—similar to those experienced by the analysand. The parallel processes between the patient and the candidate analyst can be observed in the supervision described by Kernberg. Racker introduced the concept

---

36 Kernberg, O.F. (2010) Psychoanalytic supervision: The supervisor's tasks. *Psychoanalytic Quarterly* 79:603–627.

of concordant countertransference identification, wherein the analyst identifies with the analysand's id based on their own id or with the analysand's superego based on their own superego. In contrast, in complementary countertransference, the analyst unconsciously adopts the role of the agency the analysand is dis-identifying with. For instance, if a patient identifies with her superego and dis-identifies with her id, the analyst, through complementary countertransference, may unknowingly align with the patient's disowned id. Conversely, if the patient identifies with her id, the analyst may assume the role of the projected superego, inadvertently reinforcing the patient's internal conflict.

Self and Intersubjectivity in Supervision

Watkins (2016)[37], adopting a self-psychological perspective on supervision, emphasizes the supervisee's learning process and the supervisor's role as a selfobject. This approach is based on three core principles: (1) Supervisee learning occurs through an ongoing cycle of self-disruption and restoration within the supervisory process. (2) Learning is most effectively encouraged when the supervisee's self-esteem and self-cohesion are consistently supported. (3) The supervisor acts as a vitalizing selfobject, enhancing the supervisee's self-cohesion and self-esteem while customizing the supervisory experience to maximize therapist development.

---

37 Watkins, C.E. (2016). Self psychology and psychoanalytic supervision: Some thoughts on a contextualized perspective. *International Journal of Psychoanalytic Self Psychology* 11:276–292.

Berman (2000)[38] argues for an intersubjective perspective on the analytic process, where the therapist's countertransference is both a clue to the analysand's psychic reality and a factor in its evolution. This perspective makes the notion of didactic supervision without addressing countertransference issues untenable. However, Berman (2014)[39] later clarified that supervision is at the crossroads of a matrix of object relations involving the analysand, analyst, and supervisor, encompassing a complex network of transference and countertransference patterns.

Essential Psychoanalysis and psychoanalytic supervision

Essential Psychoanalysis endorses the concept of broad countertransference, emphasizing the active roles of both the analyst and the analysand as participant observers. The idea of parallel processes between therapy and supervision suggests that supervision dynamics can mirror those of the patient-analyst relationship. Consequently, interactions between the supervisee and supervisor can provide valuable insights into the patient's psyche and their relationship with the analyst.

However, these insights are merely initial clues. Observations from the analyst's countertransference or the supervisor's experiences mainly serve as a basis for developing hypotheses that lack the evidential weight of the patient's direct expressions, such as free associations, play, or behaviors. Hypotheses based on countertransference might suggest patient identifications, object relations, or defenses, but they remain speculative and must be tested through patient engagement and

---

38 Berman, E. (2000). Psychoanalytic supervision: The intersubjective development. *International Journal of Psychoanalysis* 81:273–290.

39 Berman, E. (2014). Psychoanalytic supervision in a heterogeneous theoretical context: Benefits and complications. *Psychoanalytic Dialogues* 24:525–531.

assessing the patient's responses over time. Their usefulness diminishes progressively if the countertransference or supervisory reflections indicate a pathological quality. The analytic impact of interventions can only be assessed in retrospect after the effects of an intervention emerge.

Psychoanalysis and supervision

Psychoanalytic supervision significantly shapes the professional growth of psychoanalysts, especially trainees. Psychoanalysis, a complex system for understanding human psychology and behavior, encompasses principles, theories, techniques, practices, and assumptions. Unconscious and transference-countertransference processes form the foundational principles of psychoanalysis, agreed upon by most analysts. These principles permeate theories such as Instinct (Drive), Oedipal-Preoedipal, Ego, Relational, Self, Intersubjective, developmental, and neuropsychoanalysis. It is possible for analysts to use a single theory exclusively or to rely on several theories depending on the situation.

Most contemporary analysts assume that the analyst and patient are active participant-observers and contribute to their observations. In contrast, traditional analysts assume the analyst is neutral and objective and can serve as a blank screen to the patient. The analyst applies their principles, theories, techniques, practices, and assumptions to recognize clinical and dynamic phenomena like symptoms, anxieties, dreams, day residues, parapraxis, resistances, conflicts, deficits, fixations, compromises, displacements, condensations, and identifications.

The previously discussed points regarding psychoanalysis are also directly or indirectly relevant to supervision. The goal of supervision is to instill in the candidate the ability to appreciate these principles, theories, techniques, practices, and assumptions, adhere to ethical standards, and promote the growth of a psychoanalytic identity. A psychoanalytic identity is rooted in an analyst's inherent application of psychoanalytic principles, concepts, theories, methods, practices, and assumptions. It primarily uses the patient's free associations and, in the case of a child, play, along with the analyst's broad countertransference, as the primary raw data for analysis.

While supervising the candidate's work, the supervisor examines the student's countertransference, whether in a general or specific context. The main goal of supervision is to steer the student towards proper therapeutic behavior. It is fundamental to the supervisor's role to assess the candidate's countertransference and its impact on patient treatment. The supervisor's evaluation and advice concerning broad countertransference, which refers to the therapist's overall emotional reaction to the patient, are chiefly directed at improving patient care and are not meant to treat the candidate. Nonetheless, the supervision process can inadvertently benefit the candidate therapeutically by enhancing their grasp of broad countertransference. Such incidental therapeutic benefits should be acknowledged, but the supervisor's primary focus should remain to oversee the candidate's treatment approach. The analysis of the candidate's treatment should remain distinct from their supervision, although there may be occasional intersections concerning the candidate's broad countertransference.

Key Aspects of Psychoanalytic Supervision:

1. **Case Discussions**: Supervision sessions typically involve in-depth discussions of the supervisee's clinical cases. Supervisees present material from their patient sessions, including observations, therapeutic interventions, and patient responses.

They are encouraged to bring forward any concerns, questions, or dilemmas they have encountered for collaborative exploration.

2. **Reflection and Insight**: The supervisor facilitates the supervisee's reflection on their own emotional responses and countertransference—the unconscious emotional reactions of the therapist towards the patient. Understanding these reactions is essential for maintaining therapeutic neutrality and effectiveness in treatment.

3. **Application of Theory**: Supervisors assist supervisees in applying psychoanalytic theories to understand their patients' behaviors, symptoms, and unconscious processes better. This includes analyzing key dynamics such as transference (the patient's projection of feelings onto the therapist) and resistance to the therapeutic process.

4. **Skill Development**: Supervision is a platform for developing the supervisee's clinical skills, including interpretation and intervention techniques. This involves learning how to manage the therapeutic frame, set appropriate boundaries, and navigate complex or challenging situations.

5. **Ethical Considerations**: Supervisors address ethical issues that may arise in clinical practice, such as confidentiality, maintaining professional boundaries, and the duty to report potential harm. This helps supervisees navigate ethical dilemmas and uphold professional standards.

6. **Professional Growth**: Through appropriate feedback and mentorship, supervisors contribute to the confidence and competence of their supervisees as psychoanalysts. Supervision is a formative experience that shapes the supervisee's professional identity and clinical style.

7. **Collaborative Learning**: Psychoanalytic supervision is a collaborative process between a less experienced therapist (the supervisee) and a more seasoned senior colleague (the supervisor), fostering a dynamic learning environment.

8. **Purposeful Development**: The primary goals of supervision are to enhance clinical skills, deepen the understanding of psychoanalytic principles, and empower the supervisee to become a competent and independent psychoanalyst.

9. **Supportive Environment**: Supervision provides a secure and supportive space for supervisees to explore both the conscious and unconscious aspects of their clinical work. This environment fosters a sense of safety and trust, which is crucial for professional development.

10. **Educational Focus**: Supervision serves as an educational platform, providing information, teaching therapeutic skills, and nurturing an ethical sensibility, helping supervisees feel well-informed and knowledgeable.

11. **Emotional Support**: Supervision offers emotional support and guidance, helping supervisees manage the emotional demands of clinical work and fostering resilience.

12. **Open Communication**: Supervision encourages honest and open dialogue about cases, countertransference, and personal reactions, promoting transparency and deeper understanding.

Psychoanalytic supervision is a collaborative and educational process that fosters the development of the supervisee's clinical expertise, self-awareness, and understanding of psychoanalytic principles. It aims for the supervisee to become well-prepared to work independently and effectively with patients.

A supervisor can help a candidate analyst appreciate the following:

1. **Distinguishing Unconscious, Preconscious, and Conscious Contents:**
   - **Unconscious**: Help the candidate recognize contents not accessible to the patient's awareness without significant exploration and may manifest dreams, slips of the tongue, or free associations.
   - **Preconscious**: Guide the candidate to identify thoughts and memories that are not currently in conscious awareness but can be brought to mind with some effort, such as forgotten childhood memories that might arise during therapy.
   - **Conscious**: Train the candidate to differentiate contents that the patient is immediately aware of and can articulate easily, such as daily thoughts, feelings, and perceptions.

2. **Narrow vs. Broad Countertransference View:**
   - **Narrow Countertransference**: Explain that this view focuses on the analyst's personal unconscious reactions to the patient, often stemming from unresolved conflicts.
   - **Broad Countertransference**: Describe this as encompassing all of the analyst's reactions to the patient, including conscious and unconscious responses that provide valuable information about the patient's inner world.

3. **Mutual Interactions between Transference and Counter-transference:**
   - Encourage candidates to see how the patient's transference (projection of feelings onto the analyst) and the analyst's countertransference (reactions to the patient) interact dynamically, influencing the therapeutic relationship and offering insights into the patient's psyche.

4. **Optimal Zone for Working Through**:
   - Help candidates understand that effective therapeutic work occurs in a balanced zone where the patient is neither too resistant to recognizing transference nor too quick to resolve it, allowing for meaningful exploration and insight.

5. **Empathic and Prediction Errors, Interpersonal Impingement, Misattunements, and Intersubjective Oversights**:
   - Teach candidates to recognize when their empathic understanding or predictions about the patient are incorrect (errors), how these impact the patient, and the importance of addressing and repairing these moments in therapy.

6. **Communication and Understanding**:
   - Emphasize the importance of clear, empathic communication that respects the patient's pace and readiness, allowing the patient to grasp the analyst's interpretations and insights.

7. **Timing, Dosage, and Tact of Interventions**:
   - Guide candidates to appreciate the importance of timing their interventions appropriately, not overwhelming the patient, and using tact to ensure that interpretations are well-received and therapeutic.

8. **Negotiations and Compromise**:
   - Teach candidates about the role of negotiations and compromises in analysis and therapy, helping patients navigate conflicting desires and impulses and fostering a collaborative therapeutic environment.

9. **Spotting Repression, Splitting, and Other Defenses**:
   - Train candidates to identify various defense mechanisms as they manifest in sessions, understanding their function in protecting the patient's psyche and how to address them therapeutically.

10. **Identifying Over-Idealization and Excessive Devaluations:**
    - Help candidates recognize when patients are over-idealizing or excessively devaluing others, including the analyst, as these can reflect underlying issues with self-esteem, attachment, or past trauma.

11. **Displaying Human Concern and Compassion:**
    - Encourage candidates to consistently show empathy, compassion, and genuine concern for their patients, fostering a safe and supportive therapeutic alliance.

12. **Identifying Developmental Patterns:**
    - Educate candidates on recognizing different developmental stages and patterns, such as attachment styles, Oedipal conflicts, and adolescence-related issues, and how these affect the patient's current behavior and emotional state.

13. **Need for Containment and Limit Setting:**
    - Teach candidates to identify when patients need containment (providing a safe space for expression) or limit-setting (establishing boundaries to protect the therapeutic process and the patient's well-being).

14. **Impulsive vs. Inhibited Decision Making and Actions:**
    - Guide candidates in distinguishing between impulsive behaviors, which may indicate a lack of impulse control or deeper conflicts, and inhibited actions, which may suggest repression, anxiety, or other defensive operations.

15. **Identifying New vs. Familiar Dynamics:**
    - Help candidates recognize when patients are engaging in familiar relational patterns versus exploring new ways of relating, which can signify therapeutic progress or resistance.

16. **Awareness of Patient's Defenses, Conflicts, Stresses, Fixations, and Strengths:**
    - Encourage candidates to comprehensively understand the patient's defenses, underlying conflicts, stressors, fixations, and strengths, allowing for a more nuanced and practical therapeutic approach.

By focusing on these areas, candidates will be better equipped to understand and manage the complexities of psychoanalytic work, enhancing both their development as therapists and the therapeutic outcomes for their patients.

Psychoanalytic Identity

In this book, I chronicle my experience as a cross-cultural psychoanalytic supervisor, detailing the developmental journey of my supervisee. I focus on the initiation and initial stages of the supervisory process, providing in-depth commentary on specific ideas and interventions. I explore the complexities of psychoanalytic supervision, including principles, theories, techniques, practices, and assumptions in the individual circumstances of a particular case. My narrative focus maintains the candidate's and supervisor's first-person perspectives, inviting readers to empathize with the experiences described. I capture the dialogue between the supervisee and the supervisor, transforming theoretical abstractions into tangible experiences. I aim to illuminate the vibrant core of supervision and the path toward clinical knowledge.

Psychoanalytic principles have the potential for cross-cultural application but must be adapted to fit the child recipient's milieu. The supervisor and supervisee must recognize the complexity of their distinct cultural backgrounds and use virtual communication to benefit children. Flexibility is critical, with the analyst adapting psychoanalytic insights to their cultural context. The supervisor guides this process, avoiding overly specific feedback that may not align with the supervisee's culture. Supervision enhances the analyst's skills, fosters an "analytic identity," and facilitates appropriate clinical treatment for the patient. The supervisor adjusts to the supervisee's learning stage, style, and culture, maintaining a supportive attitude. Since the inception of psychoanalysis, a shift from classical to contemporary analysis has occurred, emphasizing reciprocal engagement in a clinical setting. This active observer perspective introduces adaptive flexibility into the system, which is vital for passing psychoanalytic knowledge across generations.

An analyst's psychoanalytic identity relies on depth psychology and, when feasible, favors non-directive techniques over direct behavioral management of the patient through didactic, cognitive, behavioral, or overtly suggestive methods to facilitate patient change. Guided by free, evenly suspended attention, the analyst listens to conscious and unconscious communications and is interactive, marked by a balance of freedom and responsibility. This freedom is not an unrestricted license but a disciplined liberty that respects the patient's autonomy and dignity. The analyst communicates freely, confident that the patient can accept or reject the analyst's opinions. The analyst's enduring interest in the patient's freedoms is coupled with relative indifference to whether the patient accepts or rejects an interpretation. The analyst's curiosity about the patient's reactions to the analyst's communication and reasons for the patient's choices and actions makes an impression on the patient. The analyst's freedom flourishes in an open dialogue and mutual respect on the journey of understanding, self-discovery, and learning from mistakes. This evolving identity enables the analyst to navigate the complexities of human emotions and relationships, transforming the analytic space into a realm of understanding transformations and facilitating growth for both the analyst and the patient.

Although primarily relying on the psychoanalytic method of understanding and interpreting the patient's free associations and actions and the analyst's broad countertransference, the analyst is aware that dangerousness, such as threats to self or others, requires interventions as per legal requirements and readily consults with other professionals when a patient's medical condition or psychopathology exceeds the scope of psychoanalytic practice. While a psychoanalytic identity serves as a guiding light for analysts worldwide, it can take on many forms, and the version I have described is my interpretation. However, for a candidate just beginning to learn and delve into a lived psychoanalytic practice and knowledge, these commonly used psychoanalytic terms may seem abstract, academic, or visionary, but they remain impractical without a context.

Differences between child and adult psychoanalysis

This book delves into child analysis, necessitating a comparison with adult analysis. Child psychoanalysis is unique in its emphasis on the immediate developmental stages of children, from infancy to adolescence, within the context of the analysis. Conversely, adult psychoanalysis explores the psychological developments of childhood and adolescence as historical events reconstructed through the patient's recollections. Environmental factors, especially familial interactions with parents and siblings and teacher educational experiences, significantly mold children's development. Conversely, adults are more influenced by their relationships in marriage or other significant bonds, adulthood, and workplace environments. Child analysts use play, verbal, and creative techniques to help children express their inner experiences, while adult psychoanalysis primarily relies on verbal, free-associational methods. Parents support any child analysis, and it is common for child analysts to have periodic information-sharing engagements with parents, often with the child's input. A child's transferences might be related to transferences stemming from an earlier period in a child's development or concurrent transferences from the significant parent to the analyst. In addition, the analyst also serves as a new object. Lastly, adults typically seek psychoanalysis voluntarily, driven by self-awareness and autonomy, whereas children and adolescents may lack this perspective, often participating in analysis at their parents' behest.

While sharing similarities with adult analysis, child analysis also introduces unique aspects due to the child's changing development and temperament. It uses playful and imaginative storytelling techniques and incorporates feelings and experiences from both past and present relationships, especially with parents, which are then transferred to the analyst. These special characteristics of child analysis can be applied to enrich adult analysis in innovative ways. For example, integrating elements such as verbal playfulness, creative storytelling methods, and using shared cultural stories, such as movies or music, can help address problems more lightheartedly, particularly when the analysis has reached a stalemate. By using characters from these sources, we can create analytical narratives that promote a more inventive and broad approach to the field, inspiring new ways of thinking and practice.

Cross-cultural considerations

While the principles of depth psychology and psychoanalysis hold immense potential for application across diverse cultures, their subtle application must fit with the milieu of the child recipient. Infusing psychoanalytic concepts into societies with minimal prior exposure to such theories presents a resistance to change and a formidable challenge. Any initial venture must recognize the complexity inherent in the collaboration between a supervisor and supervisee from distinct cultures, utilizing virtual communication to benefit children.

Flexibility is crucial at every step if the goal is to provide global clinical benefits to children through supervision. As the key player, the aspiring analyst is responsible and best equipped to adapt psychoanalytic insights to their unique cultural context. As a supervisor, my role involves guiding the delivery of psychoanalytic wisdom, always acknowledging the supervisee's pivotal role in reinterpreting and adjusting the supervisory input to create clinical interventions that suit the patient.

As a transformative process, supervision enhances the treating student or analyst's analytic skills and conceptual abilities, fostering an "analytic identity." It also monitors the quality of the supervisee's treatment efforts, playing a crucial role in safeguarding patient care and attempting to harmonize treatment with the cultural context.

Beyond what the supervisor provides for the student and patient, the supervisory process involves self-reflection and adaptability on the supervisor's part. The supervisor adjusts the supervision to the supervisee's learning stage, therapeutic style, and cultural background. Flexibility in applying theory and technical principles is vital, as is maintaining a respectful, supportive, and nonjudgmental attitude toward the supervisees, ensuring they feel valued and respected.

The Active Participant Observer and Adaptive Flexibility

Since the inception of psychoanalysis, a significant differentiation has developed between classical and contemporary psychoanalysis. Classical analysts adhere to the ideas of objectivity and the neutral, privileged analyst's ability to interpret the patient's psyche accurately. On the other hand, contemporary analysts consider these ideas false assumptions and instead advocate that both the patient and analyst are participant observers. Contemporary analysis emphasizes all parties' reciprocal and mutually influential engagement in a clinical setting.

These distinctions have an important bearing on supervision. The contemporary view shifts the focus away from a privileged analyst to the recognition that all observers in such a relationship are active and contribute elements of their personalities that become attributed to the objects of observation. It lays the intellectual groundwork for non-privileged human relationships while acknowledging the expertise of the supervisor and the distinct roles of the patient, candidate analyst, and supervisor.

In a traditional supervision model, if a supervisor demands the supervisee follow their instructions strictly, the supervisee has little flexibility to change the instruction, essentially making the supervisee a passive conveyor of the supervisor's directives. However, in a modern supervision model, even if the supervisor wants to instruct the supervisee's actions, the active observer perspective inherently involves each participant's contributions, introducing uncertainty and adaptive flexibility into the system.

When cross-cultural dynamics come into play, this perspective welcomes adaptability. Even within the same culture, people differ significantly, making the active observer perspective useful regardless of cultural homogeneity among the supervisor, candidate, and patient.

All beings are hardwired, in many areas, to do as they wish rather than how others would wish them to act. Therefore, my lessons, even if intended to be rigid, are automatically mixed with the will and execution of the candidate and will be somewhat different from what I intended. The candidate's freedom will ultimately shine through, and they will automatically execute their plan unless they become enthralled by idealization or over-identification with me.

In any relationship that interfaces consciousnesses, each person, as an active observer, inevitably modifies the contents of the supervisor's words and actions. The supervisor's intent then undergoes interpretation through the lens of the candidate's psyche, introducing inherent flexibility. This adaptability plays a crucial role in transferring psychoanalytic knowledge across generations.

Psychoanalysis and society

Psychoanalytic practice has to conform to the law, ensuring patient confidentiality according to appropriate guidelines and reporting suspected child abuse or neglect; in some states, the duty to warn is a legal obligation that requires mental health professionals to warn potential victims of a patient's violent threats, and when applicable, providing court-demanded testimony. According to the American Psychoanalytic Association (APsA) Code of Ethics, the code applies to all APsA members across all classes and categories, including those in training in all affiliated institutes or organizations. It states that "APsA Code of Ethics Psychoanalysis and psychoanalytic therapy offer children, adolescents, and adults with emotional and mental disorders methods of treatment that attempt to reduce suffering, disability, and enhance personal growth and autonomy...Respect for patient autonomy and authority, beneficence, non-malfeasance, veracity, fidelity, and justice are foundational ethical principles for all work within psychoanalysis."

Summary

This introduction summarizes many psychoanalytic constructs for prospective students or individuals exploring psychoanalytic supervision or psychoanalysis. I wrote this book to show those seeking an understanding of psychoanalytic supervision from supervisory process notes. It provides detailed accounts of supervisory sessions, including dialogues between the candidate and me about the patient and the context. This first-person, descriptive recounting hopes that it will evoke a better heart-felt understanding of the supervisory process. By offering a moment-by-moment narrative rather than a summary, the reader can visualize events and feel emotions as if they were their own, making the narrative more engaging and immersive. This detailed storytelling diminishes the gap between participants and readers, fostering a deeper connection and understanding. I hope readers gain a nuanced understanding of the supervisory process, bringing these ideas closer to the heart.

Supervision is the glue that connects generations of analysts and helps both the continuity and evolution of psychoanalysis. Psychoanalytic supervision goes beyond merely imparting knowledge; it creates a space where supervisees can delve into their own thoughts, feelings, and reactions to their patients. This reflective practice enhances their understanding of patients and allows them to customize their therapeutic approaches to meet individual needs. Supervision is a collaborative effort to maintain the integrity of psychoanalytic practice and equip future psychoanalysts to support their patients and advance the field. The ultimate goal is to cultivate empathy, understanding, and a commitment to continuous learning, enabling future psychoanalysts to make significant contributions to both their patients' lives and the field of psychoanalysis.

Supervision: 1

Supervision

I am Bhaskar Sripada, a child supervisor at the Chicago Psychoanalytic Institute. Before our initial supervisory session, Leo Sparrow, a senior candidate from Beijing, China, contacted me about starting his first child case. He shared his apprehension about initiating child work, expressing, "I have a FEAR toward starting child work. I wish to commence my supervision with you when you're available and start by discussing my struggle." Supervision in cross-cultural child therapy and analysis presents unique challenges and opportunities. Overcoming geographical and cultural disparities to engage in the supervisory process involves practical aspects of video teleconferencing and understanding each other's accents; these present new challenges worth exploring. The primary objective of a supervisory collaboration is the transfer of psychoanalytic knowledge and techniques. Hence, it's crucial to create an environment where trainees can freely express their concerns and supervisors can offer guidance and support considering their cultural backgrounds and experiences. My goal is to enhance the effectiveness of the child's treatment by the candidate, facilitate the candidate's learning in the supervision, and foster his ongoing development.

Leo, a man in his forties with a youthful appearance, appeared on the Zoom call. He wore a simple outfit of an unassuming black T-shirt and a grey sweatshirt. A neatly trimmed beard and glasses framed his face, and jet-black hair covered his head. Despite looking anxious, he greeted me with a warm and genuine smile, visibly relieved to establish contact through Zoom, the virtual platform.

Behind Leo, a modern wall hanging depicted a black bear, rendered in an impressionistic style, clutching about seven heart-shaped helium balloons. The balloons floated above the bear in a heart-shaped formation, tethered to the bear by vibrant strings. Behind the bear was a nondescript grey mountain and a bluish-grey horizon. A real-life black and white cat strolled casually in front of the bear on the wall hanging. It was late evening, and Leo was back home after a hard day's work.

I started the session by saying: "I am glad to meet you on Zoom. I know that you have many feelings and concerns about starting to see children in treatment."

> Leo responded, "Dr. Sripada, nice meeting you. I am from Beijing. I am a sixth-year candidate. A teacher at the Institute, M. W., influenced me to become a candidate at the Chicago Institute for Psychoanalysis. I hesitated. Sometime before, I had broken up with my ex-girlfriend and could not foresee what the loss would mean, so I postponed joining the Institute. I feel irritated with my current spouse. I feel she is not empathic to my cat. She is harsh with my cat. Maybe I may have the same problem myself. I'm afraid of meeting a child patient or the child patient's parents. I wonder. What will I say? What should I say? I fear I may not have the proper words to communicate with a child or a child's parents."

At this moment, Leo reached for a sleek black e-cigarette and placed it between his fingers. He took a drag, and the soft LED light at the end faintly glowed as he inhaled. After a few moments, he exhaled a wispy cloud of vapor. His face relaxed, offering seemingly a moment of calm amidst the excitement of the supervision.

"Could you be more specific? What is it about saying that is a problem for you?"

> "It is hard to explain, but I will try. I can say things in English, but it is harder to say what I want in Chinese. That is all I can say."

Leo stayed silent for a while.

"I will give you my thoughts. Let me know if it makes any sense. Do you know the word "*kowtow* (I pronounced KOW TOW exaggeratedly so he would understand)?"

> "I do not know what you are trying to say."

"You live in Beijing. Before the days of Mao, Chinese Emperors lived in the Forbidden City. People had to *kow tow* when they approached an Emperor." I bowed my head and began to mime, kneeling and touching my forehead to the ground.

> As soon as I started, Leo pronounced *kow tow* in Chinese (something like Kou tou). "Now, I understand the word."

"Correct me, this is my speculation. Maybe, when you approach parents or elders in the Chinese language, you are supposed to show respect, somewhat like *kow tow*. Some angry words may be inappropriate. So speaking and analyzing them is hard."

Leo began to smile and appeared to feel that my idea was worthwhile.

"That is correct. In Mandarin, it is hard to say you are angry with your parents. Or that your parents made you sad. He attempted to say something in Chinese and gave up after trying. Uh, I am even having a hard time pronouncing angry in Chinese. I can easily say in English, "You are angry at your parents. Your parents made you sad." But I cannot say it in Mandarin."

"Do you have any similar problems with using the Chinese language with your adult cases?"

"Many of my adult patients also speak English. I just realized that we all can communicate such feelings better in English. The problem is not with communication but with language. It is easier to express anger in English than in Mandarin."

"If we consider both English and Mandarin, you seem to have no problem discussing anger. However, it is hard to speak of certain feelings when you speak Chinese. Is that correct?"

"Yes. You taught me that you can understand something even if you cannot speak it. I need to focus on under-standing a child's feelings. Even without using Chinese words, we can somehow play or show the child and overcome problems. Maybe the problem is not language but culture. I feel that it makes me feel more ready to start child work. I know I must work through difficulties to work with children, but I want to go there and work with children."

I spoke exaggeratedly, " 'Go to hell!' In English, easy; in Mandarin, hard!"

"Not only anger but disappointment is more challenging to say in Chinese. You hit the point! You hit the point!"

I asked Leo, "Do you know what babysitting is?"

"Yes."

"Did you ever babysit?"

"Yes. I was a babysitter for my cousin, my uncle's son. My uncle told me many times I was a good babysitter. He said I was patient."

"Was the job easy?"

"Not always. My younger cousin was not easy. My cousin would get frustrated and angry with me and shout (Leo raised his voice), "UNCLE you ba—d——."

Leo spoke loudly with feeling and with a pronounced accent so that I could not understand what he said. I thought I heard the word "bastard," but I knew from the cadence of his speech that my impression was wrong. So, I asked Leo to clarify what his cousin said.

Leo laughed at my question and probably his cousin's insolence.

"My cousin was angry at me many times. He shouted, 'You badass.' Sometimes, he picked up his toy phone and pretended to call the Chief of Police. He would say into his toy phone, 'Police. Come and take my brother to jail.'"

Leo continued, "You led the way for me to understand. From my cousin's example, I know that in my own life, I am familiar with even the words of anger, disappointment, and sadness in spoken Mandarin. You soothed my anxiety. Now, my decision to proceed seems easy. It feels natural, and I believe I can work with children. I want to continue to work with you. You are patient."

"You mean like your uncle said you were!"

Leo was surprised by what I said and then replied, "Yes. At any rate, the next job is to get a child case. I have sources to get child cases. I can also try other therapists for referrals and social networks. My ex-wife works with children in kindergarten, and we are on friendly terms. I can get a child case. But before I begin work with a child, I need to ask you more questions, like how to set up my office and related questions."

"It is time for us to stop."

"Yes. I will see you next week."

My Musings

In my discussion with Leo, three main factors stood out regarding my supervisory role. First, each Zoom session centers on Leo's work with a Mandarin-speaking child from China, immersing me in a new cultural context that I need to navigate thoughtfully. Second, my supervision focuses on the practical application of theory relevant to Leo's treatment of this child, avoiding formal psychoanalytic instruction, which is reserved for the Institute's theory classes. Finally, I must address Leo's anxiety through basic educational strategies, staying clear of his personal therapeutic issues, which I understand are an important part of his own analysis and introspection. These guidelines help shape my supervision, ensuring I support Leo's clinical understanding and contribute to the child's growth and development.

I wrote my reflections following several supervisory sessions to convey my perspective on the psychoanalytic supervisory process. These reflections, included occasionally, extend the ideas discussed during supervision, introduce new associations, or explore related issues. They offer deeper insights into the complex process of supervision, which blends theory and treatment but focuses more on practical application than theoretical instruction.

Supervision is not just about teaching theory; it involves tailoring psychoanalytic concepts to help the candidate manage a specific patient. Broad countertransference is critical to understanding the dynamics between the patient and analyst, and, at times, the supervision mirrors the therapeutic relationship. This dynamic reflection offers valuable insights into both the supervision and treatment processes. Details about the candidate's personality often emerge during supervision, and these insights help the supervisor guide the candidate's understanding of patient dynamics and treatment.

Though supervision may sometimes have therapeutic benefits, such as easing anxiety or addressing conflicts, it is not meant to replace personal analysis. My reflections after supervision are part of my supervisory debriefing process. They are my private thoughts that build on the session and offer a deeper look into the ideas and interactions that occurred, often guided by Leo's insights, which play a crucial role in shaping our future supervision sessions.

My first step was to get to know Leo. I met Harold Balikov, an innovative instructor of child analysis at the Chicago Psychoanalytic Institute. He had a groundbreaking approach, preferring straightforward language instead of complicated psychoanalytic jargon. His attentive and gentle demeanor and clear teaching style emphasized the importance of learning beyond textbooks. Before practicing child analysis, I participated in his foundational course with a small group of fellow child psychologists and psychiatrists.

We shared our impressions to gain an empathetic understanding of a child's feelings when interacting with an analyst, which can also apply to any two individuals in a relationship. Even after over forty years, I remember the core lesson about "getting acquainted." Balikov paired us with colleagues and instructed us to alternate, lying on the floor while the other stood over us. This exercise likely triggered different reactions in each of us. It evoked feelings of smallness, helplessness, and powerlessness; my partner's shoes seemed like boats, and their face felt distant, like the moon. This experience taught me the significance of perspective in shaping perceptions and emotions.

Analysts need to recognize that, from a patient's viewpoint, they can easily occupy a position of privilege and must always be mindful of the patient's vulnerabilities and strengths. In any human relationship, especially a therapeutic one, the guiding principle should be to "handle with care and compassion."

As a supervisor, I strive to meet my supervisees' educational needs while supporting their professional growth. Building a supervisory relationship with Leo from the start is challenging due to his anxiety about working with children, his lack of prior clinical experience in this area, cultural differences between us, and the remote nature of our supervisory interactions.

Having practiced in the U.S., I am unfamiliar with Chinese culture and practices, a limitation that will continue throughout our supervision and has practical and real-life implications. For example, I lack awareness of disciplinary practices in Chinese culture. Are boys and girls disciplined differently? What are the cultural and legal boundaries of acceptable parenting? At what point does a form of discipline become culturally and legally unacceptable in China? Leo's role in navigating this complex terrain is crucial, and my guidance will be a blend of psychoanalytic knowledge, common sense, realism, and concern for a child who may be facing physical or emotional abuse from a disappointed mother.

Supervisors encounter unique challenges in remote, cross-cultural video supervision due to their unfamiliarity with the supervisee's cultural context. Even with their expertise, applying their knowledge in an unfamiliar cultural setting requires a reciprocal learning process. This mutual learning is not just beneficial but essential. The supervisor must convey psychoanalytic theory and technique while gaining insights into the cultural realities of the supervisee's practice. This situation demands caution, a willingness to learn from mistakes, and mutual learning between both parties. While success is not guaranteed, this collaborative approach can enrich the supervisory relationship, respect the patient's background, and promote culturally congruent treatment by honoring the supervisee's autonomy.

Through Leo's email communications, I became aware of his anxiety about beginning to work with children. Guiding a professional like Leo through these initial stages requires careful supervision. However, my role was that of a supervisor, not a therapist. It was essential to create an environment where Leo could develop new skills and apply theoretical knowledge to practical situations when working with children. This hands-on experience would help him grow professionally and alleviate his anxiety through increased confidence and competence. Part of this process might include understanding the role of broader countertransference about his patients. However, the reduction of his anxiety is incidental and does not change the supervisory relationship into therapy. Managing and working through these anxieties is the domain of his own analysis and personal reflection.

Another important aspect of this supervisory process was documenting and reporting Leo's proficiency in English. While Leo spoke fluent English, his accent and the rapid pace of his speech sometimes made it difficult for me, especially given my hearing challenges. I frequently had to ask him to repeat certain words for clarity. I took notes during the supervisory process, though I could not always capture his exact wording or syntax. My supervisory reports aim to represent his speech and ideas as accurately as possible, but I generally omitted instances of repetition and informal conversation. It is also worth noting that Leo conducted his sessions with his child patient in Mandarin, and he occasionally used Google or a dictionary to find the correct English translations.

When Leo provided a first-person account of what his patient said, I used quotation marks to indicate direct speech. I kept my supervision notes distinct from my personal commentary, which I included toward the end of each chapter. In my reports, I smoothed out minor discrepancies in our communication and refined the dialogue to minimize distractions for the reader.

Supervision: 2

Leo and I exchanged several emails as the session's start time drew near. Leo informed me that his Zoom was inaccessible due to heightened restrictions imposed by the Chinese firewall on Zoom communications outside China. He explained that he had to use a proxy server to bypass the Chinese firewall and reach me. Because of this setback, we frantically made alternative arrangements and were able to connect via Skype for our session. I, a computer novice, had to get assistance to install Skype on my computer. This adjustment underscored the importance of flexibility and adaptability in navigating cross-cultural supervision amidst technological challenges.

Finally, a frantic-looking Leo appeared on the screen.

> "I was sweating. I am so sorry for all the inconvenience. It is irritating that the Chinese government raises the firewall without warning."

"The Chinese government and the internet are beyond your and my control. Thanks to your efforts, we can now see and talk to each other here."

> Leo, obviously relieved that we overcame the communicational problem, settled down.

"Yes, I am eager to get started. But, before beginning child therapy, I want to discuss any special equipment I need, such as toys, children's books, and games. Do you have any comments?"

"When furnishing your office, it is crucial to carefully consider your preferences and the type of therapist you want to be. You have to provide toys and other items based on their age and treatment stage. For example, many children love playing games and being creative with drawing paper, crayons, or colored pencils. You can consider providing clay, a material used for centuries in China to promote creativity and relaxation. By thoughtfully selecting and providing these items, you can create a welcoming and comfortable environment for your clients to explore feelings and emotions and playful actions whose meanings you can interpret."

Leo got excited and imagined children making shapes with clay and mimed the clay-making activity. He quickly jotted down what I presumed was "clay" and "drawing materials" on paper.

"I assume I will be talking with parents to understand a child's problems for some time. I can afterward make my office ready for a child."

"Yes. However, it may not be a bad idea to furnish your office with child material so the parents can see you are ready to be with a child."

"Yes. Yes. When I imagine how I will start, I think I will talk with a child's parents first to understand the child's problems. I assume that a child will mostly be numb and silent. The parents may encourage the child by saying, 'Here is Leo. He will help you. Talk to him and play with him."

I asked, "Will the mom or dad be in the consulting room, or will you talk to the child alone?

"Not sure. Maybe parents will be in the room for a long time."

"Child work may occur when children accompany their parents to the office. However, child therapy involves meeting with the patient one-on-one and maintaining confidentiality unless the patient reveals any self-destructive or dangerous ideas. You meet with the parents periodically to provide a general update on the treatment and receive feedback. You are not the parent's agent to inform them about what the patient says or does with you. You are the child's agent. In therapy, the child may start by being numb and not talking. This resistance may continue for some time. Then, a child may play or talk about their symptoms and concerns. You relate this to the patient's symptoms, your relationship with parents, siblings, friends, and finally, anger, disappointment, or sadness with you and play characters. A child explores anger, disappointment, sadness, etc., in relationship to feelings for the therapist. You start by analyzing the symptoms, which may be the disguised representations of the problem. The goal is to have a child express the problem from a child's perspective, understand it better, and find a better compromise."

"You may come home one day and discover water on the floor. That is like a symptom. Later, after you investigate it, you may discover that a faucet was left open. Of course, in the beginning, you know only the symptoms—the overflowing water. Only later will you discover the reason for the symptom. That is just an example. Of course, there may be other reasons for the water spill."

Leo was attentive as I spoke. "Yup."

"What does 'Yup' mean?"

"I used to see a mother in therapy. She told me that her main problem was her thirteen-year-old daughter. According to my patient, her daughter mostly used aggressive silence. Always ready to fight and get into an argument. My patient wanted me to see her daughter. I said to the Mother that I was not a child and adolescent therapist. I met the girl once and talked to her about the refusal words, such as 'No,' that she uses with her Mother. The girl said, 'You don't know how hard it is.'"

Leo continued, "No. That is a powerful word. But talking with you makes sense to me. I have to learn to metabolize fantasy. Last week, before we spoke, I was afraid to start child work. Now I feel more ready. It is not so bad. Talking to you made me have the reverie about my patient's daughter. I also remembered my nephew, who is going to primary school. The words he used are popular internet words. (Leo uttered Chinese phrases that I presumed his nephew uses). These are harsh, high-tech stuff from the internet. The words are about criticisms of the food industry, which uses advertisements and tricks to get people to eat some foods."

"Coming back to starting to see a child. My office does not have good soundproofing. If I ask parents to be in the waiting room, they may hear what my patient and I talk. Maybe I can ask them to leave and return at the session's end to pick up their children."

"There are all good questions. You have to figure out what works best for you. Some people put music or white noise in the waiting room."

"Yes. I cannot wait to get started."

"You are advancing fast. Last week, you were fearful about starting. This week, you can't wait to get started."

"Yes. Moving fast, thanks to your help. Now we have to talk about your fee for my supervision."

"Yes, you have to pay me for supervision. I will do my best to teach you about psychodynamic analytic work with children. I know nothing about how treatment works in China and your financial situation. What do you think is a reasonable and fair fee per session and one you can afford."[40]

---

40 Traditionally, analysts viewed fee setting, establishing policies regarding vacations, sickness, and gifts, and announcing the rule of free associations as integral to laying the foundation of the analytic contract between patient and analyst. Setting fees in private practice is just part of any standard business practice. An analyst may set a fixed fee as part of a business proposition and expect the patient to comply and be in treatment. Analysts considered these aspects of the analytic contract exempt from scrutiny regarding unconscious, transference, and countertransference factors and devised fee settings as part of the initial contract that escaped analytic scrutiny.

However, other analysts view negotiating fees and the contract for psychotherapy and psychoanalysis as not just a practical aspect of the therapeutic relationship but also an integral part of the therapeutic work itself. Analyzeable unconscious, transference, and countertransference factors operate in such areas. Having trained for many years to become

Leo seemed thunderstruck and attempted several times to say something but could not bring himself to say anything.

---

its practitioners, analysts expect and deserve compensation for their services. For this group of analysts, whether a patient can easily afford or has difficulty affording the analyst's fee, a process of negotiations is involved in establishing the fee. Negotiating therapy fees is a delicate process that can influence the therapeutic relationship. Transference and countertransference issues related to money and fee negotiations are complex and multifaceted. An analyst might feel undervalued when a patient, in his opinion, chooses to advocate for a lower fee despite having the means for higher payment, reflecting on the patient's tendency to haggle as well as the therapist's sense of worth.

Conversely, therapists may experience guilt when setting or raising fees, especially with patients in financial difficulties but needing treatment, possibly due to their own beliefs about money and its association with personal values or societal status. Appreciating such dynamics might help them understand the specific transference or countertransference during the treatment. Analysts and therapists must navigate these feelings professionally to maintain the integrity of the therapeutic space and ensure that financial discussions promote the analysis and do not hinder the treatment process.

I was born into a Brahmin priestly caste, but for several generations, most of my family elders worked in professions such as medicine, education, and government service. Although my family moved away from traditional priestly duties generations ago, I was aware of their traditional role, which gave me a different perspective on payment for services provided. Brahmins, like those in my ancestral lineage, relied solely on voluntary donations (*daan*) and did not set fees for their services. They accepted whatever the individuals in the community offered, reflecting a cultural ethos of acceptance. My style of fee negotiations reflects my cultural background and is a source of personal satisfaction. I find great satisfaction in involving my patients in fee-setting, and I believe they treat me fairly in return. I have often considered a patient's financial situation and have devised a voluntary compromise that satisfies all parties involved. When patients actively participate in fee negotiations, they are less likely to feel like the fee was imposed on them. This facilitates better opportunities for analyzing the transference-countertransference dynamics concerning fees and money.

Accepting voluntary donations as payment for services rendered has deep cultural and historical roots in many societies. This approach reflects a profound ethos of trust and mutual respect between some service providers and the recipients of services. It can help foster a community spirit where each individual contributes according to their ability and receives according to their need. In modern professional settings, this philosophy can translate into a compassionate understanding of one's patients or supervisee's and the analyst's financial interests. Such practices honor the past's " services " traditions and enrich the present's analytic relationship, leading to a more personalized and empathetic approach to fee negotiation.

I applied my clinical-style approach to fee-setting and supervision. I initiated an open-ended discussion, which fostered a sense of active partnership with Ching, particularly in addressing the issue of supervisory fees. This collaborative environment allowed both Ching and me to openly explore different perspectives and work together towards a mutually beneficial resolution. This instance further validated the practicality and effectiveness of my fee-setting approach.

"Looks like you are having difficulty saying what's on your mind. Is there something said that you do not understand?"[41]

"No. I understand you perfectly. I understand the word afford. I am shocked by your kindness. I pay my other supervisor $ 100 per session. You have already helped me so much, and I treasure your input. I charge $ 80 for my adult patients. Maybe I will charge $ 25 for a child patient. I want to pay you at least the same, but that rate is nearly unaffordable. Part of me wants to say, 'How about $ 100 per session?' Part of me wants to say, 'How about $ 80 per session?' I have a hard time saying both these sentences."

"How about we settle for $ 80 per session?"

Leo, relieved, said, "Thank you. Maybe as I can afford more, I can increase it to $100."

---

41 I sensed that Ching was conflicted, unable to articulate his thoughts regarding what he wanted to pay me versus what he could afford. Similar to situations where he couldn't express negative emotions in Mandarin, he seemed unable to communicate with me. In Ching's inability to speak, a conflict was evident in his supervisory transference toward me. However, as Ching was progressing in taking steps to start a child case (which was his priority), the analysis of this conflict in his supervisory relationship with me seemed unnecessary. I noted it in my memory as an example of Ching's conflict. When the occasion arises, I could use it to help him better understand a patient's conflictual experience.

Supervision: 3

I fumbled with Skype's unfamiliar interface, trying to locate and accept Leo's call as the phone's distinct ringing echoed through the room. Finally, after a few moments of confusion, I found the accept button.

Leo's surprise was evident as soon as the call connected. "Very interesting."

"What is interesting?"

"You have colored stones in your background."

"What are you talking about?" I asked, genuinely puzzled.

Leo patiently explained that an artificial background with colored stones was behind me in the video call.

It wasn't until I zoomed in on my image and took in the now-expanded screen that I understood what Leo was referring to. Indeed, Skype had placed me in an island scene, with unrealistically vibrant colored stones behind me, reminiscent of an otherworldly landscape akin to something from Star Wars.

"I have no idea how this background got set. I do not know where the background button is. Can you help me?"

With Leo's guidance, I navigated through the settings and eventually changed the background, replacing the surreal island scene with the familiar surroundings of my own office. It was a moment of relief.

> "I prefer this one. I like you with your office in the background."

"I agree."

> "I spoke with a male and a female colleague to draft an advertisement notice to announce that I can see child patients in treatment. I am starting to equip my office so I can begin to see children. I got dolls, clay, wood sticks, and other items suitable for play. I am building the office in *my* (emphasis) way to suit my personality.

I recalled Leo's recent comment expressing his preference for seeing me with the background of my own office. "I am glad because you have to feel comfortable in your office. You have to be in *your* office."

> "I am working on my advertisement. When I finish it, I will send it to you. I am thinking of the practical realities of seeing a child. I am busy and have to figure out times in my schedule. I started thinking about my early life and felt a little nervous. As I began to prepare in my life to work with a child, I remembered the pain of my childhood because I did not have too many friends. I was not so good at play as a child. I was isolated. I became self-conscious about play."

"Recently, I played with my cat with a moving electronic toy. It is her favorite toy. We had great fun and loved to play. I had great fun. The "Little Me" came out, and I had fun. I thought I did not have much fun playing, but I was surprised because I had a lot of fun. The Little Me was like a bit of self-analysis.

"My analyst is George Schneider. I am starting to deal with the Little Me. When I was in primary school, I felt criticized by teachers. I isolated myself. But I am beginning to realize that I might be good at playing. I enjoy board and card games. I like to read children's books. I am ten years older than my cousin. We made up a "Finish the sentence" game when I played with him. One person says, "I am …" The other person or the first person can finish the sentence. I completed a sentence like this. 'I am brother Leo and am wonderful.' He completed it by saying I am an 'asshole.' We had fun playing."

"I am a little afraid because I cannot play with dolls. Maybe I will get some help from my ex-wife. I want to go back to my advertisement. I asked my Chinese colleagues working with children about the common symptoms parents bring them for treatment. Most problems seem to relate to difficulties in schooling and studies. A child may be breaking the rules at school or having difficulty adapting because of peer bullying. Many parents wait during primary school, hoping their children will grow out of their problems and seek help in secondary school. Some have trouble focusing at school. That is just a sample of problems. Do you have any comments?"

"Yes. It is essential to know the limits of your profession. Some troubles relating to difficulty focusing might be anxiety, in which case you can help them as a therapist. However, if the problem is primarily attention deficit or hyperactivity..."

"I understand. If the symptoms are primarily related to a medical problem, I must refer the child to a child psychiatrist."

"Yes. Because such a problem may require medications. Similarly, a child psychiatrist may be better suited to treat a child with severe depression and who is suicidal. Also, severe autism may require specialized school interventions."

"I need to be mindful of the problems I can treat and those that require other consultations."

"Right on. We are coming to the end of our time today. Making your office *your* own is a good idea. But I wanted to ask you about your name. Is your name the same in Chinese, or do you have a different Chinese name?"

Leo laughed. "You know me as Leo Sparrow. That is my English name for America. I picked up Leo from Leonardo Decaprio, and the name Jack Sparrow from the Disney movie 'Pirates of the Caribbean.'"

"Do your Chinese friends know your American names?"

"No. Chinese people do not appreciate my type of humor."

We both laughed.

"What is your Chinese name?"

"Ching Kong"

"What does your name mean?"

"Kong is the Chinese character for 'empty' or 'voidness' in Buddhist philosophy. This concept represents 'dependent origination' and aligns with serendipity. Ching is the Chinese name. When two Chinese-speaking people communicate in English, they might spell it as 'Ching,' but both understand that 'Q' is pronounced 'Ch.' However, for more accurate English pronunciation, the spelling is 'Ching.' "

If OK, Ching, we must be stopping."

"You have to give me your PayPal ID."

"We can take care of it after I get someone to help me figure out how to set it up."

My musings

Edelman's (1989)[42] biological theory of consciousness focuses on the concept of an 'active observer,' which challenges the detached 'God's eye view' found in Cartesian thinking and classical objectivity. His theory relates to psychoanalysis by acknowledging human individuality, the dynamic nature of experience, and the mind's capacity for adaptation and self-organization. Edelman (1992, p. 243)[43] described our universe as an "unlabeled world," where the signs, symbols, and names we use in language are arbitrary. However, they are crucial in linking our conceptions with our experiences and memories.

Labeling and naming the world is one of the foundational steps in organizing our reality. But what's in a name? From a cross-cultural perspective, names carry much more than their function as identifiers; they hold deep personal, cultural, historical, and adaptive significance. Names reflect the traditions, religious beliefs, and linguistic features of the societies they originate from. Cross-cultural psychology shows that while names can create common bonds across cultures, the processes and meanings behind naming vary significantly, shaped by cultural contexts. This diversity in naming processes can enrich our understanding of human experience, influencing behavior, motivation, self-esteem, social interactions, and communication.

In a globalized world, names can embody meanings that are self-initiated or assigned by others. Names are powerful elements of identity, representing both the interconnectedness of our global society and the uniqueness of individual cultures. They serve as a powerful tool in

---

42 Edelman, G.M. (1989). *The Remembered Present: A Biological Theory of Consciousness*. New York: Basic Books.

43 Edelman, G.M. (1992). *Bright Air, Brilliant Fire: On the Matter of the Mind*. New York: Basic Books.

creating a shared human experience that transcends cultural differences. A name often marks the beginning of a deeper journey, revealing layers of meaning that go beyond the surface. For example, Leo Sparrow (an assumed American name), Qing Kong, and Ching Kong are all different facets of the same individual, reflecting this complex interplay of identity and culture.

Supervision: 4

Wearing a casual gray t-shirt, Ching appeared on Skype, eager to begin our session. As soon as we settled, Ching spoke.

> "I have started equipping my office for child work. I want to show you my office." He gestured towards an upright couch covered with a modern, multicolored quilt with a pleasant and repeating pattern. "This is my favorite couch," he declared proudly. Ching then shifted the camera's focus to a rug on the floor showing a world map showcasing all the continents and oceans. "This is where the patient and sit can sit on the floor and play. I could ask a child, 'Where are you?' Or, 'Where would you like to go?'"

Next, Ching turned the camera to a stuffed dinosaur figure.

> "I got this at IKEA. It was a little expensive. Look at its big, sharp, and ferocious teeth," he remarked. "I believe it will be good to channel some aggressive feelings." Finally, Ching revealed a pink-colored stuffed girl doll with a smiley face. "I feel some discomfort with it. It has a smiley face and may be easy for a child to play with. Nice and smiling, but maybe too nice." He then looked at me to see if I had some comments.

"Maybe you are trying to say something like this: A movie actress may have a smiling face and show a positive smile on the screen, but in her private life, she may feel sad. Perhaps your discomfort is because, in the treatment, you want to uncover a child's true feelings. You want a doll to help a child express true feelings and not mask true feelings."

"Yes. But a child will know how to put others' feelings and meanings onto a doll."

"That's what I mean, Ching."

"You hit the point even without knowing it. For example, I advance because of our conversations. Now I am thinking the following. If I smile too much, like the doll, am I somehow modeling smiling to a child? A child may be more sincere, real, or true, and my smiling could make it hard for a child."

"You are concerned that a smiling doll or your smile may influence a child. Your frown, emotionless face, or any expression will also influence patients. However, you learn to work and try to understand how you influence a child. Last time we spoke, your cat enjoyed playing with you, and you enjoyed playing with it, too."

"I can play with dolls, toys, maps, or word games. I also put in an order to get a small child's table with a chair so that a child will have a reliable place to draw or play. I also got a stuffed dog so a child would feel like a friendly companion to protect them from scary feelings. I think you are trying to tell me that going behind the surface is important. There are many ways to do that. When I was four or five years old, my maternal grandparents cared for me when my parents went to work. In those days, there were no kindergarten schools in Bejing. I remember my grandparents were rich and had color television and a refrigerator. Those were luxuries that, in those days, most people did not have them. However, there were not too many programs on TV, but the Bejing Opera played on TV most of the time. I watched the Opera a lot. The Opera was grand. It only used a few objects but in a very creative manner. For example, a chair or a table turned sideways or upside down could represent a mountain, a ship, or a bed. I remember playing with objects in the house and imagining they were something else."

"I think you have had a long life of getting experiences and have many ideas for playing. From what you said, you could play at home and with your grandparents, but you became less playful at school because of teachers' criticism."

"In our conversations, you have already helped me to see things differently. I know anger, but you taught me about disappointment. Recently, I started seeing an adult female patient. Her parents were only interested in her studies and always asked how school was going. She wanted them to know about her feelings and real Self, but they were interested only in her study. I told her that maybe she was disappointed in her parents. She suddenly felt relieved and agreed and said, 'Yes. I feel sad. They knew so little about me. They focused only on my learning and not me.'"

"Good."

"My ex-wife is an excellent teacher. We were classmates in secondary school. She became a teacher, and I continued my studies. She is warm-hearted. I spoke to her. She knows about autism and is good at guiding parents through disappointments if their child has autism. She told me that since China started allowing two children per family, the second child has often had many problems. It may be anger, difficulty making friends, nervousness, or focus problems. I don't know what parents have children when they do not have the energy to take care of a child's emotions. They often are over-preoccupied with a child's education. They deny problems in primary school and won't seek treatment for their children early in development. Then, they feel upset when severe problems emerge in secondary school. My ex-wife, who keeps in touch with the parents of her children, tells me that parents who deny problems earlier cry after such problems emerge later in a child's life. I am imagining getting a four or five-year-old child for treatment. Who knows, maybe I will get an eight or nine-year-old child."

"Well, we never know what's in store for us. But for today, how do you feel about our supervision?"

"I feel you give me room and space. I feel I am developing with your help. You listen. You confirm my ideas and so build my confidence. I feel more sure of myself. What you said about the true Self beneath the smiling is a great idea.

Only the treatment process will show what is beneath what is happening now."

Well, you are progressing one step after the other. Soon, you will have a patient."

Supervision: 5

Dressed in a T-shirt, Ching began the supervision session enthusiastically, as if we were continuing from the previous one. He wanted to review an "advertisement" promoting his child therapy practice. Ching informed me that the original was in Chinese, which he had translated into English to get my feedback. He then shared his screen, displaying the English version of the advertisement. After explaining the reasoning behind his choices, we engaged in a discussion in which I suggested some minor adjustments. Ching incorporated these changes into the screen in real-time as we spoke.

> "I recently saw an impressive new anticancer advertisement that promised to detect cancer early and help treat it before the tumor grows. Similarly, my child therapy advertisement aims to identify emotional issues early on, enabling prompt treatment to prevent major problems in the future. I want to emphasize that our goal is to help children develop so that their curiosity drives their growth rather than obedience to parents or adherence to societal expectations."
>
> "I spoke to a lady colleague who works with children. She emphasized that the main problems seen in children in China are fighting and violence. I wondered what I would do if a child would try to kick me in the first session."

I said, "Your advertisement came from planning, effort, and teamwork. Here, most people start by saying their name and who they are. Of course, I do not know the standard operating procedure for how Chinese professionals introduce themselves."

"Good idea, I will make the change."

"You have much imagination about starting child work. If possible, it is good to do child therapy without getting kicked. However, such anticipations keep you on your toes and keep the job of child therapy or child analysis interesting. While promoting child therapy, you have to find your own way to deal with situations as they occur!"

"Yes. With your help, I feel things will work out. Still, it is a new kind of job. Before I started to work with CAPA (China American Psychoanalytic Alliance) and the Chicago Psychoanalytic Institute, I used to be in business. Now, I want to learn more about child therapy and analysis."

I said, "It is a change, which may explain your previous nervousness. You seem more settled and ready to explore working with children."

"Yes."

"I agree with your plan and understand what you want. Moving on, I want to discuss a different topic. I value our supervision sessions and want to provide as much knowledge and guidance as possible to help you become a proficient child therapist and analyst. I want to help you start your own practice, assist with clinical work with children who face challenges, and guide you in your interactions with their parents. Moreover, as our supervision has unique cultural and linguistic nuances, I'm interested in writing about it and presenting some ideas about our experiences. I'm also keen on helping the Chicago Institute for Psychoanalysis in its dealings with other candidates like yourself."

Ching responded as soon as I stopped, "Of course. I am thankful that you want to remember what we discussed and that you want to write about it and share it with your colleagues to help other candidates and the Chicago Psychoanalytic Institute. I agree. Do I need to sign some paper that shows my agreement?"

"Yes. I will send you a paper that you can look over and revise. You understand the consent is not final or cast in stone. You can change the consent document and offer modifications if you wish."

"I understand what you are saying. Please send it. I am willing to say, 'Yes.' I try to recruit candidates to join the Chicago Psychoanalytic Institute because I'm pleased with their high-quality teaching. I have already advised some of my colleagues in China to seek supervision from you or other skilled analysts at the Institute."

"We are coming to the end of today's session. So far, in our supervision, we talked about my anxieties about starting child work, setting up my office, getting toys that match my personality, mental preparation for meeting children and parents, and setting aside times when I can see a child."

"You are taking a series of steps to move the process to working with children."

> "In my previous job, my colleagues nicknamed me the 'gear' because I was known for helping to keep the process or job moving smoothly, much like interlocked cogs in machinery."

Reflecting on the various meanings of his name and what his friends called him, I said, "You know that Serendipity is Lucky; so, OK, Lucky Gear, we have to stop."

Ching laughed and said, "Goodbye."

Consent

Between the last and this supervisory session, I sent this draft of the consent to Ching.

The Child supervisee's consent for the use of material from supervision

Supervisee: Leo Sparrow (Ching Kong)
Supervisor: Bhaskar Sripada, M.D.

I, _____, confirm that I grant permission to my child supervisor, Bhaskar Sripada, M.D., to utilize the material discussed during our supervision sessions to study the supervisory process and for any presentations or publications related to this endeavor. In addition, I authorize Bhaskar Sripada, M.D., to provide supervisory feedback to the Chicago Psychoanalytic Institute, especially to increase cross-cultural awareness in the treatment and supervision of children.

Purpose of Consent

This consent supports Bhaskar Sripada, M.D., in studying supervision processes. In child psychotherapy and analysis, the candidate learns the clinical practice of child analysis or therapy under the guidance of a supervisor (supervising child analyst). They examine specific cases, focusing on the child's symptoms, conflicts, and family dynamics. The objective is to comprehend emotions, conflicts, and parental worries, aiming to craft suitable treatment strategies that promote children's growth and development. Supervisees strive to gain deeper insights into emotional dynamics, conflicts, transference, and countertransference within the analytic context while appreciating and addressing parental concerns during the analysis process.

In long-distance learning, where supervisors and supervisees come from different cultural backgrounds, negotiating cultural differences is an essential aspect of supervision. Since videoconferencing-based supervision is a new form of learning, there is a great need to understand cross-cultural supervision of child analysis, therapy, and supervision dynamics better. Providing detailed accounts of supervision sessions, particularly in how cross-cultural differences are addressed and navigated, is crucial for studying cross-cultural supervision in child therapy and child analysis. A description of child supervision can help gain valuable insights into the complexities of cross-cultural supervision dynamics by documenting the strategies, challenges, and successes in bridging these cultural gaps. These insights can contribute to developing guidelines and training programs that promote culturally competent supervision, ultimately improving the quality of care provided to diverse populations of children and families. Although psychoanalytic supervision is a necessary part of training, there is a lack of published material concerning the description of this process. This consent will aid in describing supervisory sessions, which can enhance understanding of the supervisory proces.

Explanation of Procedures

To help me start seeing a child patient, Bhaskar Sripada, M.D., will supervise me roughly weekly. If the case is suitable for conversion to child analysis, I will convert the child therapy to child analysis under supervisory guidance.

Description of Risks and Discomforts

Bhaskar Sripada, M.D. informed me that he would use my case material and our discussions to understand cross-cultural child therapy and child analytic supervision. Furthermore, Bhaskar Sripada, M.D. may use this material in presentations and publications concerning supervision for child therapy and child analysis. He has informed me that I may experience anxiety or be somewhat uncomfortable, knowing that he might use my supervisory case material and the contents of our discussion for presentations and publications.

Description of Benefits

My consent may contribute to understanding child therapy and child analysis supervision, particularly regarding cross-cultural dynamics and teleconference-based distance learning. This consent supports the Chicago Psychoanalytic Institute in devising improved teaching approaches, especially for candidates from diverse cultural backgrounds. I will not personally gain from giving this consent; however, this consent has the potential to advance the psychoanalytic study of child supervision and benefit future trainees.

Confidentiality

In any presentations or publications, Bhaskar Sripad, M.D., will not use my name; he will disguise the identity of all concerned parties.

Noncoercive Disclaimer

I understand I can refuse to consent at any time. Even if I refuse this consent, Bhaskar Sripada, M.D., will continue supervising me.

Monetary compensation

I will not receive any money for providing this consent.

Offer to Answer Questions

I have been encouraged to ask questions about my consent at any time, and Bhaskar Sripada, M.D., has offered to answer any questions concerning this consent.

_____

Supervisee's signature (Sign and date)

_____

Supervisor's signature (Sign and date)

Supervision: 6

Before starting the supervisory session, I sent Ching a copy of the draft of the consent document.

> Ching initiated the session by stating, "I read your document and have a question. The consent talks about converting a psychotherapy case into a case of child analysis. My question is, what if, for whatever reason, I cannot convert a case from psychotherapy to psychoanalysis? Then, it would be regretful because I would have spent a lot of effort without having a child psychoanalysis case. I also want to continue with your supervision."

"There is always some risk that you cannot accomplish what you want to do. Therefore, it is essential to carefully assess a child before commencing treatment. You may remember that we previously discussed that patients with severe conditions such as schizophrenia, severe autism, suicidal depression, or other organic problems are better suited for treatment by child psychiatrists or the school system."

> Ching nodded and said, "The initial child assessment is critical."

Ching also shared his experience with advertising. Ching revealed that the advertisement had about 102 viewers on the first day and 170 viewers over the week. However, no one had contacted him. He chuckled as he remarked that he had overestimated the influence of his advertisement. He planned to consult a colleague for potential referrals. He reflected on the societal challenges in China, where there is a significant need for children's mental health support but a lack of parental recognition of the problems their children face.

> Ching said, "In China, there is virtually no public recognition of children's issues on television, the internet, or daily life. It is a tragedy."

I replied, "Every society struggles with sufficiently recognizing children's problems." Ching concluded the session by affirming his persistent personality and reassured me that he would find a patient and do his best to help that child.

Supervision: 7

Between the previous and this supervisory session, Ching sent me an email confirming that he had a chance to read the consent form and liked it. I had drafted a consent to get his permission to use material from our supervision for future presentations or publications. I clarified that his consent would help in understanding video-based cross-cultural supervision of child psychotherapy and child psychoanalysis. In the email, Ching asked me whether he should sign his name in English or Chinese and use his Chinese or American name. The reader may recall that Ching used the nickname Leo. He also informed me that, in response to his attempts to get referrals, a parent contacted him to help her daughter.

Ching was wearing a denim shirt and looking relaxed.

> As soon as he came on the screen. Ching greeted me and asked, "How should I sign my name for the Consent?"

"Do you have any preference?"

> "First of all, I like the consent and agree to it. Like you, my previous supervisor also asked me what to call me when we started our supervision. Since I was a baby, my parents called me Ching Kong. That is who I am. But for my American psychoanalytic education and to make my name easy for others, I took on the name of Leo."

I said, "This consent is between you and me. I know you are giving consent, whatever you call yourself."

"I think any consent must be understandable by all parties and make sense. How about I sign my name both in English and Chinese? You will know it is me because of my English signature, and I will feel my true Self is consenting because I sign in Chinese."

"So, we have a deal?"

"Yes."

"OK. From now on I will call you Ching"

"OK."

———

Ching paused, hinting at a change in direction for our conversation.

"In our last session, you mentioned that reaching out to colleagues for patient referrals and advertising might prove beneficial. I took your advice and contacted one of my colleagues, who subsequently sent me a referral. As a result, three parents have contacted me, and I've already had a lengthy telephone conversation with one of the mothers. I genuinely believe this could be a promising case."

Ching shared his recent experience with a mother during a preliminary phone appointment. He could sense her palpable anxiety across the phone line.

"She explained, 'My daughter is eight, and in second grade. She had no issues in primary school, but now she is struggling. I am considering whether to have her repeat second grade or even go back to first grade.' "

"I asked the mother, 'What are the manifestations of your daughter's problems?' "

Ching, speaking as if he were the Mother, conveyed the depth of her distress, "My daughter cannot understand mathematics. Her classmates bully her, calling her 'stupid' and 'dumb.' I am ashamed of my daughter. I feel helpless. Recently, I slapped my daughter and said to her, 'Maybe you are stupid.' " The anguish in Ching's tone reflected the Mother's turmoil, highlighting the severity of the situation and the urgent need for support and intervention.

In the Mother's voice, Ching continued, "I know what I did was wrong. After I slapped her and called her stupid, we hugged each other and cried together. My daughter doesn't know how to make friends or play with other children, even those who don't bully her. She wants to play with a nice girl but feels rejected even before she tries to be her friend. Recently, she came home and started saying that the other girl was 'shitty.' I told her that maybe she was nervous because I knew she wanted to play with that girl. Then my daughter and I started talking, and she came up with a game in which she played the role of that girl's Mother, and I played that girl. My daughter, acting like that girl's Mother, scolded me for not being nice. My daughter needs help. If she sees you, how do you work?"

Ching reported that he told the Mother, "It could be that your daughter is upset because she wants to play but does not know how to play. She feels left out because her friends do not include her. By engaging in play together, your daughter and I can hopefully start to understand her problems. We can meet regularly to discuss her progress and develop plans to support her. However, it would be beneficial for you and me first to meet in person so I can explain how we can assist your child and address any questions you may have."

"We agreed to meet tomorrow to discuss further details," Ching continued, "but the Mother had a few additional questions. She asked if she needed to bring her daughter. Assuming the Mother would come alone, I replied, 'Maybe you and I can talk without your daughter.' Even over the phone, I could sense an increase in her tension. She explained, 'In the past, both my husband and I used to work. But after my daughter started having problems, I stopped working, and my husband is working extra hours. He's very busy and unable to help with our daughter's care. I'm the only one available to take care of her. I will need to bring her to your office.'"

Ching's understanding of the Mother's situation deepened as she shared her family's challenges.

Ching said, "My immediate reaction was that I would somehow accommodate to seeing both. It might be hard.

I must accommodate the Mother's anxiety and help the child."

"The Mother said, 'My daughter is a good girl. I will bring an iPad, and she will play on it alone. She will be quiet, too.'"

Ching said, "I will see them probably together, so we will all three be in the office at the same time."

I responded, "You remember when we discussed setting up your office? You said you wanted to set up your office in your own style. Similarly, do therapy in your own style. What do you think will earn the girl's trust: knowing what her Mother is saying to you and being able to comment on it, or being alone in the waiting room and imagining what you and the Mother are talking about?"

Ching was pleased and said, "Of course. We are all in the office together at the same time, so she can see what is happening."

I chuckled in response to Ching's cultural observation. "This is a kind of joke, remembering the world map carpet in your office," I remarked. "You wanted to ask a child: 'Where are you, and where do you want to go?' You will only have that chance if she is in the office with you! Not if she is playing alone on her iPad in your waiting room. What I mean by a joke is that I remembered what you said; it does not mean that is what you should do."

The light-hearted exchange added a moment of fun to our conversation. I intended to reaffirm that each therapist's approach is unique and tailored to the patient's needs. Ching nodded, but his relatively blank expression suggested he did not know what I was talking about. So,

I said, "Although you nodded, your face did not change. I am not sure if you got what I was saying."

> Ching nodded, acknowledging my previous comment. "I understood what you were saying," he began. "You were referring to the carpet with the world map, and how I envisioned interacting with a child patient." Then, he shifted the conversation to a lighter note, sharing a cultural observation. "This is also a kind of a joke, but true. In China, it is typical not to show your feelings on your face. That is automatic in Chinese culture. It is what I call the 'Natural Masquerade.' I have understood it after many supervisions and exposure to the West. I have it, but I'm aware of it." Ching paused, his expression thoughtful. "There's a more serious case of Chinese Masquerade, though. In this case, people smile even when they feel sad inside. Fortunately, I do not have this second condition."
>
> Ching continued, "What if the girl is so shy that she does not participate in the conversation with her Mother and me? Maybe I should prepare with paper and colored pencils so she can draw."

I said, "There are no fixed answers to such hypothetical questions. Your personality will shine through whatever you do during the treatment."

> Ching responded, "My babysitting history is returning to me. You have to play with the child and satisfy the parents!"

"Right on. We have to stop soon. What happened today?" I asked

> "I enjoyed today, especially when you confirmed my intuition that I should see the child and Mother together. It is what, in Intersubjectivity, they say is an 'encounter moment.'"

"Yes, in anticipation of encounter moments with the Mother and child."

Supervision: 8

Ching began the session, "I have had the chance to see the girl twice now. After the first session, I admit I was a bit nervous. However, after the second one, I started feeling more hopeful that I could help her. As we discussed last time, the Mother said she couldn't arrange for someone to watch the girl, so she had to bring her along. I thought it might be a good idea for us to meet together so I could also build trust with the girl. But when they arrived, the Mother whispered to me, 'I don't want her to listen. Let her wait outside.'"

"Yet, the girl could not resist. She peeked into the office, eyes wide with excitement, and exclaimed, 'Oh, toys! Oh, clay! Oh, pencils!' She grabbed them and went to the waiting room, staying occupied without any trouble."

"After the Mother entered my office, she provided a brief overview of the current situation and the girl's developmental history. She began by recounting her troubled marriage with the girl's father, which ultimately led to divorce. When the girl was just eight months old, her Mother, the girl's grandmother, fell seriously ill. In response, the Mother left her daughter with her husband and left town to care for her Mother. This separation lasted eight months, by which time the girl reached sixteen months of age. Upon the Mother's return, she found her daughter difficult to manage and unsociable. Concerned, she had the girl tested for conditions like autism or ADHD. Reflecting on our previous conversations, I couldn't help but feel a sense of apprehension. While I empathized with the Mother's worries about potential disabilities, I also pondered whether the girl's challenges stemmed from the unintended absence of her Mother during her crucial developmental months. I felt more optimistic after our second session. I'll share more about that session soon."

I added, "As we discussed, assessment and diagnosis are important and based on combined symptoms, history, social and family situation, and your feelings of optimism or pessimism as you gather all this information."

"Yes. By this point in the session, I was growing concerned about the girl alone in the waiting room. So, I politely excused myself from the conversation with the Mother to check on her. When I peeked into the waiting room, I found that the girl had arranged all the toys around her in a circle, like they were her audience. Meanwhile, she had made a clay fish, which the dolls seemed to admire."

Ching reached for his cell phone, quickly navigating through his photo gallery until he found the picture of the clay fish. With a subtle smile, he turned the screen towards me, revealing the colorful creation that had captivated the girl and her toys. At a glance, I could see the outlines of a multicolored clay fish and her capacity for play.

Ching said, "I told the Mother she had done a clay project, which I showed her. The girl entered the office and started exploring the area around my desk by herself. She saw a box and opened it, only to find another box inside. Since there was nothing in the second box, she moved on. Then she spotted another box and pointed to it, asking, "What is this?"

"I replied, 'It's a tea box.' "

"She then glanced at my cabinet and asked, 'What is this?' "

"I answered, 'My cabinet.' "

"She boldly opened it, revealing its contents, and exclaimed, 'What a mess!' "

Ching then said that the Mother chimed in and asked her daughter, 'Is it messier than our house?' "

Ching continued, "The girl moved on to another box and inquired, 'What is this?' "

"I told her, 'It's my cake.' "

"She continued, 'Where did you get it?' "

"I replied, 'At the supermarket.' "

"Chi asked, 'How much did the cake cost?' "

Ching continued, "The Mother then told her daughter, 'You're looking around all his things without asking permission. Maybe you want some cake.' "

Ching continued, "The Girl said, "See, my mom understands me."

"We stopped soon after that, and I am glad the girl felt her Mother understood her. Aware of the Mother's eagerness for another meeting, we scheduled an appointment before I could talk with you. I consulted with a colleague specializing in child psychology. Together, we devised a plan for the upcoming session. I proposed that the Mother wait in the reception area while I spent 15 to 20 minutes alone with the girl. I would tell her Mother to observe her behavior independently and see if she could play and talk because these are necessary for any treatment. Then, we would all meet and talk things over. Additionally, I planned to involve the girl in tidying up the office before her Mother joined us. It was a simple task to gauge her ability to follow instructions."

Ching began his second session report, "I outlined my plan to spend around twenty minutes alone with the girl before meeting with both of them together. They both seemed to grasp and agree with the arrangement. I explained to the girl that we'd tidy up the toys after our playtime before inviting her Mother in, to which she readily consented. As we commenced the session, the girl engaged briefly with the toys, clay, paper, and pencils. However, she quickly declared that she knew all the toys, and requested to know what else I had in my office. Recalling something from the waiting room, she described a bird made of folded and cut paper as a pretty bird. She wanted to make one herself and asked, 'Uncle, who made it?'"

I asked, "Who is Uncle?"

Ching replied, "Oh, she calls me Uncle. My girlfriend made the bird, but I did not want to reveal it to her. So, I hesitated to answer. Surprisingly, the girl confidently declared, 'I know who made it. Aunty made it.' Impressed by her guess, I praised her, saying, 'You are a smart girl.' "

"We moved from the bird talk to another part of my office, where she discovered a box of cars that I had thought might interest boys. However, she became incredibly excited upon seeing them and began enthusiastically playing with cars. We raced with the cars, and I noticed she was quite competitive. I remarked, 'You seem to enjoy competitions,' and she nodded eagerly."

"Amidst all the action and excitement, I couldn't help but break a sweat. She immediately said, 'This place is stinky. I'm not stinky. I had a bath just before I came here to see you. So it must be you who is stinky.' I chuckled and admitted, 'Yes, all the action makes me sweat.' "

At this point, Ching shifted his narrative from the session to address me directly. "I'm nervous. I want to behave like an analyst. I want to remain calm. I am calm when working with my adult patients."

I responded, "Child patients often evoke those feelings. You're there to help her understand, 'Why are you here?' "

Ching then asked, "Why am I (meaning Ching) there?"

"I mean, 'Why is *she* there?'," I clarified. "You will have to find some way to make her realize that she is there not simply to play with you but to understand that playing with you is a means to help understand her difficulties in playing with her friends. She is there not merely to play but to use play to work out her problems. Sometimes, your nervousness may be like her nervousness when wanting to play with her classmates who seem not to want to play with her. It will take some time before you can start translating the happenings of the session as relevant to her life outside of the sessions."

> Ching grew pensive. "I mentioned to you before that I was away from my Mother for some time and lived with my maternal grandparents. So, I, too, experienced some abandonment and had nervousness in life."

I responded, "So, maybe you have had the experiences that enable you to understand her pain."

> "Today was excellent," Ching remarked. "I felt the chaos of her life. I gained some insights into how her life and mine may be similar. I feel I can grow to help her understand the intrapsychic aspects of abandonment and anxiety. I ended the session with the girl and the Mother, saying that although the girl has problems with mathematics, she has other strengths. She can play and put away toys. I reminded them of the next appointment."

Supervision: 9

Ching, dressed casually in a grey T-shirt, started the session by saying, "I need your help." He continued by recounting the session he'd had with his patient. "I could see a smile on the Mother's face as soon as she opened the door to my office. The girl was also excited and shouted and waved her hands 'yes, yes, yes' to coming into my office. Putting her finger to her lips, the Mother motioned to the girl to calm down and said, 'Sh. Sh.' "

"I felt comfortable before the session, and looked forward to receiving her. I was in a calm mood. She came in and started to look at the various toys and play materials, and I waited for her to choose what she wanted to do. To improve the soundproofing of my office, I changed the door to my office. Because I had no time to dispose of it, the old door was still leaning against a wall in my office. My patient started to scold me by saying, 'Why is the door still there? You should have removed it.' She looked at the dolls in my office and said, 'I am not interested.' "

Ching then explained that he had purchased several Oragami paper projects, in which the girl had expressed interest in the previous session.

"There were several boxes of such projects, and about ten paper shapes were in each box. She was truly excited and asked if she could play with them. I told her that I got the paper projects so she could play with them. However, she opened the boxes, took out the paper projects, and went on to the next project without completing the previous project or reading the instructions. When my patient discovered the Origami paper projects, she told me her father visited her. They worked on paper projects, and he started to work on a paper parrot. However, the project was so challenging that he fell asleep and couldn't complete it. I thought she was having trouble managing too many options. Then she gave up on the paper projects."

"My patient then stumbled upon some toys that were new to her. Her excitement grew palpable. 'Look, Mommy cat. Look, Daddy cat. They are a couple.' She played with the cats in a manner that, to me, seemed like erotic involvement. Soon, she lost interest and made up a game with a car and a dinosaur. The dinosaur chased the car fast. It quickly caught up and looked like it would eat the car."

"When she played with the car and the dinosaur, she wanted me to play along. I did not know what exactly to do. I wondered if my play with her was too much. I did not feel comfortable. She noticed my change, and she also lost interest in the game. She went back to the paper projects. She found a bird project she liked. She is a girl who is careful about her manners and asked if she could take that project and work on it at home. I agreed. Then, she said her Mother would not let her play with projects before homework. She put it aside to take to her home when she left."

"My patient's interest changed more to ask me about our sessions. She asked, 'How much time do we have to play when I come to see you?' I said, 'Fifty minutes.' She said, 'That's not enough time. I need more time.' She went back to playing with some rabbit toys. She made up a story about a rabbit family. 'This is Father Rabbit, and this is Mother Rabbit. They have babies.' She started to make dinner for the Rabbit family. She asked me to help with the dinner. As she played, her forearm and my arm touched. She tugged my beard. I reacted and stiffened. She withdrew."

"We went back to playing with the car and the dinosaur. I wondered if the car should fight back or flee. I did not know how to continue the game. She noticed and engaged me by behaving and playing with the paper projects we had already played. This time, she wanted to do a peacock. She had trouble reading and understanding the instructions. She said, 'I cannot understand the instructions. Why don't you get your cell phone, scan the QR code, get instructions, and do the project?' Then she asked, 'Do you have a daughter? How old is she? Does she play?'"

Addressing me, Ching said, "She has so many questions. I felt she engages in difficult play or projects, then withdraws and tries to escape. She told me that her Mother said that she had too many questions. She asked me how much time we had left in the session. I said we had about ten minutes. She wanted to read the instructions to understand the peacock project. It was too hard for her. She wants to be superior but feels frustrated because she cannot do what she wants."

At this point, Ching took a drag of his e-cigarette and puffed a vaporous cloud.

"After this session, I briefly spoke to the Mother in the waiting room. The Mother said, 'She gets easily frustrated and withdraws from activities. She wants the Mother to complete projects for her. She relies on me too much. She often asks me, 'Will you always love me? Will you dislike me if I can't do it?' "

Ching addressed me, saying, "That's about it for this session. Do you have any comments?'

I said, "You started the session by saying, 'I need your help?' What is it you need help with?"

"How can I get her to stop withdrawing when she is frustrated, and to take on a challenge? Maybe I am too idealistic and expect too much."

I said, "You want to help her very much. We all want our patients not to get frustrated and take on challenges. Even with our help, change is something for a patient to decide. We do not control our patients' change but try to help them. We can tell them what we see, think, and feel that may be useful."

I continued, "What you have already told me is that she wants to come and see you, and she can play with you. She feels fifty minutes is not enough. Her Mother also smiled when she saw you. You have many ideas about her. She gets frustrated, like when she cannot read. She talked about playing with similar paper projects with her father and you. She seems interested in playing with mother and father rabbits and having babies. In foreign movies, the subtitles at the bottom of the screen give a running translation or commentary about what is happening in the movie. During the session, you can convey your ideas to her. For example, when she cannot read, she gets frustrated and switches to another activity. You felt uncomfortable playing her dinosaur-eating-car game. One play technique you could try is to think of yourself as an actor and your patient as the director. Ask her how the dinosaur is supposed to behave and do as she instructs."

Ching seemed delighted and clapped his hands to applaud my suggestion.

> "I feel strongly supported by you. You confirm my insights. I should not play spontaneously. I can ask her, 'What is the dinosaur supposed to do? How does dinosaur feel?' Excellent idea. I should watch her play, ask how she wants me to play, and comment on the play. Also, there may be similarities between her father and me. Thank you."

"OK, see you next week."

Supervision: **10**

"The last time I met my child patient, she started not being in such a rush to check out, and was losing interest in the boxes of toys and playthings in my office." Ching started as though we were in the middle of a continuing conversation.

I raised my left finger, indicating that I had something to say. Ching immediately noticed it, stopped talking and waited for me to speak. I said, "I think She, the little one, needs a name."

He paused a moment to ponder. By this point, we both recognized the importance of maintaining a patient's identity while using a pseudonym for therapeutic and supervisory communications. We also understood the complexities of Chinese names and the benefits of using a simple name for clear communication.

"Of course. 'Qi' is an excellent Chinese name for a girl. As I explained before, for English-speaking people, it would become 'Chi' in English Chinese for its proper pronunciation. Or, we could settle for 'Angel' for the Americans.' "

I laughed and said, "It is your call."

"Qi means Jade."

As a boy growing up in Hyderabad, India, I often visited the Salar Jung Museum with my family. Its Jade Room boasts one of India's public displays of jade. I remember the Jade Room included a fruit knife of Mughal Empress Noorjahan and a hunting knife belonging to Mughal Emperor Jahangir. The fruit knife is especially notable for its intricate design, with one end of the jade handle decorated with enamel to represent a parrot's head. Sir Thomas Roe, an ambassador of King James I of England, arrived at the Mughal court in 1615 and successfully negotiated with Emperor Jahangir, securing rights for the English East India Company to establish factories (trading posts) in Surat. As they say, the rest is history; this trading post subsequently expanded, and India became a British colony. China, too, endured the Opium Wars, which devastated the country. Perhaps I unconsciously tried to connect Ching and myself through the similar fates of India and China at the hands of the English. Yet, through the peculiar twists of history, I was now teaching Ching psychoanalysis using English. I did not share any of these thoughts with Ching.

Ching said, "Let us go with Chi."

"OK. Chi is a beautiful name."

"Initially, Chi relaxed when we met, and did not rush from one box to another. Maybe because I did not say or do anything, Chi seemed to get a little nervous and asked, 'What are we going to play?'"

Ching continued by remembering what we had spoken about in the last session, "I remembered that you said that she was the director and I was an actor, and it may be best to let her decide. I said to her, 'Not sure. What is your idea?' She got nervous and began to pour out all the dolls and anxiously said, 'What is new? Where is something new? Is there something new?'"

"I wanted to interpret that she was looking for something new. I said to Chi, 'You want something new?'"

"Chi was slightly startled by what I said but replied, 'We can play with what we have. Do you want to play?'"

"I replied, 'Of course. What do you want to play?'"

"Chi said, "How silly you are. Put this doll here, and that doll there.' Gradually, she organized my office like a classroom and said, 'I'll be the teacher. You be the student.'"

"We played many animal life games. Mommy Cat, Daddy Cat, Baby Cat, and similar animal games. After we finished, I said to her, "You like animal family games.'"

"She replied, 'Yes.'"

"That was mostly the session. Contrary to my initial fears, I feel quite comfortable. Your idea that I should let Chi direct me has helped me."

I replied, "Good. You have been seeing Chi and her Mother for diagnostic sessions, and it may be a good time for us to think of how to wrap up the diagnosis. I am not sure how they transition from diagnosis to treatment in China. But I will ask a few orienting questions, and you can answer them in any manner that makes sense. So, what is your understanding of the case? What are Chi's presenting symptoms? Are there any hints of Chi's transference? What are your recommendations?"

Ching seemed ready to respond as I spoke about his understanding and Chi's symptoms, but when I added the questions about Chi's transference, he became anxious.

"May I take some time to think?"

Surprised by his sudden anxiety, I burst out in laughter and added, "Relax. I did not mean for you to come up with some understanding you do not possess; what I mean is just to summarize in a one-two-three-point manner what you already know. Such an outline of your diagnosis is necessary when you meet and talk to Chi's Mother."

> Ching explained, "Chi struggles with anxiety and emotional development, especially related to safety and attachment. The mother's anxiety about Chi's math difficulties has grown into frustration, causing her to slap Chi out of exasperation. The mother knows physical punishment doesn't promote learning, and she feels self-conscious about her actions. This situation has made Chi anxious and fearful of her mother. So she asks her mother to help her and asks her mother too many questions."

I added, "Exactly. Additionally, between the ages of 8 months and 16 months, Chi and her mother were separated when the mother had to be away in a different city to care for her own seriously ill mother. I believe the mother loves Chi but feels embarrassed by Chi's problems and ashamed of her inability to manage the situation."

I continued, "Now, what are Chi's symptoms?"

Ching said, "Chi has anxiety. She gets easily frustrated; when she gets frustrated, she gives up and does not persevere. She has an inappropriate dependence on her mother and wants her mother to complete her tasks. Her anxiety has turned into a learning problem."

"Good. Has Chi's transferences manifested in any manner?"

Ching seemed anxious and said, "I need help figuring it out."

I said, "Chi referred to you as Uncle, and thought Auntie made the bird in your waiting room; that is your spouse. She asked if you had any daughters, and mentioned that she does origami projects with her father, similar to the ones she does with you."

"That is fantastic. You linked everything. Chi is curious about me. Maybe she has a father transference and wants to be like my daughter. Suddenly, I understand transference! She wants more time with me; she feels fifty minutes is insufficient! The process of discussing my impressions with her mother has already begun. After my last session with Chi, I spoke to the mother, and we are setting up an appointment to discuss my recommendations. Chi's mother sent me an article she read about parenting. The article dealt with problems with learning at school. The article said mothers may feel the problems are related to I.Q., but the real problems may be emotional. The article said that going to school for a child can be like going into a desert. When a child feels support and love from a parent, the child feels the desert has oases and that they can survive. However, children may panic at school if they do not feel supported. The mother wants to use psychological ways to use the mind. I feel the article is like a golden idea. She wants to discuss the article also when we meet."

Ching continued, "I feel hopeful that I can help Chi. I will tell her we can start treatment and negotiate for the best number of sessions the mother wants to bring her. I think the mother is not blocking me. She is working to find the best solutions for Chi. Today, I feel happy. I believe, thanks to you, I have begun to understand transference."

———

In psychoanalysis, transference and countertransference are crucial concepts. Supervision aims to facilitate the application of these concepts in real-world situations, and to the case at hand. A systems perspective reveals many parallels between supervisory and treatment processes. For example, facsimiles of the transference and countertransference between patient and analyst can also manifest in the analyst-supervisor relationship. This perspective facilitates developing ideas for explaining the patient's transference or the analyst's countertransference from supervisory events. Exercising optimal supervisory judgment is essential because excessive conjecture in supervision can be as counterproductive as excessive zeal in therapy. Therefore, tailoring, testing, and modifying these ideas according to the specific treatment scenario is critical.

I wanted to help Ching organize his thoughts before talking to Chi's mother. I asked him to summarize Chi's case, her presenting symptoms, diagnosis, transference, and his recommendations. In response to my query, Ching looked like a deer caught in headlights, asking, "May I take some time to think?" I laughed at his response because it was unexpected and contrary to what I intended.

It occurred to me that Ching's anxiety about responding to me might be related to a broad countertransference identification with Chi. At school, Chi experienced panic when dealing with math. Could Ching's frozen anxiety during supervision be related to his unconscious empathic identification with Chi? The way I understand my patients often relies on similar constructs. When I am in a session with a patient, I use what I see, hear, think, feel, and remember as an imaginary laboratory to explore the patient's Self. Of course, I must communicate any insight to the patient through a sentence or action. Clarifications help me establish simple ideas before using them in an interpretation. Patients may be surprised if their analyst interprets their symptoms or conflicts based on empathic identifications without adequate clarifications. Over time, I must teach Ching about using himself and countertransference identifications to understand a patient. For now, I let my speculation about Ching's identification with Chi's math anxiety rest and did not communicate it to Ching.

Supervision: **11**

King began the session, "This was Chi's third week of treatment. Chi and her mother arrived about ten minutes before the session time. I was taking down notes from my previous patient. I could hear Chi singing in a very loud voice through the closed door of my office. Her mother, concerned that she was too loud, was trying to shush her to be quiet. Chi quieted for about three seconds and then continued to sing loudly. Then, the singing ceased. After I finished my notes, I went to the door and said, 'Come in.'"

"Chi was in the adjoining bathroom, and her mother went in to fetch her, apparently getting her out before she finished her business. When anxious, I thought Chi might get involved in activities to calm herself down, such as singing or going to the bathroom. We sat down on the carpet. I felt relaxed and faced her. Perhaps Chi's business in the bathroom was not quite finished as she put her finger inside her sandals and smelled her fingers. I remembered that in the first session, I was sweating, and she referenced the bad smell not coming from her. Today, she seemed self-conscious and enjoying the bad smell of her feet. She then asked me for some tissue to clean the soles of her feet and the inside of her sandals."

"Looking sad, Chi said, 'After I saw you, a new baby brother was born. He lives near Beijing.' She went to the boxes with my dolls and threw all of them down, saying, 'Out, out. Get out.' She then got two rabbits, one with a skirt. She took the skirt off one of the rabbits and wanted me to put it on the other. As I was a bit slow, she called me 'stupid.'"

"She changed the topic and asked me, 'Did you get the paper to make the paper bird in your waiting room?'"

"I told her, 'Not yet. I ordered it, but it has not come.' I thought at that moment, 'I could purchase a bird's origami project and give it to her as a gift.'"

"She decided to play with the paper projects I had in the office. The paper project for a Penguin was simple, but she wanted me to start and complete it for her. I think this is how she plays with her mother. She asks her mother to do things for her."

"As I helped Chi with the project, she seemed happy. I told Chi, 'You feel happy if you can get me to help you.'"

"Chi replied, 'Very happy.'"

"Chi quickly added, 'How do you know so much about how a child feels?' Do you have another child patient after you see me?' 'How hard is it to become a therapist?'"

"After asking these questions, she was doing some calculations. I said, 'It looks like you are doing some calculations to see how much money I make.'

"Chi replied, 'How smart you are.' She then added, 'How old are you?' She then asked, "Why do people die?'"

"I said, 'Looks like you have many questions.' I added, 'Are you wondering how close to dying I am?'"

"Chi then lost interest in the questions and started building a large-sized clay nest. She used scissors to cut pictures of stars and animals and put them in the nest. She was cautious with the scissors and very proud of her cutting; she showed me her work and tucked the pictures inside the nest."

"Chi then asked, 'Do you like me?' She added, 'I like to play with you.' In an instant, she became careless about cutting the pictures, became violent with her project, and destroyed the nest. She then said, 'My mother beat me.'"

Ching demonstrated it by showing a slap on his forearm. Based on this demonstration, I understood the word beat to mean slap or hit.

Looking at me, Ching said, "I became sad and said to her, 'It must have hurt you.' She nodded"

I asked, "How do you understand your sadness?"

Ching replied, "I feel my sadness is something similar to what she feels. I feel there is something similar between her and me."

I said to Ching, "I agree, but what?"

"When I was a boy, maybe about eight or ten years old, my mother also beat me."

Overcome with feelings, Ching removed his glasses, reached for tissue paper, and wiped tears from his eyes. Enacting his mother hitting him, he took his right hand and slapped his left forearm.

"When my mother slapped me, I did not feel pain. I felt numb. Maybe she wanted me to be frightened. I feel that is how Chi feels when her mother punishes her."

I said, "You are right to say that Chi reminds you of your own life."

"Yes."

"You feel Chi, and you are similar. But you do not know how or where the similarity is. You need details of why Chi's mother punished her and how Chi felt. If Chi says she felt sad, you will have the words to interpret her sadness."

"Yes, you are right. I need exact data on what happened between Chi and her mom, and how she felt. I need to be scientific. Mark Levy says to be empirical. You are teaching me how to understand the similarities between her and me.

I said, "You mentioned that you thought you could give Chi the origami project of the bird. Your job is to facilitate treatment and stock your office with therapeutic materials. Her parents provide food, clothing, shelter, basic care, love, and gifts. That's not your job."

Ching said, "Thank you for that clarification. I did not have time to discuss my conversation with Chi's mother in this session. After our last supervision, I spoke to Chi's mother and communicated my understanding of Chi and my treatment recommendations. She agreed, and we decided that we would start the treatment and increase the sessions after some time."

My Musings:

This session provides a unique opportunity to delve into the profound clinical significance of Chi's words, transference patterns, and Ching's countertransference memories. Chi's therapeutic journey is a testament to her growing engagement and trust in Ching. Her use of familial terms like 'Uncle' for Ching and 'Aunty' for the bird display creator, whom Ching interpreted as his wife in Chi's imagination, underscores Chi's ability to form transference connections within the therapeutic relationship, a clear sign of a budding relationship with Ching.

In this session, Chi appeared sad, and spoke about the birth of a baby brother who lived near Beijing. After sharing this, she playfully created a large clay nest, filling it with star and animal paper cutouts. As she engaged in this nesting play, Chi expressed her feelings for Ching by asking, "Do you like me?" and then added, "I like to play with you." These statements emphasized her growing attachment to Ching and her desire for a positive, reciprocal response. However, her mood soon shifted, reflecting the complexity of her emotional state. She became agitated, destroyed the nest she had carefully built, and revealed, "My mother beat me." In this way, Chi demonstrated her trust in Ching by expressing positive emotions and revealing her vulnerability and destructive impulses, likely stemming from her mother's punishment.

During our discussion, Ching shared a personal memory from his childhood when his mother slapped his arm as punishment. This emotionally charged recollection highlighted his connection with Chi, suggesting he identified with her experience. This memory, shaped by countertransference, offered insight into Ching's empathic identification with Chi.

There are multiple ways to interpret this rich session. The analyst's personality and theoretical framework will shape these interpretations. Chi's destruction of the nest could be seen as a way of testing Ching—would he react like her mother did? This dyadic interpretation, which focuses on the dynamic between two individuals, explores the mother-child relationship, the patient-analyst interaction, and the theme of maternal transference.

A triadic interpretation, which involves the analysis of the relationship between three individuals, is also possible. Chi's sadness might reflect her response to the birth of a baby brother, a complex situation involving her father, and the new addition to the family. Dyadic and triadic explanations are not mutually exclusive. An Oedipal matrix, with unconscious feelings of rivalry and anxiety, could also explain her sadness and sense of loss related to her sibling's birth, as well as her fears of punishment tied to her provocative behavior.

The unconscious competition inherent in triadic themes—represented by human, rabbit, and cat babies in her play—could provoke anxiety. Returning from such triadic conflicts to a dyadic scenario, such as being physically punished by her mother, seems plausible. Chi's provocative and destructive behavior during the session invites the possibility of limits or punishment from Ching. His countertransference memory, combined with Chi's communication about her mother's punishment and her provocative actions in therapy, suggests that the theme of punishment is ripe for further exploration and interpretation.

Chi's play in the session with cats and rabbits engaging in sexual behavior, along with her displaced interest in the bird displayed in Ching's office, reflects her unconscious fantasies and the triadic dynamic at play. Readers may recall that Chi referred to Ching as "Uncle" and said that "Aunty" (his spouse) had created the bird. Addressing and working through these dynamics would require engaging with her fears of punishment and Oedipal conflicts. Although Chi's immediate focus was on the physical punishment she recently received from her mother, the underlying triadic dynamics likely surfaced due to the birth of her brother. This emergence, however, did not indicate Chi's readiness to address these themes in treatment fully. There were early signs of deeper issues, but they were not ready for analytic exploration. Addressing such dynamics gradually and carefully would require extended treatment and multiple clarifications. Dyadic and triadic interpretations may be considered independently or in an interconnected way.

I believe that Ching's identification with Chi, especially through his sense of similarity to her experience of punishment, was the most significant area for him to explore. I agreed with Ching's reflections, reinforcing this shared experience regarding the theme of punishment. His recollection of his mother's discipline, an immediate and first-person memory, could serve as a key insight, guiding his most effective approach with Chi. Ching's acute sensitivity to Chi's needs offered the best compass for determining when and how to intervene. Furthermore, an analyst's professional growth is best fostered through their own self-exploration and application of meaningful insights rather than simply following supervisory instructions. This approach helps to shape a more competent and authentic analytic persona. Ching could begin charting his own course, merging his clinical acumen with a student's eagerness to learn.

The psychoanalytic technique is a complex and subtle process, requiring the therapist to follow the patient's free associations, play, and transference while simultaneously reflecting on their own countertransference. The objective is to contain, work through, and interpret the unconscious meanings of symptoms, inhibitions, anxieties, and conflicts that impede adaptation. This process aims to reduce symptoms and anxieties, enhance insight, promote development, and improve relationships and life adjustment. This intricate work demands many small steps and a nuanced understanding of transference. The analyst's broad countertransference—the immediate, felt responses to the patient—often provides a reliable guide for making decisions about long-term goals and next steps. Unlike sporadic supervisory guidance, this personal insight is ever-present. Ultimately, an analyst must trust their own insights to navigate the therapeutic process effectively.

My reflections in this session concern understanding clinical transference and countertransference dynamics, where the therapist has primary decision-making power. However, Chi's disclosure that "my mother beat me" may introduce an additional dimension.

As a consultant to shelters supporting mothers and children affected by domestic violence, I have become keenly aware of the connotations of the term "beat" within urban American contexts. It often refers to physical abuse, frequently involving a male partner hitting his spouse, sometimes resulting in serious injuries. From my experience working with women who have endured such violence, I have learned that the term often implies being struck with a clenched fist, leading to visible injuries like black eyes or busted lips. However, the meaning of "beat" in other cultures, such as China, was unclear to me. Still, it raised concerns, leading me to reflect on the responsibilities of an analyst or supervisor when encountering such statements.

In some cultures or families, the word "beat" might refer to a form of physical discipline that falls under parenting and boundary-setting practices. In these contexts, it could be an unfortunate but common aspect of childhood, often summed up by the adage "Spare the rod, spoil the child." Alternatively, the term could indicate abuse, which requires legal intervention and brings the matter into the realm of child protection laws, surpassing clinical considerations.

Within the scope of psychological treatment, distinguishing between discipline and abuse is essential. While some forms of discipline may reflect attempts to set boundaries, they can sometimes cross over into abusive behavior, which presents legal and ethical concerns. Professionals must carefully assess these situations, ensuring the child's well-being is the top priority. If there is any indication of abuse, it is the professional's responsibility to follow legal and ethical protocols to safeguard the child's welfare. This is not only a legal obligation but also an ethical and professional duty.

I have worked extensively as a consultant for the Department of Children and Family Services in Illinois, and as an administrator of a hospital for adolescent patients. Through frequent collaboration with attorneys addressing child welfare concerns, I learned the importance of adhering to legal standards, which ultimately guide child welfare decisions within the judicial system. Professionals must be prepared to justify their clinical decisions in court, ensuring they align with clinical considerations and legal expectations.

Mandatory reporters—such as physicians, psychologists, social workers, and teachers—must report suspected abuse or neglect, not confirmed cases. Judges make the ultimate determination based on findings from child protection services. Therefore, failing to report after a child mentions being "beaten" constitutes a serious dereliction of duty. This standard applies not only in the U.S. but also in other countries with similar child protection protocols.

Historically, psychoanalysts have focused on intrapsychic dynamics, often minimizing the roles of interpersonal and societal factors. My reflections here take a different path, addressing broader societal concerns which may feel unfamiliar or too straightforward for some traditional analysts. However, psychoanalytic supervision, particularly in cross-cultural contexts, requires the ethical application of psychoanalytic theory, considering both the patient's and supervisee's societal and legal environments. Ethical treatment involves a fiduciary responsibility to the patient, ensuring actions that uphold trust, confidentiality, informed consent, beneficence, non-maleficence, autonomy, and justice. These principles are essential for maintaining trust and prioritizing the patient's welfare in every aspect of care.

Societies define legal terms to ensure a common understanding, transcending individual experiences with discipline or translation challenges. Establishing these definitions is crucial for maintaining clarity, unity, and fairness in both legal and clinical settings.

The State of Illinois defines child abuse as follows (https://www.ilga.gov/legislation/ilcs/documents/032500050K3.htm):

"Abused child" means a child whose parent or immediate family member, or any person responsible for the child's welfare, or any individual residing in the same home as the child, or a paramour of the child's parent:

(a) inflicts, causes to be inflicted, or allows to be inflicted upon such child physical injury, by other than accidental means, which causes death, disfigurement, impairment of physical or emotional health, or loss or impairment of any bodily function;

(b) creates a substantial risk of physical injury to such child by other than accidental means which would be likely to cause death, disfigurement, impairment of physical or emotional health, or loss or impairment of any bodily function;

(c) commits or allows to be committed any sex offense against such child, as such sex offenses are defined in the Criminal Code of 2012 or in the Wrongs to Children Act, and extending those definitions of sex offenses to include children under 18 years of age;

(d) commits or allows to be committed an act or acts of torture upon such child;

(e) inflicts excessive corporal punishment or, in the case of a person working for an agency who is prohibited from using corporal punishment, inflicts corporal punishment upon a child or adult resident with whom the person is working in the person's professional capacity;

(f) commits or allows to be committed the offense of female genital mutilation, as defined in Section 12-34 of the Criminal Code of 2012, against the child;

(g) causes to be sold, transferred, distributed, or given to such child under 18 years of age, a controlled substance as defined in Section 102 of the Illinois Controlled Substances Act in violation of Article IV of the Illinois Controlled Substances Act or in violation of the Methamphetamine Control and Community Protection Act, except for controlled substances that are prescribed in accordance with Article III of the Illinois Controlled Substances Act and are dispensed to such child in a manner that substantially complies with the prescription;

(h) commits or allows to be committed the offense of persons as defined in Section 10-9 of the Criminal Code of 2012 against the child; or

(i) commits the offense of grooming, as defined in Section 11–25 of the Criminal Code of 2012, against the child.

Conclusion

In this situation, distinguishing between discipline and abuse is crucial. Discipline aims to guide and teach a child, but when it crosses the line into causing harm or distress, it becomes abusive. The therapist must carefully evaluate the intent, the nature of the actions, and the outcome to decide the best course of action. This evaluation must include cultural sensitivity, recognizing that practices vary across societies. However, the child's safety and well-being must always come first. Any form of punishment that causes significant physical or emotional harm should be carefully scrutinized, and the child's mental health must remain a priority.

In advising Ching, it is essential to assess whether Chi's experience represents child abuse or a form of exaggerated but culturally common discipline. If abuse is suspected, following societal protocols, such as notifying child protective services, is imperative. If it appears to be normal but excessive discipline, Ching might guide the mother in adopting safer and more effective parenting strategies, which would ultimately promote Chi's emotional and physical safety. Regardless, therapy for Chi could be beneficial in addressing her anxieties—not only those related to mathematics but also her emotional reaction to the "beating" she mentioned. Therapy could provide a safe space for her to express and manage her feelings.

Ching's role as a therapist is not just about interpretation. It's about prioritizing ethical considerations and ensuring that Chi's best interests are upheld. Despite his cultural unfamiliarity, Ching must err on the side of caution when it comes to Chi's experience. His responsibility is not only to reflect on the psychoanalytic meaning of Chi's experience but also to follow the legal and ethical protocols regarding child welfare. Child therapy can offer a way for Chi to process her feelings, especially around themes of punishment and anxiety, fostering emotional resilience and trust. The gravity of the situation should underscore the importance of following these protocols.

Ching must pay close attention to Chi's communication about her "beating" and her mother's guilt, which might indicate the mother's awareness that her actions were inappropriate. In cultures where physical discipline is common, guilt often accompanies the recognition that the punishment may have crossed a line. Thus, this situation could represent an opportunity for Ching to work with the family to address healthier ways to discipline Chi and alleviate her anxieties. Regardless of cultural differences, ensuring the child's safety and emotional well-being must be the highest priority. This potential for positive change should motivate Ching and the family to work towards a healthier and safer environment for Chi.

The text *The Best Interests of the Child* by Joseph Goldstein, Albert Solnit, Sonja Goldstein, and Anna Freud provides important psychoanalytic insights into child welfare. It underscores the idea that no child's cry for help should be ignored, regardless of cultural or societal context. Ching must, therefore, take Chi's words seriously and assess her situation thoroughly. By doing so, he can act in Chi's best interests, ensuring her safety and supporting her psychological development that aligns with legal obligations and ethical standards.

Supervision: **12**

Ching began the session, "I have a report and a question. Which option should I choose first?" He looked at me to see if I indicated any preference. Noticing that I did not, he continued, "O.K. Report goes first."

"Gradually, there isn't much new to report. Chi plays less chaotically now and is calmer. She is less hyperactive. Chi is more like a typical eight-year-old girl who is more used to me and my office routine. She comes into the office. She takes off her shoes. She sits on the rug. She plays. A few days ago, she came to see me in the office, sat on the couch, and wanted to talk. 'I saw my little newborn brother,' she said. As Chi spoke, I realized it was her cousin, not her brother. Her maternal aunt had a baby boy. In Chinese culture, brothers and cousins are referred to by the same name since they are from the same generation."

I said to Ching, "Thank you for that clarification. Last session, I thought that a baby brother was born to Chi's father."

"I, too, was confused. Returning to this session, the more we talked about the baby, the more curious she became.

She asked me, "What did you look like when you were born?"

"I said to Chi, 'I do not know because I cannot remember that far back.'"

"Then Chi asked, 'How did your daughter look when she was born?'" She was very curious, and I had previously told her I had a daughter.

"Chi fired away several similar questions, like 'How many children do you have?' And 'How many other child patients do you have?'"

"As you know, Chi is the only child patient I have. I told her that she was very curious."

"She wanted to play but could not find much interest in playing with the dolls, animals, Origami projects, or clay. I keep a small glass jar of peanuts in my office. Before Chi came to the session, I threw an empty glass jar of peanuts in the garbage can. She looked around for things to play with and found this empty glass jar in the garbage can. Chi wanted to play with it and make the drink "Coke." She started by putting clay in it, and the process dropped bits of clay on the carpet. Now, she wanted to put some water in it and shake it. I knew it would get messy, so I suggested she put imaginary water, play with pretend water, and drink it with a pretend straw. She was agreeable, played with making an imaginary coke concoction, and talked about various topics."

"Chi was curious about the other kids I treat. I couldn't give her an answer. I do not have any other child patients, and I have not responded. She said, 'Why don't you answer me?' Then she asked if I enjoyed playing with her.

I told her, "Yes." After that, she started thinking about AI (Artificial Intelligence). She said that someday, AI might take over my job."

"I then asked Chi if she was worried that AI might make me jobless. How would life be if she could not visit me anymore?"

"Chi's talking and mood became playful. She wanted to play a game with a cat and a car toy. She gave me the cat toy and told me to try to catch the car toy in her hand. But whenever I almost caught it, Chi quickly hid the car toy behind her. The game became more active. And when I tried to make the cat toy reach the car toy, she pushed me away firmly with both her feet."

"I had a thought and shared it with her. I said, 'This game where the Cat chases the Car is similar to your struggle with math. When you play, you're actually pushing me away and covering up how scared you are of facing math.'"

"Chi said, 'How can you be so smart to know my mind and how I hide my problems? But now, I want to play with a paper project.'"

"Chi took out an Origami kit. It was in a plastic bag that was hard to open. She got frustrated and tried to tear the plastic with her teeth. I noticed she seemed mad because she couldn't open it. I said, "Because you can't open it, you are angry.'"

"Chi shook her head 'No' when I said this. Then I guessed she wanted to show she could open it herself and told her so. Chi agreed. Then, she asked for my help to open the plastic, and I helped her. Afterward, Chi was calm, read the directions, and folded the paper according to the instructions. She made four folds, but then it was time to stop. I suggested she take the Origami home; maybe her dad could help her finish it. She was glad, and left the session with a smile on her face."

"I noticed that working with Chi is useful in understanding one of my adult patients."

I asked, "How so?'

"Many years ago, I began treating a nineteen-year-old woman when she started. She was involved with a man who seduced her into a harmful and controlling S and M relationship. She became a sexually enslaved person, and he was sadistic toward her. She felt she had no control in this relationship as if someone else's hands were molding her like clay. However, as time went on, the man started to depend on her, which, in a way, gave her some control back.

"In the treatment, she realized that her submissiveness gave her power; it was through her submissiveness that she made him dependent on her. I interpreted this as her clay technique, being submissive to him on the surface, which gave her power over him but kept her in a bad relationship. During my treatment, she was able to break away from the relationship. She's now with a new boyfriend and in a healthier situation, and without any sadomasochism. She is now struggling because she is unsure if she should share her past struggles with her new partner. I feel that both Chi and this patient invite, or allow, a controlling relationship to maintain attachment unconsciously."

I asked, "Yes. You began today by saying you had a question. What is your question to me?"

Ching replied, "Can I interpret Chi's worry that I will not punish or put her down because of her misbehavior?"

"Why do you have this doubt?"

"I am not sure whether it is possible to interpret a child's conflicts. Maybe positive experiences, in treatment, rather than interpretations, are a better way to solve problems."

I said to Ching, "You've asked a good question. Understanding Chi's actions and problems is based on her development, emotional issues, family life, and your ability to explain your thoughts clearly. For example, when she kicks you or breaks something valuable, she may be trying to get your reaction; this expectation may be similar to what she expects from her mother. But it's important to remember that psychoanalysis is a talking cure. It's a method that uses conversation to heal. For us, talking and playing are the best routes if they are available."

"I understand." Reaching for a tissue, Ching wiped off the sweat from his brow.

"We do not have much time available. I wanted to bring up something. In the last session, you reported that Chi said that her mother 'beat' her."

"Yes, I remember."

"Chi talked to you in Chinese while you were together. I'm not familiar with the Chinese language, culture, or traditions. The term 'beat' can mean different things when used by a girl. For example, Chi might be overstating if her mother tapped her wrist and scolded her not to do something. Alternatively, Chi might actually mean that her mother struck her forcefully. Which situation do you believe it was?"

Without any hesitation, Ching said, "It was a violent slap. And the mother had hit her many times in the past."

I said to Ching, "In Illinois, a state in the U.S., certain professionals like doctors, therapists, psychologists, social workers, and teachers are required by law to report if they suspect a parent, guardian, or anyone else is abusing a child. It means that if such a professional notices any signs of physical or sexual abuse or neglect, or if they hear about it from the child or someone else, they must immediately report it to authorities. The Department of Children and Family Services will then check to see if the child is indeed being abused or neglected. This rule is in place to help protect children from harm."

I continued, "You were present and heard Chi. There's a saying in English that goes like this: 'If a tree falls in a forest and no one is around to hear it, does it make a sound?'"

Ching paid close attention and replied, "I understand. It cannot be that after Chi has spoken, it is like nothing happened. I heard what she said and will never forget it. I've had so much to share with you but didn't get to talk about my time with Chi's mother. I apologize for that.

Here's a brief account: When I first met her, she confessed to hitting Chi and was remorseful. She wanted to stop this behavior. Her decision to get help for Chi was partly to deal with her own issues of losing control."

"I spoke to Chi's mom and said, 'You love Chi. You cannot bear it when Chi struggles at math and gets teased. You can't hide your disappointment and feel powerless, just like Chi. Being a single mom is hard, and you carry a lot of stress. You don't mean to hurt Chi; you're looking for ways to stop it. You could use some support, too. Remember, hitting doesn't fix anything; it makes Chi more anxious and scared."

"Chi's mother is working on not hitting Chi anymore. She promised to keep me updated on her progress by sending messages. Since our agreement, she hasn't hit Chi, and she continues to send updates. I plan to discuss this with my colleagues working with children to understand how they handle similar cases. Additionally, I'll research the legal aspects of these situations."

"I'm pleased by your follow-up. What did you learn from our session today?"

Ching continued, "Well, first, it seems you agreed with my interpretation that Chi is keeping secrets about the car and pushing me away, like when she kicked me."

"That's right. It's good you're sharing your observations with her. If you're right, she'll confirm it. If not, she'll correct you, and that's how you'll learn."

"Your idea about interpreting her fears in the treatment is good. I could tell Chi after she makes a mess, 'Maybe you're worried I'll judge you like your mother does or embarrass you like she does.'"

"Exactly. Right, Ho."

My musings

When I began this reflection, I aimed to adopt a conversational yet insightful tone, offering readers a window into a supervisor's thought process during psychoanalytic sessions. However, it soon became clear that supervision touches on many critical aspects of psychoanalysis. I reflected on the profound contributions that have shaped the field, which weighed heavily on my mind. Initially, I intended to write freely, expressing my thoughts and feelings without overthinking.

However, the desire to honor the teachers and pioneers who have contributed to psychoanalytic literature around process and interpretation somewhat stifled that freedom. I became concerned that my writing might become overly formal, burdening the reader. As a result, this reflection feels more labor-intensive than I had hoped, though it explores supervision's clinical intricacies in sufficient detail. For ease of reading, I opted to omit citations, pointing readers instead to the rich body of psychoanalytic literature that exists for further study. I divided my thoughts into sections, breaking the experience into distinct parts.

As a supervisor, the pivotal task is to discern when a candidate's growth is best supported by building upon their own insights and approaches, and when it is necessary to introduce new concepts or ideas. This responsibility carries significant weight, as the former approach requires an understanding of the candidate's personal frameworks, while the latter involves presenting knowledge or techniques unfamiliar to the candidate.

Readers may recall that after session eleven, I reflected extensively on Chi's account of her mother beating her, even referencing the Illinois definition of child abuse and the obligations of mandatory reporters to act on suspicion alone. In this session, I alluded to Bishop George Berkeley's question, "If a tree falls in a forest and no one is around to hear it, does it make a sound?" Ching's quick and thoughtful response reassured me.

Understanding the complex dynamics between a parent's unresolved trauma and how it manifests in their relationship with their child is essential for promoting healthier family interactions. While such reactions may be deeply entrenched and difficult to change, acknowledging these patterns, developing better communication, and adopting new coping strategies can lead to meaningful improvements in parent-child dynamics, instilling a sense of hope and optimism.

This does not mean that deeply rooted trauma is insurmountable. I have witnessed abusive mothers with long histories of intergenerational trauma gradually reduce, and sometimes even cease, their punitive behaviors through therapy. Acknowledging and understanding these patterns is a crucial step in the therapeutic process. Still, I understood that managing Chi's mother's pattern of punishment would be no simple task. To prepare Ching, I asked him what he would do if Chi mentioned again that her mother had beaten her.

In this session, Ching shared a game Chi played with him. She challenged him to find a toy car she was holding, but when he tried, she hid the car from him. Ching interpreted this as Chi concealing something from him. This was an interpretation of her overt play, though it did not delve into the underlying emotional content. By bringing attention to the meaning behind her actions in play, Ching helped Chi realize that her behaviors held significance. He intended to explore her underlying concerns later, specifically her worry that Ching, like her mother, might judge or embarrass her. He also believed I shared his interpretation.

What is a psychoanalytic interpretation? What is an interpretation in the context of psychoanalytic supervision?

The debate surrounding the value of interpretations in psychoanalysis is a nuanced one. Some analysts view interpretations as essential tools that unlock deeper understanding and insights for the patient. These interpretations serve as milestones on the psychoanalytic journey, creating connections between previously disjointed aspects of the patient's psyche. On the other hand, some argue that the therapeutic relationship and the experience of being analyzed carry a profound transformative power, potentially more significant than the interpretations themselves. This view prioritizes the process over content, suggesting that simply engaging in psychoanalysis can bring about a powerful change in the patient's internal world.

At this point, a comparison between a photographer and an analyst might be instructive. To capture a portrait, a close-up, or the night sky, a photographer chooses from various lenses and settings to present the subject in the most favorable light for the intended picture. Similarly, a psychoanalyst selects the most appropriate theoretical framework, considering their expertise and the patient's circumstances, to shed light on a patient's situation. Each theoretical framework functions like a lens, sharpening focus on certain areas while blurring or obscuring others. This deliberate choice aims to enhance understanding and facilitate insight—whether in photography or psychoanalysis.

In both photography and psychoanalysis, chance plays a significant role, and the outcome remains uncertain. A subject may blink, resist, or simply accept an interpretation, while an analyst may misjudge the timing or intensity of their intervention. Yet, the analyst's ability to choose the right "lens," or interpretation, is critical. When successful, it can lead to profound insights and significantly advance the therapeutic process, adding an element of unpredictability and excitement to the journey.

A single situation can yield multiple interpretations. Analysts may view the same scenario differently with their unique personalities, favored theories, and individual perspectives. This diversity of views resembles a marketplace of ideas, where debates among analysts—and between analysts and patients—add to the richness of understanding. Such discussions ultimately refine interpretations to better resonate with and assist the patient. This plurality enriches the interpretative process, deepening our grasp of complex situations.

Interpretations consciously bridge known ideas connected by unconscious links. They bring coherence to otherwise disconnected thoughts within the analysis. Through this process, unconscious material is made conscious. A simple interpretation connects two established elements, building on previously clarified and mutually understood meanings. It's akin to fitting two puzzle pieces together where the connection is already well-defined.

Complex interpretations, however, uncover deeper layers of meaning. Here, the analyst must weave a more intricate web, linking multiple elements that may not have immediate conscious connections. This involves navigating a network of associations, emotions, and thoughts, and constructing a narrative that captures the multifaceted nature of the subject's experience. Whether simple or complex, interpretation is a dynamic, evolving, and iterative process, with each new insight building on the last, guiding the analysis toward greater clarity and progress.

In psychoanalytic theory, dyadic and triadic interpretations serve as frameworks for understanding the intricate emotional dynamics within relationships. Dyadic interpretations, focusing on two-person interactions, often shed light on the foundational elements of trust and dependency, reminiscent of the bond between parent and child. Here, the emphasis is on the parent's ability to empathize with and manage the child's emotional states, such as distress, discomfort, and anguish. On the other hand, triadic interpretations introduce a third party, bringing to the fore the multifaceted dynamics of competition, affection, and rivalry typical in a family setting involving a child, mother, and father. For practitioners in training, it is essential to approach these interpretations not as orthodox beliefs but as testable ideas. When evaluated and beneficial, they are integrated into the method of analysis. All interpretations aim to achieve psychological insight, heal traumas, and promote growth and development.

While an interpretation is expressed as a sentence or utterance by the analyst, its effectiveness is deeply rooted in the conditions that exist before and after the interpretation. The pre-interpretation conditions, such as the atmosphere of the analytic relationship and the patient's psychological mindedness, play a crucial role in shaping the impact of the interpretation. The patient's ability to use free associations and express themselves freely significantly influences the effectiveness of an interpretation. The success of the post-interpretation exploratory process often hinges on the dialogue and well-tuned compromises between the patient and analyst, allowing the patient to shape a more suitable course of action and potentially fostering a more adaptive organization of the self.

Some interpretations may be successful immediately after being presented to the patient; this is often rare in analysis and sometimes may represent mere compliance by the patient. Immediate acceptance of an interpretation does not necessarily equate to a deeper understanding or integration of the insight. In psychoanalytic practice, the process of interpretation is complex and multifaceted, requiring time for the patient to reflect and internalize before any meaningful change can occur.

An interpretation introduces a novel perspective that may lead to patient insights, sparking uncertainty, surprise, and curiosity; this can trigger new predictions and memories in the patient. However, the effectiveness of the analysis is not solely dependent on the patient's readiness to explore their unconscious motivations. Equally important is the analyst's skill in negotiating and managing the implications of an interpretation, which can significantly influence the outcome of the analysis.

It is essential to note the difference between interpretations in clinical and supervised analyses. In clinical psychoanalysis, the analyst's interpretation is deeply rooted in the familiar grounds of the analyst's Self, and is automatically in tune with the analyst's belief and prediction systems. The analyst is intimately familiar with details of the patient's history and associations, and is a personal witness to the transference-countertransference dynamics. This differs significantly from supervised analyses, where a supervisor typically influences the analyst's interpretation and involves an external presence that, although helpful and guiding, is not internally derived.

The supervisor's role is of utmost importance in assessing and enhancing the candidate's psychoanalytic education. Their focus on a specific patient case, rather than instructing them in psychoanalytic theory, is a crucial aspect of their work. While transference toward the supervisor may emerge, the candidate's communications in supervision are not free associations; the relationship is framed as a learning-teaching mentorship, not a therapeutic one. Analyzing the candidate's transference falls outside the supervisor's scope and belongs to the candidate's personal analysis or self-reflection.

However, the supervisor may still consider the candidate's overall countertransference as a valuable perspective on the case. The candidate's countertransference may reflect the patient's self or object representations. This perspective, when considered, can provide useful insights into the case. Occasionally, the candidate's transference toward the supervisor can parallel their countertransference toward the patient, revealing dynamics at play in the treatment. When such parallels are evident, the supervisor might bring them to light to assist in understanding the case. Yet, these insights remain somewhat theoretical and may not always be directly applicable due to their distance from the patient-analyst relationship.

Sometimes, a candidate may idealize the supervisor's viewpoints and feel compelled to adopt suggested interpretations, especially due to the supervisor's extensive clinical experience. This can lead the candidate to try interpretations without fully grasping their implications. Even without idealization, the desire to succeed in their training may result in compliance. For instance, Ching interpreted Chi's hiding a car as reflecting her desire to keep secrets from him. Ching also believed I endorsed his interpretation, an assumption rooted in a history of idealization. In supervision, such idealizations are typically left unexplored unless they interfere with the case or the supervision process.

From a systems perspective, it's possible to identify a parallel process between treatment and supervision. In this view, the dynamics between Ching and me in supervision could mirror the treatment relationship between Chi and Ching. Ching's expectation of my agreement might echo Chi's desire for Ching's approval. This assumes a parallel identification between Ching and Chi, where I stand for Ching. Based on psychoanalytic and systems theories, such theoretical formulations require Ching's communication and application in treatment to determine their relevance or applicability.

Psychoanalytic or supervisory events can be understood from various perspectives. A topographic lens differentiates between unconscious, preconscious, and conscious processes. A dynamic lens explores underlying conflicts. A structural approach focuses on the id, ego, and superego. Object-relations theory examines activated internal representations, while self-psychology emphasizes empathy, idealizations, selfobjects, and self-concept. Intersubjectivity highlights the shared psychological space between supervisor and candidate, while a genetic perspective traces the historical roots of present dynamics. Resistance interpretation uncovers patient avoidance, and hermeneutics seeks to decipher underlying meanings. The transference perspective reveals how past relationships shape present ones, while an adaptive perspective evaluates how these dynamics affect real-world functioning. A developmental lens links personal growth to developmental milestones, and a neuroscience-based economic view compares predictions and sensory input to assess prediction error or surprise. Together, these perspectives offer a comprehensive framework for understanding psychoanalytic supervision.

In supervision, intellectual and emotional autonomy is crucial for candidates. While supervisors offer insights and interpretations, these should spark independent thought rather than serve as directives. Candidates must critically evaluate these suggestions, weighing them against their own research and theoretical inclinations. This fosters a dynamic intellectual exchange, ensuring the candidate's analytical approach remains robust and personally authentic.

Supervisors face the delicate task of tailoring interpretations to the candidate's level of experience. While they must introduce new interpretative techniques, they must also ensure these methods are well-understood. Overly complex interpretations risk being applied prematurely or superficially. The true success of supervision often becomes clear in the long term, reflected in the patient's progress and the lasting impact on the candidate's development.

A supervisor may propose an interpretation that surprises the candidate or differs from their perspective. While the supervisor's interpretation may be theoretically sound, the candidate might struggle to implement it effectively if unprepared or disagrees with its rationale. Thus, it is often more beneficial for the supervisor to help the candidate cultivate a pattern of interpretation that aligns with their analytic style.

My goal as a supervisor is to enable Ching to offer Chi meaningful insights based on his understanding of her situation. Following an interpretation, a dynamic process called "analytic working through" occurs between patient and analyst. This phase helps transform the interpretation into practical insights. As patients assimilate these changes, they demonstrate new patterns of memory and behavior. The analyst's role extends beyond offering interpretations—it involves maintaining an ongoing dialogue to support the patient's exploration of new perspectives. A successful post-interpretation process often involves dialogue and compromise, allowing the patient to choose the most appropriate path forward.

In summary, the candidate's communications in supervision provide insight into their understanding of the patient, the patient-analyst relationship, and their level of empathy. These communications also reveal important personal information about the candidate, which helps uncover broader countertransference dynamics and object representations. While such communications are rich in psychodynamic content and may include transference toward the supervisor, they remain distinct from free associations.

The supervisor evaluates the candidate's grasp of psychoanalytic theory, ability to apply theory in clinical practice, and empathy for the patient. The supervisor also assesses the candidate's capacity for self-initiated interpretations. This evaluation helps determine the balance between encouraging the candidate's independent analytic efforts and introducing new theoretical approaches.

Supervision: 13

When Ching's Skype screen opened, no one was there. In a few seconds, Ching appeared and, as he sat in front of the screen, said, "Sorry. It just started to rain, and I was closing the windows. Chi's mother called me the evening before her appointment to tell me that she was sick and running a fever, and needed to cancel Chi's appointment. Because I do not have any sessions to report, I will take this opportunity to talk about Chi's mother."

Ching then delved into a detailed account of Chi's mother, highlighting her complex nature. He initially perceived her as anxious and distant, a perception that was reinforced when she shared about her unsuccessful marriage with Chi's father. The conversation also touched upon the extended period of separation between Chi and her mother, during which Chi's mother had to care for her seriously ill mother.

"After I started seeing Chi, her mother seemed overinvolved and said, 'It is hard for me to entrust my child to someone else.' She discussed Chi's problems at school with math and mentioned that Chi often sought attention from others, insisting that they help her with tasks she could do herself. Chi is finishing 1st grade, and her teachers recommend that she enter 2nd grade. However, her mother feared Chi would become more dependent and considered having her repeat her 1st grade."

"After I saw Chi a few times, I told her mother that Chi was highly anxious, likely related to the long separation they experienced when Chi was an infant. She did not have hyperactivity; her school problems were probably a manifestation of her anxiety. I recommended starting treatment with me initially once a week, increasing to three or four times a week."

"Chi's mother agreed. After Chi told me of the beating, the mother and I talked. She said that Chi's overdependence makes her impatient and sometimes annoyed. 'I get outraged with the little bastard and slap her, and this is the main problem between us.'"

"I agreed. The mother was getting annoyed and impatient with Chi, which was a problem. I felt that she had to wake up. This pattern is destroying Chi's confidence and makes her anxious. I told the mother, "I know how hard it is to be a parent. I, too, have a daughter." After a discussion, we both agreed that hitting does not help a child. We decided that she and I would somehow figure out how to help Chi, but she had to stop hitting her. I told her to communicate with me when she is upset. After the discussion, I felt that Chi's mother trusted me."

"She sends me occasional texts and communicates with me, though she mentioned that I do not need to respond. She said that Chi's father is egocentric. Despite his desire to help, he is a limited man. Chi sacrifices herself trying to earn his love. She advised Chi not to give up her dignity to please him, stating that he has not done enough to deserve her love. She also said that Chi's situation reminds her of her own childhood.

I said, "Yes, there are similarities between Chi and her mother, which annoy her. In contrast to adult cases, the mother and father are concretely present in any child therapy or analysis. You are doing therapy with Chi. You are providing good parental psychoeducation to her mother, helping her avoid punishing Chi, which you must do, but you can only do so much. You cannot perform alchemy!"

"You read my mind. I wish I could help Chi more and make her change faster. However, I feel her mother is changing. She texted, saying she had decided not to focus so much on Chi's school studies. She wants to be nicer to her and spend more time playing with her. She does not want her anxiety to become a burden on Chi. She also mentioned wanting to exercise and maybe try to lose weight instead of over-focusing on Chi. 'If I want Chi to become a free girl, I need to become a free mother.'"

"Good. What will you do if Chi tells you that her mother beat her again?"

"I want to respond based on the emotions of the moment."

"Could you give an example?"

"I could say, 'It is sad that your mother beat you.' I could say, 'Maybe you are frightened of your mother.'"

I said, "Yes. Maybe you could also ask Chi, 'What do you wish me to do?' You can make your final decision after that information."

"Yes. I spoke to a colleague who works with children about this case. We talked about transference. I told him that maybe my child patient sees me as her father figure— perhaps the new boyfriend of her mother—who knows."

I asked, "What did your colleague say?"

"Keep an open eye and be open-minded."

What did you get from today's supervision?"

"I will remember if the topic of Chi's punishment comes up so we can talk about how she feels and maybe what she wants me to do."

Supervision: **14**

At the beginning of the session, Ching stated, "This week, I met Chi's father. Chi's mother wanted me to meet him and facilitated my meeting with the father. She also sent me a Word file summarizing the family dynamics from her point of view. I will first summarize what she wrote."

"Chi's mother reported that she was traumatized by her ex-husband's family and by him. She said that before her marriage, she was a trusting person and trusted him and others. She described her ex-husband as being controlled by his mother and highlighted the tensions between herself, her mother, and her mother-in-law. The drama mainly involved Chi's mother and Chi's two grandmothers."

"According to Chi's mother, the two grandmothers were conflicted about caring for Chi. The paternal grandmother was aggressive and forced the maternal grandmother to retreat. The maternal grandmother became angry and stressed out. She was eventually hit by a 'stock.'"

I could not understand the term 'stock' and wondered if Ching was referring to a stick. Not being sure I was following him, I asked, "What is a stock?"

"Let me look up Wiki and let you know. Ah. She got hit by a 'paralytic stroke.'"

"Oh. So, Chi's mother had to take care of her mother because of a stroke."

"Yes. Chi's grandmother's problem was serious; she needed someone to nurse her. At this time, Chi was eight months old. When Chi's mother decided to leave Beijing, she moved to the town where her mother lived. During this time, the paternal grandmother became verbally and physically aggressive towards Chi's mother. The paternal grandmother said, 'You should not leave to care for your mother. Who cares if your mother lives or dies? You should be here to take care of Chi.' Despite this, Chi's mother decided to leave to take care of her mother and stayed with her mother away from Beijing."

Ching continued, "Chi's maternal grandmother gradually recovered, and Chi's mother returned after an absence of eight months when Chi was sixteen months old. Upon returning, she found Chi was aloof, anxious, and not socially responsive. Chi's mother feared that Chi might have autism, but Chi's father and paternal grandmother denied any problems."

"Chi's mother strongly felt that Chi had issues, while Chi's father and his mother did not, leading to conflicts. They started shouting at each other, and then Chi's paternal grandmother became physically aggressive towards Chi's mother. Chi's father also became violent towards her. One day, Chi's mother used her cell phone to videotape the verbal and physical aggression from her husband and mother-in-law. This evidence was crucial in the Court granting Chi's mother a divorce."

Ching reached for his e-cigarette, positioning it between his fingers so they almost covered it. He took a drag and, after a few moments, exhaled a wispy cloud of vapor.

"I feel Chi's father is manipulated by his mother. He is cornered by two women; he cannot handle the conflicts between his mother and wife.

I asked, "During the eight months that Chi's mother was away, who cared for Chi?

"Chi's father and mother cared for Chi. Now I will come to Chi's father. He is smart. He wants to win my support and wants to appear friendly and cooperative. However, he wants to deny Chi's problems and say there are no problems. He is vigilant with me. He is a computer coder. When I asked him about his occupation, he seemed irritated and said, 'Let's come to the point. What do you want to know?' "

"I said, 'The reason I asked you about your profession was that I wanted to know a little about you and your background to understand your daughter. Let us talk about your daughter.' "

"Chi's father He asked me point blank, 'Do you think my daughter has problems?' "

Ching continued, "I wanted to avoid being judgmental and try to agree with him. But (pointing a finger to a voice in his head) Dr. Sripada's voice was on my mind[44]. I remembered how we talked about Chi."

He continued, "I said, 'Yes. Chi needs help. When she was an infant, her mother was unavailable for eight months. Chi is anxious, has trouble playing and forming friendships, and struggles with understanding math in school. I am here to help.'"

"Maybe because of my frankness, Chi's father agreed that Chi has problems. However, he is inclined to downplay them. He mentioned that Chi's mother tends to exaggerate her issues."

Ching paused and said, "I just remembered that Chi's mother expressed feeling helpless and angry in her letter. She wants help and wants me to assist in persuading Chi's father and paternal grandmother to acknowledge and address Chi's problems. Chi's mother wrote that Chi's paternal grandmother says, 'Your stupidity is because of your mother's fault. She enrolled you in a stupid idiot's school. Your problems are not your father's fault. Your problems are my fault.'"

I said, "Clearly, not everyone agrees about the seriousness of Chi's problems. You clarified to the father that Chi has difficulties that need treatment. The mother sees the need for treatment, and my question is, will Chi's father also support the treatment?"

---

44 This is an example of Qing's transference to me and the concrete manner in which he felt my influence. In an analysis, such an association might warrant analytic scrutiny. In supervision, there can be many views on how to manage such a situation. I felt that unless it became the nodus of a countertransference resistance that blocked his ability to work with and interpret analytic events, there was no need for me to draw attention to the situation he had pointed out.

"Chi's father knows she has problems but would like to deny them. He feels the issues are not as significant as the mother believes. He will not block treatment, but he thinks the need for it is less urgent. Chi's mother feels strongly about the need for treatment and relies on me to assist her daughter. I believe she trusts me."

"Although Chi's father wishes to deny her problems, he did acknowledge something significant. He said, 'There has been a big improvement in Chi's situation since she started seeing you. Her teachers are not calling us every day with complaints. Chi has not been so upset at school. She connects better with her teachers and is not as terrified by math as she used to be.'"

Despite his initial anxiety about working with children, I felt that Ching had effectively worked through his fears about starting a child practice, and had furnished his office accordingly. He announced his practice and began treating Chi, a child with anxieties about relationships and school, who had trouble playing and forming friendships. Ching identified several family dynamics contributing to the child's anxiety and symptoms. Through good history-taking, Ching identified a period of maternal absence for eight months that contributed to the child's pathology. Additionally, the child struggled with her mother's own sense of inadequacy and shame, which led to the mother devaluing Chi and being punitive in her style of punishment. Ching noted that analytic treatment required a deeper understanding and working through Chi's trauma of early separation and fear of punishment. Just as her father tended to deny her problems, she did not want to feel her anxiety (math or fear of being beaten), but she felt the anxiety, and denial did not work for her.

Furthermore, Chi and Ching developed the potential for a good working alliance with clearly identifiable transference and countertransference concerns. Chi liked him and was concerned whether he liked her too. She had started to elaborate fantasies concerning the bird display in his waiting room, connecting them to her imagination of Ching's wife. He was beginning to interpret her tendency to keep secrets and push him away. Chi and Ching were a good fit, and the conditions for initiating a child analysis were present. So, I discussed these with Ching, and we started a discussion about transitioning the treatment to a child-analytic treatment.

I discussed many of these concerns in my musings after Session 12. Using these ideas, I used this occasion to review what he said to Chi's father and add to his impression that Chi had significant problems that needed child analytic treatment.

Ching pondered over what we discussed. He said Chi felt that fifty minutes was not enough to be with him and wanted to see him more often. Chi was open to the possibility that her play had meaning and was curious about what was happening in the treatment, indicating she was ready for deeper involvement. Chi's mother was keen on the treatment. Although the father wanted to deny Chi's problems, he acknowledged that the treatment was helping Chi.

> "My thinking was solidified when you brought up the subject of transitioning Chi's treatment to a child analysis. I trust your word and judgment, but I also believe that starting to see Chi three times a week would provide a greater sense of continuity and offer opportunities to deepen the relationship and make more meaningful connections and interpretations about her anxieties and fears." Additionally, he considered that starting a child

analytic case would make him one of the pioneers of child analysis in Beijing. He said, "Becoming a pioneer in child analysis in Beijing is a big step. Analytic cure cannot take place seeing a child once a week; I will start seeing her three times a week."

I said, "You want to help Chi and her family. Additionally, you also want to advance your career. It can be a win-win situation."

Ching appeared pleased and resolute, somewhat nervous, but ready to become a pioneer child analyst in Beijing.

Supervision: **15**

With a furrowed brow, Ching came onto the screen.

"I have good news and difficulty. According to Chi's mother, Chi's father liked me. He thinks I am smart and interesting and wants Chi to continue her treatment with me. I asked the mother if he could interfere with Chi's treatment. She said, 'No.' She has full legal custody of Chi and is fully responsible for her daughter. The mother said that Chi has generally improved. She is less fearful at school and less afraid of being with friends."

"Usually, Chi is withdrawn and hesitant to be with friends. Last week, her friends invited her to a party. One of the fathers invited the children to come on stage and sing songs in the arena. She volunteered, went on stage, and sang a song. Chi was happy. I spoke to the mother about starting child analysis and increasing sessions to three weekly. She agreed to three sessions a week."

I replied, "I am your supervisor and not in charge of Institute administration. You should contact them to get confirmation from the Institute about the number of sessions a week necessary for your treatment to count towards analysis."

"I understand you are a supervisor. You teach very well."

"That is good, and that is your opinion. My point is to get official clarification concerning minimum requirements for analysis."

"You mean the Institute may say I must see Chi four or five times a week?

"It is best to get official clarification and know the formal expectations concerning analysis."

"I understand. I will get the administrative manual for candidates and confirm it."

"Now, coming to the difficulty, it was in the session. When I opened the door, Chi sat on the couch. Usually, she comes in and goes to the carpet to play. I thought maybe Chi had something to say. She said nothing. After a while, she asked me what I wanted to play. Because we normally play what she wants, I did not respond and waited for her to decide. I sat down on the carpet. She came and sat near my knee. As she reached over to the cupboard to get toys, she looked down at my penis and said, 'Little chicken.' I was surprised. She then again said, 'Little chicken.' It was unmistakable she was referring to my penis."

"I immediately felt this session was different. Maybe something happened, and I felt that Chi was anxious. I wanted to say something, but my tongue could not say anything. After a moment, I said, "Oh, maybe you realized I am a man. I have a chicken.""

"She did not respond. I felt that I did not give the response she needed. Last week, she played with intricate origami paper projects. Today, she took out dolls and toys and threw them everywhere. Then she asked if she could get paper cups from the waiting room and made imaginary Coca-Cola in the cups. As she made it, she started to hum a tune: Na, na, na.....Na, na, na, na, na, na, na. She repeated the tune Na, na, na.....Na, na, na, na, na, na, na, several times. However, she hummed the tunes somewhat tensely. So, I told Chi, 'The way you are singing, you look a little nervous.'

"Chi did not immediately answer me. Then she said, 'My mommy slapped me again.'"

Looking at me, Ching said, "Before I could respond to Chi, I remembered that you and I had spoken about what to do if the mother slapped Chi again. But I could not remember what you said!"

"At the start of this supervision, you said there was difficulty. That was the difficulty. You could not remember what I said." I chuckled in a manner hopefully to suggest that we would try to make the best sense of his forgetfulness and that it would all work out.

"Yes. So, I had to speak independently, without remembering what you said. So, I said to Chi, 'You got slapped because of some math problem at school.'"

"Chi responded immediately, 'No, you stupid idiot.'"

I told Ching, "Good, you tried clarifying what happened. So slapping was not related to math and school."

Ching continued, "Chi said her classmates told her, 'You are away from school and missing some classes. We had enough of you.'"

I asked Ching, "Did she miss some school because she was coming to see you?"

Ching replied, "No. Mother was taking Chi out of school classes to get her extra one-on-one tutoring."

I asked Ching, "What does 'We had enough of you' mean?"

Ching repeated a phrase in Chinese. "It means, 'You are too much.'"

I said, "Perhaps her classmates were saying her irregularity was too much of a disruption at school. They want her regularly in school."

"Yes. Chi's classmates said they had had enough of her irregularity at school. It was not Chi's decision. Her mother took her out because she wanted Chi to catch up with her academics."

Talking to me, Ching continued, "When I am with you, I can pull myself together, and things make sense. But when I was with Chi, I forgot, became jumpy, and felt lost. When I was with the China American Psychoanalytic Alliance (CAPA), I read an article about child analysis. It said there is a risk for the child part of the child analyst to come alive. I became like a child. It was like there were two helpless children in the office.

I said, "You may have forgotten what we discussed; that was a negative. However, the positive was that you felt directly for Chi. You had an automatic empathic understanding of her feelings. That experience is the best guide to help you treat her. You felt her helplessness."

> "Yes. Then I told Chi she was feeling helpless. She began to hum the tune she had previously sung in the session. I recognized the song and became aware of its lyrics."

At this moment, Ching seemed relaxed and began to hum and then sing the Chinese song Chi had hummed. He then translated the lyrics for my benefit.

> "The song is about a person singing about wanting a protective hero to rescue her."
>
> Explaining what he did in the session, Ching said, "So, I told her, "You want me to be a hero and save you.""
>
> "Chi then said, 'Wonderful, how do you know?'"
>
> Ching continued, "I have concordant feelings for Chi."

Ching seemed less tense than he was at the start of the session. In general, I have clarified that I do not dwell on Ching's transference for me unless it interferes with his treatment of Chi. In this instance, his inability to remember what we previously spoke about did interfere with his treatment. So, I asked Ching, "Do you now remember what you forgot from our supervisory session?"

> Ching laughed anxiously, "I am still in the broken mode. My mind is blank."

I laughed and said, "That is why psychoanalysis is called the study of the unconscious. We discussed: If a tree falls in a forest and no one is around to hear it, does it make a sound? You heard her cry for help. She wants a hero to help her, and you know how she feels. We discussed whether the mother's physical punishment was within the range of normal parenting or whether it was bordering on abuse. We also talked about asking Chi what she wanted you to do."

"Now I remember."

"If it is a trauma within her ability to manage, you can decide to manage the situation solely within the analysis between her and you through play, containment, and interpretations. However, if the problem is significantly stressful, you can try to manage it separately with the mother through understanding and support, psycho-education, or the law. You can also manage the situation by including Chi in your discussions with the mother. We talked previously about having a word with Chi before you act, which gives her a chance to offer her point of view."

> "At the end of the session, I walked out with Chi to the waiting room where the mother was seated. The Mother got up. I looked at Chi and asked her, 'Did your mother slap you again?'
>
> "Both Mother and Chi were surprised by my question. Chi's mother responded, 'Because Chi had to make up academics at school, I decided to enroll her with a tutor during her class period. I got so anxious about her school that I slapped her. It was my fault."

Ching said, "Disapprovingly, I shook my head No. Although I wanted to say it, I did not verbally say, 'Not good. Not helpful.'"

Ching continued, "Chi's Mother lowered her head in shame and avoided my eyes. I ended the session by saying, 'This week, we start three times a week for Chi's treatment.'"

"I identify with Chi. I must also identify with the Mother and develop a comprehensive strategy for appreciating and understanding all parties. Just now, I remembered an incident I witnessed about ten years ago. I was walking to my parked car and on my way to get breakfast. I saw a violent father dragging a small boy who was late getting ready for school. The father was yelling at the boy and hitting him repeatedly. I was about to open the door to my car when I stopped, walked over to the father, and said, 'Stop it. You are a coward. You are picking on a boy because you feel powerless. Help the boy get ready in time and find some way to be a real father.'"

Ching recalled the incident with passion. The session was almost over, and I wanted to make some summarizing comments.

"You have a good heart and feel for children. You got angry and shouted at the father for being excessively mean to his son. During this session with Chi, you were under stress. You could not remember what we had spoken about previously and had to act independently. You addressed the slapping in a timely fashion with both Mother and Chi. You showed presence of mind."

"Chi's Mother was slapped by her mother-in-law (I slapped my forearm to indicate the violence and her hurt). Her ex-husband slapped her (I slapped my forearm again). She hates herself for allowing them to abuse her. Her daughter's failures remind her of her own shortcomings. Fate has slapped her with a daughter with her own failings (I slapped my forearm). She loves her daughter but feels trapped by her daughter's problems. She feels helpless. When confronted with Chi's problems, she can only treat Chi as fate has treated her. So, she ends up slapping Chi (I slapped my forearm). She regrets it but cannot help herself. Mother's self-hate and hatred for Chi are a repeating cycle. How can your verbally slapping Mother help the situation?"

"Chi wants you to be a hero and rescue her. You were bold and brought the matter up with the Mother in her presence. That is a great start. In this situation, good enough is pretty good."

I told Ching, "You have a good heart. In my heart, I also shook my head and thought 'No' when I heard that she had slapped Chi. Our job is to try to find the best action we can muster. It is hard to know the right action in difficult situations. Whether an action accomplishes its goals, you cannot know immediately. You can only answer that question after you follow up and understand the results. Follow the laws of abuse according to China. Chi disappoints her Mother. She cannot bear her daughter's failures. When upset, the Mother seems unable to show compassion or care for Chi. From a therapeutic point of view, Chi's situation makes the Mother feel helpless and powerless."

"Chi's Mother loves her daughter, but that love comes out in twisted actions. When you can show her the love in her intentions, maybe she will grow to show more love. She hugs her daughter, but often only after she strikes her. Maybe she can do it before. To learn from life's disappointments and failures, Chi's Mother would benefit from understanding them, not just knowing them. You need to help the Mother understand that you appreciate that she loves her daughter but cannot tolerate her daughter's failures. Mother feels helpless and tries to act powerfully, slapping Chi out of her own frustration.

I thought of Ching's numbness when his mother punished him. When Ching remembered the beatings he had suffered from his own mother, tears welled up in his eyes. Therefore, I had to not scold Ching for his anger and disapproval when Chi's mother punished her daughter or when he yelled harshly at the father on the street.

I should offer my feedback and criticisms as compassionately as possible. I hoped my criticism would not be too painful for Ching. Telling others what to do is easy. I had to practice what I preached. I said to Ching, "The situation needs truth and compassion. What you know and feel about Chi's Mother is correct; communicate it to her like Confucius!"

Over time, Ching and I developed a comfortable method of sharing thoughts. I never intended to mold him into a philosopher; my goal was for him to remain simply true to his nature—be himself. I sought for Ching to understand that Confucius' teachings, combined with the vast heritage of Chinese civilization—its long-standing history, culture, wisdom, and ethical codes—could greatly enrich his journey through psychoanalysis. The current situation was his opportunity to blend China's essence with psychoanalysis's discerning perspectives to benefit not only himself but also Chi and her Mother.

Therefore, I was not surprised that Ching's eyes brightened after I mentioned Confucius. "Yes. I understand and agree. You helped me start to work with Chi. I want you to know I want to work with children; this is my test and wish. However, I have to understand children and also parents."

My Musings

Over fifty years ago, as a medical student, I was part of a close-knit group of friends who often gathered at each other's homes. One friend's father, a knowledgeable and generous man, took a keen interest in our reading habits. He would lend us books from his vast library and guide us based on our interests. On one occasion, he lent me a philosophy book by Will Durant, though I cannot recall its exact title—it may have been *The Greatest Minds and Ideas of All Time*. This book introduced me to some of Durant's thoughts on Confucius, which left a lasting impression on me, even if I can no longer remember the specifics. What resonated most was Confucius' focus on human relationships over concerns of the afterlife or the soul. He categorized relationships between ruler and subject, parent and child, husband and wife, elder and younger siblings, and friends. His grounded, common-sense approach to life struck a deep chord with me.

Growing up in predominantly Hindu India, I observed how many people fixated on reincarnation, often more concerned with past and future lives than with the immediate hardships and opportunities of the present one. Even at a young age, I was struck by how this focus on the imagined beforelife and afterlife often overshadowed the very real struggles and suffering that demand our attention in this life. This awareness ignited my desire to address human needs and suffering, ultimately guiding me toward a career in medicine.

Similarly, psychoanalysis is deeply concerned with human experience, seeking to heal through understanding without focusing on spiritual concepts like the soul. The method relies on tools such as free association, play, fantasy exploration, dream analysis, detailed examination of unconscious motivations, and transference and countertransference dynamics. Through these tools, analysts aim to help patients gain insight and make meaningful changes by uncovering previously hidden connections between their minds and behavior.

As beginners in psychoanalysis, candidates are eager to learn, though they are often unfamiliar with the complexities of the treatment process. I use terms like candidate, supervisee, trainee, mentee, and novice analyst interchangeably throughout this book to avoid repetition. The level of guidance a candidate needs depends on their personality and prior experience with patients, particularly children. Practical matters like setting up a practice, handling billing, vacations, illness policies, confidentiality issues, and understanding the ethics of professional conduct are all areas where a candidate may initially need support. For instance, a child analyst must also be prepared to report suspected cases of abuse or neglect, a duty that adds another layer of responsibility to the practice.

Child analysis, while rooted in the same principles as adult analysis, presents its own set of unique challenges. Creating a child-friendly therapy space, selecting suitable toys, and navigating the delicate balance of engaging with parents while maintaining boundaries with the child are all critical considerations. In some instances, the supervisor may need to implement setting limits (parameters) and follow with clarification and interpretation of the meanings of the intervention itself. In some instances, collaboration with schools or other professionals may become necessary. External agencies may need to intervene to manage or prevent harmful behaviors when imminent danger exists. While these approaches may not align with traditional psychoanalytic methods, they are essential for maintaining a safe therapeutic environment. Supervisors play a pivotal role in teaching these techniques, ensuring candidates understand when such interventions are necessary, particularly in the context of child analysis.

Practical, widely accepted knowledge in psychoanalysis—such as ethical standards, privacy rules, and established regulations—is easily accessible and shared among analysts. It is foundational and applies to all cases. However, therapeutic interventions like clarifications, confrontations, interpretations, limit-setting, and play techniques are case-specific and require more nuanced, personalized guidance from the supervisor.

Supervision in training is a delicate balance between providing direct instruction and offering broader guidance. Supervisors must offer direction without overshadowing the trainee's development, allowing space for personal growth and the evolution of their own methods. The supervisor's role is to foster a learning environment where the trainee can apply their knowledge, make independent decisions, and learn from experience while having support when needed. This approach helps trainees cultivate skills, build confidence, and provide quality patient care using their unique strengths and understanding. Effective supervision requires knowing when to lead and when to step back, ensuring the trainee's journey toward professional autonomy is both supported and self-directed.

The purpose of supervision is not to demonstrate how the supervisor would handle the case the trainee is working on, as that would reduce the trainee to a mere extension of the supervisor. The trainee's approach does not need to mirror the supervisor's; however, when a situation exceeds the trainee's experience or capability, more direct guidance may be necessary. The ultimate goal of supervision is for the trainee to develop self-sufficiency and confidence in their individual approach, maximizing their inherent talents to ensure the best patient care. This emphasis on self-sufficiency in trainees fosters a sense of empowerment. This is achieved under the broad guidance of the supervisor, with the trainee retaining the freedom to determine specific interventions. Supervisors often blend directive and non-directive approaches, adjusting to the circumstances as needed.

Trainees should not rely solely on their resources when feeling uncertain, nor should their independence be forced into rigid conformity. Supervision seeks to empower trainees to rely increasingly on their judgment, fostering a style that reflects their individuality while prioritizing the patient's welfare and remaining open to feedback. Recognizing the trainee's autonomy becomes especially important in cross-cultural supervision, where the supervisor may lack familiarity with the candidate's or patient's cultural context. As the saying goes, "I did not know Confucius nor the price of tea in China." Supervisors vary in their approach; some supervisees resonate with and adopt aspects of their supervisor's methods, while others develop entirely new approaches over time.

In the current scenario, Ching is tasked with managing Chi's circumstances, in which her mother appears to use punishment out of frustration. Navigating the complexities of different cultural approaches to discipline requires careful judgment. Parents are responsible for guiding their children's behavior in a manner that aligns with societal norms and avoids abuse. Each situation is unique, challenging the balance between honesty and tact. While the outcomes of combining truthfulness with consideration may not be immediately apparent, their effectiveness often becomes evident over time.

Cross-cultural supervision shares similarities with earthquake-resistant architecture. A building's foundation is made flexible with shock absorbers and damping systems to handle stress without breaking while remaining anchored to the ground to prevent toppling. Likewise, cross-cultural child supervision benefits from adaptable teaching methods that accommodate the complexities of diverse cultural contexts.

In such cases, the supervisor may know psychoanalysis but not the culture, while the trainee understands the culture, and the patient experiences the immediate pain of their problem. The aim is not to enforce rigid norms but to create a resilient space that embraces the dynamic interplay between depth psychology and cultural nuances. Psychoanalytic treatment extends beyond theory to integrate the patient's cultural and familial influences, ensuring the therapy remains relevant to their unique life and psychological circumstances.

Ching's clinical responsibility is to address Chi's questions, anxieties, and concerns, especially given the high pressure of her living environment and her overburdened mother. While love is necessary, a child also requires attentive, caring behavior. Furthermore, it is essential to blend Chinese cultural subtleties with the complexities of my Indian heritage and Western lifestyle. Ching cannot always rely on consulting me during active sessions; thus, he must become adept at using his own judgment, periodically seeking guidance when necessary. Empathy and readiness to respond immediately are crucial for any competent analyst.

After the session, I briefly researched Confucius and found myself drawn to his concept of Ren. Ren, central to Confucian philosophy, is often translated as "benevolence," "humaneness," or "compassion." It represents the ideal way of relating to others, emphasizing empathy, altruism, and ethical behavior.

Ching was conflicted between empathizing with Chi and disapproving of her mother's harsh discipline, which echoed his childhood experiences. This inner conflict challenged him as he grappled with the situation's complexities.

Upon reflection, I realized my earlier guidance to Ching—urging him to be like Confucius—was too vague. Though unfamiliar with Chinese philosophy, I sensed that Ching could draw from the richness of his cultural heritage, particularly the principle of Ren, to benefit both Chi and her mother. I sent Ching a message encouraging him to integrate his Confucian (Chinese) wisdom with psychoanalytic guidance. I included the symbol for Ren, hoping it might resonate with him as a source of inspiration.

仁

Readers will undoubtedly notice that the symbol of *Ren* is prominently displayed on this book's cover. I want to clarify my intention in referencing Confucius's concept of *Ren* about Ching. My goal was to illustrate how foundational psychoanalytic principles—such as the unconscious, transference, resistance, and other critical concepts—should guide Chang's treatment of Chi in a way that is congruent with the supervisee's capacity, tolerance, discretion, and individual style. Unless there is a matter of vital importance, such as dangerousness or ethical considerations, supervision should enable these principles to be meaningfully experienced and integrated by the supervisee rather than imposed by the supervisor as abstract intellectual constructs lacking emotional resonance. In this instance, I found the Confucian principles embodied in *Ren* to be a fitting vehicle for transmitting psychoanalytic thought and technique, as they resonate with the familiarity of Chinese cultural symbols.

Ren symbolizes the integration of the idiom and experiences of any supervisee and their patient within the appropriate cultural and familial context. It underscores the supervisor's role in fostering the supervisee's development as an analyst in a manner that aligns with their unique circumstances while respecting the supervisee's chosen techniques and therapeutic decisions. Crucially, the supervisee's approach to learning often diverges from how the supervisor might handle a similar case, reflecting the individualized and evolving nature of their growth within the dynamic supervisory process.

Did I, or any supervisor, truly succeed in guiding supervisees according to their unique circumstances rather than imposing theories or modeling the supervisor's approach? Naturally, opinions on this matter will vary among supervisors, supervisees, and readers alike. Individual experiences and expectations shape each perspective, and the art of supervision lies in embracing and learning from these diverse and sometimes contradictory interpretations of the supervisory process.

Supervision: **16**

Ching started the session by saying, "To tell you the truth, I was anxious before I saw Chi. She went on a vacation with her mother by the seaside. I felt a little empty and dull before the session."

"Why?"

"I asked myself the same question several times. I got this answer: Maybe Chi was getting a repetitive pattern playing with origami, dolls, and clay. I thought that a different activity might help, so I got some cards and garden string from my house."

Ching reached into a cupboard and brought out a roll of brown twine. It was light brown, textured, and tightly twisted with a rough, hairy appearance—the material commonly used for packaging and binding.

"When we first met, you asked me if I babysat. I used to play cards when I babysat, but I used the cards to teach numbers to my baby cousin. I used the cards from 1 to 8 to teach addition, subtraction, multiplication, and division."

"After Chi came in, she sat on the couch and noticed that I had put cards and string on my table. She said, "My dad knows how to play cards. I am not so good with it.""

Ching said Chi moved on to the string and played Cat's Cradle. He demonstrated the game with a piece of string, showing how players use a long string loop to make complex figures with their fingers and hands. The game can become intricate as more shapes can develop. Cat's Cradle ends when a player makes a mistake or creates a dead-end figure that cannot change into anything else. Chi frequently made mistakes, bringing the game to an end. Ching tried to explain, but she could not understand his instructions. Then, he helped her by guiding her fingers with actions, helping her better play the game.

I told Ching, "I think you got the cards and string because you got nervous. I have an idea about why you may have gotten nervous, but I am unsure if it is helpful."

"Your ideas are welcome."

Ching gulped a few sips of tea.

"At the end of the last session, you arranged a brief discussion with Chi and her mother. You asked Chi in her mother's presence if her mother had slapped her."

"Yes. So, any punishment Mother gives Chi is an open fact between Chi, Mother, and me. It is no longer a secret."

"Maybe you were anxious about the consequences of your intervention."

"Yes. For half the week, I was wondering about it and whether I should send Mother a message. Remember, you told me it would be useless if I slapped Mother."

I asked, "Did you get my e-mail?"

"No. Let me check. Now I see it." Ching laughed as he pronounced the Ren Chinese character included in my email.

I laughed and said, "I am trying to teach you something I cannot even pronounce!"
We both laughed.
I said, "The Mother wants Chi to succeed so much that she cannot tolerate her daughter's failures."

"During the week, I wondered how Mother might react to our discussion after the session. I wanted to tell her, 'We are all here to help Chi. Be careful.' It was tiring to have such thoughts. Then, I realized that this was not the time for me to talk to her to soothe or encourage her. It might provoke negative emotions from her. I will act when Mother is ready enough to receive my thoughts."

I told Ching, "I shared with you a general idea that slapping Mother might not be helpful. I am not directing you to take any specific action. The decision is yours when you feel it is appropriate."

Ching replied, "Thank you. I appreciate your perspective. The timing and actions are for me to decide. I need to determine how involved I will be with Mother."

Ching continued, "I would like your opinion on our young patient. She can be quite critical of me. She complained against me for bringing coarse garden twine and said, 'You should have brought a children's string like they use for birthday parties.'"

I said, "I had an idea—Chi's criticism was like her mother's criticisms..."

"Yes. It was my fault."

Ching took a drag from his e-cigarette.

I continued, "I am considering a two-step approach to address how she treats you. First, you could mimic her critical tone and say, 'You do not like the unfashionable coarse string I brought you to play with.' The second step would be to say to Chi, 'You disapprove of me in the way your mother disapproves of you.' Both steps need careful timing."

Ching smiled. "Yes. Repeat the first step several times, then move to the second step."

He continued, "I would like to discuss another behavior. When Chi was playing with some rabbit dolls, she tried to put the clothes of a small doll on a larger one. Despite knowing they wouldn't fit, I felt she repeatedly asked me, 'Help me. Help me.'"

Ching continued, "I thought she was pretending to be helpless so she could ask me for help."

I said, "When Chi was an infant, her mother was away caring for her own mother for many months. It must have been a difficult time for Chi. Although she likely does not remember it, she wants her mother or you to be close to her and not abandon her. Managing such early traumas is challenging."

Ching said, "Chi knows her mother had to leave for a long time when her own mother was ill. So, Chi's problem is hard-wired. Do not go too fast. It will take time."

"I think you have good ideas about how to help Chi and her Mother."

Supervision: **17**

"I think increased sessions help Chi. She continued playing with filling clay in a jar, which I call the Coca-Cola game. This past weekend, I met some colleagues working with children associated with the Tavistock. We discussed our respective cases. I talked about Chi's clay-in-the-jar Coca-Cola game. My colleagues associated with Tavistock understand the concept of the 'Container' to describe the dynamic relationship between the therapist (or parent) and the patient (or child). According to them, the 'Container' provides a holding environment for emotions. They commented that the container might be a mother, analyst, or even the womb. Such wonderful fantasies!"

I added, "I am glad you are engaging with your colleagues; it is a great way to exchange ideas. However, I want to highlight the differences between clinical and theoretical approaches. I prioritize what the patient says, focusing on a clinical perspective. For instance, in Chi's case, clay in a jar games represent her attempts to manufacture Coca-Cola. It is so because she said so. In the future, she might associate Coca-Cola with her father, who loves it; her mother, who forbids it; or herself, if she likes it."

I continued, "Sticking to the patient's words and actions in your interpretations keeps you connected to real-life events in the treatment, providing a reference point to return to the patient and the initial analytic context. Relying heavily on theoretical interpretations offers a broad range of possibilities, but these interpretations can seem distant or surprising to the patient because they diverge from the patient's experience. For example, associating a girl putting clay in a jar with the concept of a womb may be theoretically sound. However, for an eight-year-old, the term 'womb' requires an understanding of internal organs. Chi was developmentally not there yet. She would rely on the analyst's words rather than her own experiences to grasp such an interpretation, which could be too burdensome for a child. The advantages of theoretical frameworks come with the risk of overextension; this applies not only to the term containment but also to concepts like the Oedipus Complex, self-object, projective identification, etc. Ultimately, the patient determines whether a theory is effective for them. If a patient does not sense the value in an interpretation, even if it is theoretically correct, you must rethink the situation."

I continued further, "Another example. Chi told you she believed your wife was responsible for the bird display in your waiting room. You told me this was factually incorrect. However, from an analytic perspective, it's still valid to interpret the bird in your waiting room as representing a psychic connection to your wife for Chi, even if it's not literally true."

Ching added, "Thank you. Discussing my case with my colleagues was good. They are vital, young, and imaginative. I understand what you are saying, and I agree with you. I like sticking to the patient's words, but such a method takes time to develop. For example, when Chi was humming a tune in the last session, I asked her what song she was humming."

I responded, "The Hero song?"

"Yes. Chi told me that she was humming a song about the Hero who is a rescuer. In this last session, she brought something in a McDonald's bag to the session. Opening the bag, she said, 'I have a gift for you.'. She took out some pink and yellow flowers and gave them to me. I was touched. She asked, 'Do you like them?' And then she asked, 'Do you like me?'

"She took some paper cups from my office and made a vase of flowers in the paper cups. Then she asked me, 'How long will the flowers last?'

"I said, 'They are fresh now and will be until you get home.'

"Chi then opened the door and saw her mother sitting in the waiting room. She took an empty paper cup and slid it to her mother. Her mother seemed annoyed by this action. Chi slid another empty paper cup to her mother. Her mother was annoyed. Chi closed the door and asked me, 'Am I a naughty girl?'"

"I thought that Chi was teasing her mother. I told Chi, 'Your mother seemed a little annoyed when you opened the door and slid the empty cups to her.'"

"Chi said, 'My mother has two cell phones. I have none. All my classmates have cell phones. Why does my mother not give me a cell phone? It is unfair.'"

"I thought Chi wanted to grow up and be like her mother. Somewhat Oedipal. Mother has two, and I have none. Unfair. Adults have everything, and children have nothing. Then Chi asked me, 'Do you like me?'"

At that time, I was sitting on a sofa. "I said to Chi...
I forgot what I said. Maybe something like, 'You want to
grow up and be like your mother.'"

"Then, Chi asked me, 'Is the sofa soft?'"

"She wanted to sit on the sofa. I moved and made room
for her. I behaved spontaneously. She sat and nuzzled by
my side. I wondered, 'In psychoanalysis, are we allowed to
be side by side? Is this physical contact with the opposite
sex?'"

"I said to Chi, 'You feel cozy?'"

"Chi said, 'Your hair is curly.'"

"I remembered from previous conversations that her
maternal grandmother was very kind and cared for Chi,
and she had curly hair. So I said to Chi, 'Your grandmother
also had curly hair. She helped you to feel calm.'"

Ching asked me, "I feel that Chi's feelings towards me
are similar to those she has for her maternal grandmother,
who took care of her, But is it a good idea for an analyst
to share a seat on the sofa with a young female patient?'"

I looked reassuringly at Ching and said, "As an analyst, we must always
be in a state of self-inquiry and ask such questions. One size fits all is not
a good motto for analysts. You have to judge based on the particulars of
the situation. Chi was anxious, and she wanted to sit by your side. You
did not choose to sit by her side. She commented on your curly hair. Your
interpretation was that your hair reminded Chi of her grandmother, who
was caring, while her mother is sometimes harsh. It seems correct, and
you tried to facilitate Chi's sense of trust and the roots of that feeling."

Ching said, "It is not military, Allowed or not allowed. The situation decides what is the best explanation."

"I feel Chi appreciates you reminding her of her grandmother, who was gentle with her. That is why she brought you the flowers."

Ching said, "I bear you in my mind when I work with Chi. I had a question I meant to ask you. After saying that I had curly hair, Chi asked me a question. "Can I bring my cat to our session?"

Ching continued, "I did not see any reason to say, 'No.'" So, I said, "Why not." Then, I thought some more and said to Chi, 'The cat might be sacred and not want to come, or the cat might want to come.' So humorously I said to Chi, 'Why don't you ask the cat if it wants to come.'"

"At the CAPA meetings, some people talked about using trained animals, for example, dogs, to help treat some patients. It is hard to figure out what to do in such cases. I want to be human. Do you have an opinion?"

I told Ching, "Whether the cat comes or stays out does not matter. I think you can take any number of positions concerning the cat. The important thing is to ask Chi how she felt about whatever way you decided. Another thought I had was that you felt Chi irritated her mother by sliding her empty paper cups. Will Chi ask her Mom to arrange to transport a cat and irritate her mother? Now, this next thought is a long-shot explanation. Do you want to hear it?"

"Yes, I do," Ching said, giving me a thumbs up!

"Because Chi's mother left to care for Chi's grandmother for eight months, we infer that Chi's sense of object constancy may be fragile. She may be irritating her mother and being naughty to ensure her mother's attention is on Chi. With poor object constancy, some children provoke parents by standing precariously on chairs, tables, or window ledges and being accident-prone. Maybe she is testing you to see if you will get irritated by asking to bring in a cat?"

"I understand what you are saying. It is hard to explain because Chi can recall events when she was an infant. Maybe all that is left is an irritating habit of being provocative to mother."

Ching continued, "This last session, Chi and mother were late. After I waited five minutes, I sent Mother a message and went downstairs to get a quick smoke because I could not smoke in the office building. I returned in a few minutes and found that Chi and Mother were waiting for me. The first thing Chi said was, 'You were late. It was so long.' This may be an example of Chi's sensitivity to me being late or gone."

"We played a game with clay, and she gave each of us a car. We buried the cars in the clay and made them invisible. Then we dug out the cars and discovered the cars in the clay. Then I told Chi, "Just like my car, you could not find me when you came.""

I said to Ching, "Right on. You understand that Chi is sensitive to people who are not there. You can work with Chi to appreciate this through analysis and reduce her provocative actions that irritate her mother. You can also directly speak to the mother about the uselessness of punishing Chi. You decide what to do."

Ching laughed and said, "You are my advisor, not my commander!" Then Ching gave me a smart salute.

My Musings

Ching's recognition of my supervision as a collection of ideas to assist him, which he can choose to use or not, depending on his judgment, is significant. I value his autonomy and ensure that I provide clear instructions when I suggest a specific course of action, leaving no room for ambiguity. Our discussion on the contrast between a primarily clinical approach and one more shaped by theory, particularly the clay-in-a-jar analogy and the idea of a 'container,' was also satisfying.

Beginning analysts often focus on practical, day-to-day clinical situations and ask questions seeking concrete solutions. For example: Should a patient bring a cat into the session? How should the analyst respond if a patient damages their office or brings a guitar to sing during the session? Can a child kick the analyst, or should the analyst call if the patient is late? When should an analyst lock up at the end of the day or end a session when the patient refuses to leave? Should the analyst accept a gift from a patient, and how much notice should be given before taking a vacation? Is it necessary to disclose vacation destinations if asked or explain cancellations due to illness?

Supervisors, textbooks, and workshops often provide frameworks for these contingencies. Novice analysts tend to seek consistency, but practice introduces variability, especially when working with children who may not grasp concepts like time. For example, explaining a vacation to a child with a limited understanding of weeks or months can require adjusting the usual protocols.

Despite the challenges, we, as analysts, agree that the practice of psychoanalysis is complex and often demands navigating situations that cannot be reduced to fixed guidelines. This complexity underscores the weight of our profession and the need for continuous learning and adaptation. I continue to work through such decision-making processes myself, acknowledging the ever-evolving nature of our field.

Regarding Ching, I advised him that whether he allowed the cat into the session or not was not the key analytic issue. His judgment in the moment was important, but what mattered more was the follow-up. The significance of post-decision analysis cannot be overstated. If the cat was allowed in, he should explore the patient's responses; if not, the same applies. This method, which I developed gradually, might not be common practice, but it has evolved from my experience over time.

I gained immensely from my time at the Illinois State Psychiatric Institute, particularly through my friendship with Merton Gill. We met weekly for nine years, and our discussions reinforced, for me, the importance of transference and countertransference for gauging clinical psychoanalytic process, while allowing for decisions that respect the patient's and the analyst's individuality. This emphasis on individuality is not just a professional principle but a reflection of the value and respect we give each person in the analytic process.

Ching has built a strong sense of trust with me, and he openly shares his concerns. For example, he compared his patient Chi's feelings toward him with those she had for her maternal grandmother and questioned whether it was appropriate for him to sit on the sofa with a young female patient. I noted how Chi pointed out that Ching's hair was curly, like that of her grandmother. Children are often unpredictable, and analysts can be caught off guard by their actions, as Ching was unexpectedly when Chi sat beside him.

This reminds me of the famous exchange between Freud and Ferenczi on the kissing technique, where Freud emphasized the principle of abstinence and the theory of infantile sexuality, protecting the boundaries of acceptable behavior in psychoanalysis.

Ferenczi, on the other hand, championed a more active and affectionate approach to psychoanalysis. He believed there could be a disconnect between how children and parents (or parental figures) communicate and how patients and analysts interact. For instance, a girl might innocently pretend to be her father's wife, seeking comfort and closeness without any sexual implications. However, if the father is emotionally unwell, he might misconstrue the girl's role-play and sexually act up. Ferenczi (1949)[45] claimed that misunderstandings between generations could result in children's exposure to violence, sexual or otherwise.

In Ferenczi's perspective, the analyst should counteract the emotional deficiencies and misunderstandings that the patient experienced in their childhood, possibly behaving like a caring parent, offering warmth and acceptance. He saw the primary risk in the analysis as reenacting the original trauma and re-traumatizing the patient, who might be as reluctant to criticize the analyst as they were their parent. Ferenczi believed that both analysts and patients could resist acknowledging the patient's repressed or suppressed criticisms of the analyst.

Ferenczi suggested that analysts help patients overcome early emotional deprivation by satisfying their longing for love and affection,

---

45 Ferenczi, S. (1949). Confusion of the tongues between the adults and the child: The language of tenderness and of passion, *International Journal of Psycho-Analysis*, 30:225–230.

even to the extent of hugging and kissing them. Freud (1931)[46] was concerned that this *kissing technique* would lead to further erotic escalation.

There are many reports of boundary violations, both sexual and otherwise, which have made analysts understandably anxious about the dangers of relationships between analysts and patients. However, analysts should evaluate each situation on its own merits, avoiding group think and the tendency to categorize diverse scenarios as potential boundary violations quickly. In this scenario, Chi chose to sit beside Ching and noted his curly hair. Perhaps she was looking for refuge and working through her fears of her mother's punishments. Despite his doubts, Ching felt Chi sought solace as she did with her grandmother. Ching, noting the similarity in curly hair between her grandmother and himself, clarified a possible grandmother transference.

Still, the question Ching asked hung in the air, "But is it a good idea for an analyst to share a seat on the sofa with a young female patient?' "

Such questions are the reason that psychoanalysis is called the impossible profession!

Each analyst has to answer that question individually.

Psychoanalysts can help children and adults identify and understand the people and situations that trigger or alleviate their fears. However, psychoanalysis carries some risk that others may misunderstand their method and accuse an analyst of a boundary violation. Psychoanalysis can help others better understand themselves and the world while making it a fulfilling profession for the analyst. Therefore, the analytic identity

---

46 Freud, S. (1931). Letter from Sigmund Freud to Sándor Ferenczi, December 13, 1931. In E. Falzeder & E. Brabant (Eds.), P.T. Hoffer (Trans.), *The Correspondence of Sigmund Freud and Sándor Ferenczi Vol. 3*, pp. 421–424. Cambridge, MA & London: The Belknap Press of Harvard University Press.

has to contain the promise of understanding people and the chance peril of being labeled as an Enemy of the People.

If pressed to answer that question, I would say, "An analyst must guard his goodness and name with prudence."

Supervision: **18**

Ching did not call at our appointed time. After nearly ten minutes of waiting, I texted him, asking if he was OK. Soon after, I received a video Skype call from Ching. He looked tired.

"Sorry, I took a nap and overslept. I set an alarm to wake me up after thirty minutes but didn't hear it go off. There are so many mosquitoes in Beijing this time of year that I haven't been sleeping well. They make noise, bite, and prevent me from getting good sleep. Thank you for your message."

"There was a prominent playful phenomenon in today's session with Chi. Yesterday and previously, she played with clay and dolls. That play was somewhat ritualistic and controlled. (Ching looked up for a reference on his screen) I would say her past play was ceremonial. Maybe you remember the last time Chi asked if she could bring her cat into the session. She asked if she could bring 'everything' into the session."

"When Chi came into yesterday's session, she brought a water gun to the office. As soon as she came in, she said she wanted to shoot the walls with it."

"I immediately said, 'Playing with the water gun inside the office is not a good idea.' I could see she was having a hard time holding back her impulses. Until then, her style of play was ceremonial and controlled. Now, the risk was that it would become uncontrolled. I could head off trouble and propose an alternate game. As I struggled to develop an alternate idea for play, she started shooting water on the walls and carpet. She wanted to shoot me with water. So I firmly said, 'No. No, you cannot play with water inside the office.'"

"Chi stopped playing with the water gun but secretly wanted to squeeze the trigger. I firmly said, 'No. The rug is getting wet, and I do not want that.'"

"Chi still wanted to play with the water gun. So I said, 'Last week you asked if you could bring everything. You can get an empty water gun, but not a toy gun filled with water. I cannot allow it.'"

"Through her eyes, Chi was saying, 'Why?' Or 'It is unfair.'"

"I said, 'You are trying to figure out what is and is not allowed.'"

"Chi heard me and said she wanted to play with pillows. She then started collecting pillows on a couch. I said to her, 'You can play, but you have to rearrange the pillows back where you found them.'"

"I was sitting with pillows on my chair. Chi wanted to pull pillows in my chair and under my arm. I said, 'No. These pillows belong to this chair where I am. I need them.'"

"Chi then played with a doctor doll, giving the child an injection. I said, 'Today you wanted to play with games that I had to say no.' I thought that my 'No' was painful to her, like an injection. However, I did not say it to her."

"I think you were right. You understand that while treatment can be helpful, it can also be painful. Chi is starting to understand this as well. One of her main issues is dealing with the physical pain from her mother's punishments. Your perspective will be useful in helping her, especially since it acknowledges the pain associated with treatment."

"All that was yesterday's session. In today's session, Chi was different. She did not play with dolls, clay, or water guns. Chi sat across from me in a chair. She pointed to her new smartwatch and said it was like my smartwatch. We talked about what we should play. I thought a change might help and suggested cars. She refused my suggestion."

"Chi decided to play with origami paper projects. She wanted to work on them herself. Chi paid attention and could follow the instructions and make folds along the guiding lines. I praised her for playing by herself and not wanting my help. That is it for today's session."

I said, "Chi provoked you during the last session to say 'No' to her play. Provoking others and not appreciating their limits is an essential dynamic for Chi. She does the same with her mother, except her mother physically punishes her. You are in the process of helping Chi understand, and she pushes others."

I continued, "Do you have any thoughts about your extended nap this evening that made you forget our session time?"

Ching said, "I am doing too many things and carrying a heavy load. It is ten o'clock. After you, I have my analysis. Mosquitoes have been killing me and disturbing my sleep."

I asked, "Do you think anything from your last session weighed on your mind?"

"Not sure I can connect it to anything. What do you think?"

"Last time you asked, 'But is it a good idea for an analyst to share a seat on the sofa with a young female patient?' I think you realize that working with Chi is a weighty job. She teaches you many things, but Chi is a mixed blessing. Do you know what that expression means?"

"No. I will look it up in the dictionary. 'Something good in some ways and bad in other ways.' That is very true."

"That is why psychoanalysis is called the impossible profession, good in some ways and impossible in other ways."

Ching laughed. "My slogan used to be 'Psychoanalysis is my lifestyle.' Now, with child analysis, the slogan has to be 'Psychoanalysis is my hard lifestyle!' I feel it is complex and unpredictable. I did not expect that a child would be shooting a water gun at my face or wanting to pull a pillow from under me."

"You said to me that you were willing to be a pioneer in China treating children with psychoanalysis. Chi needs help, but she is impossible at times!"

> Yes, both Chi and her mother need help separately. They need to talk. But, not like Trump with his 'fight, fight, fight' mentality." (Ching raised his hand and pumped his fist as Trump did after being shot in Milwaukee just before his confirmation as the Republican party nominee in 2024.)

My musings

In the previous session (Session #17), Chi displayed affection and chose to sit next to Ching on the sofa. The situation made Ching question, "Is it appropriate for an analyst to share a sofa seat with a young female patient?" In this session, Chi, armed with a water gun, exhibited disruptive behavior. That much is clear. The cause of this shift, however, remains uncertain. I wondered if Chi had sensed some anxiety from Ching. Supervisors who are not directly involved often find it easy to generate ideas. These ideas may or may not be helpful to treating analysts, such as Ching, who was warding off water gun attacks! I chose not to share this thought.

Supervision: **19**

"This week, I consciously followed our discussion. I wanted to help Chi understand her feelings and actions. For example, last week, she fell apart with the water gun and had many provocative questions. Monday was the start of this week. She sat on the sofa and said, 'This is a big, soft, and nice sofa. It has lots of room for you and me. We can sit on it and talk.'"

"I said to Chi, last week you provoked me. The weekend passed. Today, you are behaving nicely and want to see if I will be nice too."

"She enjoyed being on the sofa. She was relaxed. She started a new game of giving me orders. It started easily and cooperatively. She politely asked me to help her transfer four dolls and two cats (dolls) from storage and put them on the carpet. I did as she asked. Then she asked me to put all the dolls on the carpet. I did. She started to ask me to do several things at once. She became upset because I was confusing cats and dolls. She yelled at me, 'Stupid, can't you see that kittens have whiskers and dolls do not have whiskers.'"

"I told Chi, 'Looks like you have many complaints and feel I am stupid."

"She said, 'Yes, you are stupid. Now, put all the dolls in a neat row, make them sit still, and make no noise; this is a school, and these are the rules.'

"I said, 'You are running your own school and making rules for the dolls.'"

"She said to me, 'Uncle, if you have rules, you also will get angry.'"

"I said, 'A child like you will get angry with rules and if you cannot do what you want.'"

"She reacted to my comment and said, 'Standstill or I will punish you with five hundred math questions."

"You sound like your mother."

"Chi said, 'Of course.'"

I asked Ching, "Looks like you are combining psychoanalytic teaching and interpretations. If, in the play, Chi is her mother, who are you?"

Ching answered, "Good question. Not sure."

"Who is being given the five hundred questions as punishment?'

"Thank you for the question. In the game, Chi was particularly upset and angry with a doll who had trouble being still."

"I think both of us agree that Chi was playing the Chi's mother's role as the punisher. There may be two options for who unconsciously plays the role of Chi in the game. Option one: She unconsciously assigns Chi's role to the doll because it sit still. Option two: She unconsciously assigns the role of Chi to you. You told Chi that she was like a child who gets angry when she cannot do what she wants. Maybe you made her angry, and now she wants to punish you. Regardless, it seems we are having an interesting discussion."

"It is interesting. Which path should I follow? I understand that semantically, Chi put me in the position of the punished person. However, I don't want to identify with a punished child. I do not want to live the life of a punished child. I don't want to fit into the shoes of a punished child. It is too painful."

In a previous session, Ching recounted instances from his childhood when his mother would discipline him through physical means such as slapping. These incidents have had a profound and enduring impact on him, frequently triggering negative emotions associated with those early years.

I responded, "I heard that in ancient China, a custom involved breaking and tightly binding young girls' feet to alter their shape and size, creating "lotus feet" which were considered a status symbol and mark of beauty. These feet wore "lotus shoes." The tradition of foot binding, seen as a sign of elegance and social standing, caused lifelong pain and disability for those who underwent the process. Nowadays, the old custom has been abandoned. I understand that no one would want to put themselves in the feet or shoes of an ancient Chinese girl. It is too painful. However, I have another theory if you want to hear."

"Sure, go ahead."

"In what I will say, I want to stay in my lane."

"What is a lane?"

"A traffic lane is a designated section of a road or highway meant for a single line of vehicles going in one direction. Each lane, demarcated by road markings, is designed to regulate traffic movements, enhance safety, and uphold order within the transportation system. Drivers stay within their assigned lanes, initiate a lane change when necessary, and provide ample warning to fellow motorists.

"I understand."

"You once told me that when your mother hit you, you did not feel pain but felt numb."

"I thought of it but did not say it. It is too shameful to say I thought of it."

"I want to stay in the supervision lane; I do not want to go into your life or analysis lane. The supervision lane contains the job of understanding your countertransference. Your shame could be related to Chi feeling ashamed to tell you that her mother had hit her. Your shame could be related to Chi's mother, who feels ashamed that she lost control and punished Chi. If I deal with such areas, your shame is relevant to supervision."

Ching clapped enthusiastically with his hands, appreciating my comment.

"I fully understand you. You are using my shame to understand my countertransference to Chi and the total treatment situation. Every feeling I have is usable to understand my broad countertransference. My shame may be related to Chi, her mother, her invisible father, and even her grandmothers."

"Right on. Countertransference is my lane. Your life is not my lane. Sometimes, they may briefly merge and appear to overlap."

"I am glad you brought it up. I agree with you. I will consider both options. In her play, Chi might be treating the doll as herself or placing me in the position of her own Self. How do I use that in the session?

"We do not need to make analysis more complicated than it is. Ask Chi if she is like her mother, who is like Chi—the doll who will not sit still or you. She may say the doll is Chi; she may say you are Chi; she may say both the doll and you are Chi; she may say neither of you are Chi. There is also the possibility that she will call you an idiot, which seems to be her occasional default response. Her answer will settle the questions. You do not have to figure it out all by yourself. Chi is glad to tell you how she feels!"

"With regards to my shame. I feel Chi's mother is not hitting Chi, but she may still be secretly giving disapproval and feels ashamed about it."

I asked, "What gives you that impression?"

"After a session, Chi used the bathroom, and I was alone with Chi's mother. Chi's mother looked angry and explained that she had overheard Chi complaining to me about herself. Chi's mother said, 'I feel Chi's accusations against me are unfair.' "

"I told Chi's mother, "Your daughter needs to say what is on her mind. That is her treatment. What Chi says does not mean it is true; it is her point of view. I want to talk to you whenever you have anything to say."

"Chi's mother said, 'When I am angry with Chi, I cannot always be logical and be in control.' "

I said, "Maybe she feels ashamed.' "

Ching clapped his hands vigorously. "I understand. Chi's mother is ashamed that she loses control of herself. She has reasons to get angry at Chi. Chi is sometimes or often provocative."

At that moment, I remembered Ching telling me that his wealthy grandparents babysat him as a child. They had luxuries like a color TV and refrigerator. They often watched the Beijing Opera, which used minimal objects creatively; for instance, a chair or table could represent a mountain, ship, or bed. This inspired Ching to imagine household objects as something else. Thinking about the current events in his waiting room, I said, "It looks like your office has become like the Beijing Opera House. All kinds of dramas are playing out in it!"

"I told the mother that we are allies in helping Chi adapt better to life. Today was a day of much learning. One valuable insight I gained is the concept of a 'lane.' As you maintain your position in the supervision lane, I will strive to stay in mine. Numerous lanes in the treatment room intersect and diverge. You taught me various aspects of high-level countertransference understanding, such as identifying who the punisher is and whom the punished. After our discussion today, I feel less apprehensive about stepping into the shoes of a victim. If a patient who is a victim wants me to empathize with her situation, I am ready to do so. I can empathize. I have a painful past, but my need to contact patients is strong and is a top priority. In you, I trust!"

"That is nice; do not over-trust me; trust yourself and Chi."

My Musings

The session provides a dynamic example of broad countertransference, a concept that has been constantly evolving and the source of much discussion and dispute. To fully understand the complexity of this example, it is beneficial to briefly review the contributions of Freud, Tower, Winnicott, Kohut, Gill, Racker, and others to the concept of countertransference. Classical and contemporary variations of countertransference exist, and their applications differ significantly. Therefore, the analyst must clarify their chosen version to avoid misinterpretations of their intentions and actions. In this musing, I will present a brief overview of the term's evolution, provide comments, and demonstrate its specific relevance to the dynamics of this session.

The classical version of countertransference rests on Freud's theory, and the practice of psychoanalysis was built on the pillars of the analyst's neutrality, abstinence, and anonymity. These principles provided patients a 'blank screen' to project their subjective unconscious, transferences, and resistances. Normally, without countertransference, the analyst's unbiased, objective observations enabled the analyst to perceive the patient dynamics accurately. Such an understanding provided an orderly certainty for the privileged analyst to accurately perceive the patient's conflicts and deficits and make compelling interpretations, thereby aiding the patient. However, these ideal conditions are not always achievable in analysis. Freud (1910)[47] states that the analyst's 'countertransference' results from the patient's influence on the analyst's unconscious, which can disrupt successful treatment. Therefore, the analyst should recognize countertransference as an analyst-based pathological influence and overcome it through further analysis.

The "classical" view, which includes a narrow view of counter-transference, posits that countertransference is typically absent. Under normal circumstances, the analyst's objectivity allows for accurate patient findings. However, countertransference emerges when the analyst is influenced by a pathological aspect of their own personality. In this view, countertransference always interferes with analysis, underscoring the need for the analyst to recognize and manage it. This perspective highlights the analyst's responsibility and accountability in the process. It also suggests that the analyst's normal objective observations provide a view of the patient's dynamics; countertransference does not exist. When countertransference is present in the narrow sense, it is an indication for the analyst to seek consultation or further analysis. It does not give the analyst any window into the patient's dynamics.

From the initial beginnings of a narrow notion of countertransference to the culmination of the notion of broad countertransference has required

---

47 Freud, S. (1910). The Future Prospects of Psycho-Analytic Therapy. *Standard Edition* 11:139–152.

several critical experiential and conceptual transformations within psychoanalysis.

Initially, analysts believed that their "blank screen" approach guaranteed a neutral stance. However, they were taken aback when they stumbled upon clinical phenomena influenced by the analyst's unconscious processes. For example, Lucia Tower's (1956)[48] unconscious oversight of forgetting a patient's session led to her influential work on countertransference. Similarly, Winnicott's (1949)[49] candid discussion of experiencing hate during a treatment highlighted the emotional range and complexity involved in countertransference. The realization dawned that the blank screen was not infallible, and the analyst's countertransference emerged as a critical subject for deeper psychoanalytic investigation.

The shift from the objective observer to the active participant-observer:

Twentieth-century scientific discoveries led to the appreciation of the active observer, especially in the study of atomic events. However, independent of developments in the physical sciences, Sullivan and others discovered that both the patient and the analyst, in an analysis, are active participant observers, highlighting the need for analysts to consider their own reactions to patients (Havens, 1976)[50].

---

48 Tower, L.E. (1956). Countertransference. *Journal of the American Psychoanalytic Association* 4:224–255.

49 Winnicott, D.W. (1949). Hate in the Counter-Transference. *International Journal of Psycho-Analysis*, 30:69–74.

50 Leston Havens. (1976). *Participant Observation*. New York: Jason Aronson.

The evolution from the traditional psychoanalytic stance of assuming objectivity, neutrality, and privilege to a more interactive and egalitarian approach has fundamentally reshaped the dynamics of analyst-patient relationships. In the past, the idea was for the analyst to remain detached, providing authoritative interpretations grounded in established theories, including the controversial concept of penis envy, which is a term used by Sigmund Freud to describe a girl's sense of deprivation upon realizing she does not have a penis. This often placed female patients in a position where they felt compelled to accept the analyst's views, given the power imbalance inherent in the therapeutic setting.

Modern psychoanalytic practices, such as Essential Psychoanalysis, challenge the traditional model by advocating for a mutual influence between patient and analyst. Here, both parties are active participants who co-construct the therapeutic experience. This approach not only emphasizes the importance of the patient's agreement with the analyst's interpretations but also, importantly, empowers the patient to actively modify the interpretations.

In Essential Psychoanalysis, the analyst's insights and interpretations are not based on the presumed authority or privilege of the analyst. Rather than being compelling due to the analyst's power or the patient's admiration, these interpretations result from a history of consistent attentive listening, empathetic understanding, and honest exchange of viewpoints. Offered as provisional yet sincere opinions, these interpretations invite the patient to consider their value. Their effectiveness lies in their relevance, significance, and practicality to the individual, presented with careful timing, discretion, and respect for the patient's freedom to modify them as necessary. This shift allows for multiple interpretations and acknowledges the analyst's countertransference responses as valuable tools for understanding the patient's experience and for initiating clarifications, questions, or interpretations, creating a sense of partnership in the therapeutic process.

This method implies that analysts must relinquish the notion of neutral and objective interpretations without bias. Instead, the patient's acknowledgment and agreement are essential, reflecting the more democratic ethos of modern society within the therapeutic journey. Such a shift in perspective levels the playing field in the therapist-patient dynamic, fostering authentic conversation, mutual comprehension, and joint recovery efforts. Additionally, it invites a process of post-interpretation in which the patient's input on any misinterpretations can lead to corrective measures and refine insights, ultimately enhancing the mutual understanding between patient and therapist.

From an objective view of transference to a wew definition of transference involving patient and analyst

In the classical Freudian view, analysts held that the transference occurred only within the patient in a relationship with a neutral analyst. However, a new psychoanalytic understanding emerged that acknowledges the patient and the analyst as active participants in the analysis. Gill emphasized the importance of transference but also introduced a shift in its concept, arguing that, unlike Freud's view, transference is not solely the product of the patient; both the patient and the analyst play an active and mutually influential role in its formation.

This shift is characterized by Gill's (1984)[51] quote, which signifies the abandonment of the possibility of objective neutrality: "Transference is

---

51 Gill, M.M. (1984). Transference: A change in conception or only in emphasis? *Psychoanaytic Inquiry* 4(3):489–523.

not only always contributed to by both participants, but each participant also has a valid, albeit different, perspective on it."

Gill (1994, pg. 47[52]) states that,

> "My thesis is that the therapist should embrace the principle that whatever he does or does not do is an action that will have its interpersonal [and intrapsychic] meaning, that he has a major responsibility to search for this meaning, and, in interpreting that meaning, to recognize that his response (and here silence is a response) is a stimulus to bring about a response on the analysand's part. And the analysand's response will not simply be an irrational reaction without any basis in the ongoing interaction."

Like numerous peers, I have moved away from striving for unattainable objective neutrality in psychoanalysis, which was once considered achievable and desirable. Instead, I embrace the idea that both the analyst and the patient are active participant-observers who influence each other mutually but have different perspectives on the same designated manifest event (Sripada and Kronman, 1996).[53] While the patient and analyst may agree on many, or even most, aspects of manifest events during analysis, their interpretations of the latent meanings assigned to these events can differ significantly.

The passage above emphasizes Gill's recognition of the interconnected nature of transference and countertransference. It suggests that the

---

52 Gill, M.M. (1994a). *Psychoanalysis in Transition: A Personal View.* Hillsdale, NJ: The Analytic Press.

53 Sripada, B. Kronmal, S.L. (1996). Merton Gill and the Genesis of a New Psychoanalytic Paradigm. *Annual of Psychoanalysis* 24:67–81.

analyst's attitudes, interpretations, actions, and even silences contribute to the transference, while both the patient and analyst co-create countertransference. Gill and some contemporary analysts acknowledged this theoretical link between transference and countertransference. However, in practice, there has often been an insufficient focus on detailing the analyst's countertransference. Analysts have tended to give more attention to transference, perhaps due to tradition or habit, without fully exploring the complexities of their own countertransference. However, there is a pressing need for more attention to the analyst's countertransference, as it plays a crucial role in the analytic process. Essential Psychoanalysis aims to address this by emphasizing the importance of recognizing and accounting for the analyst's broad countertransference, which includes aspects of the analyst's childhood and life experiences that influence the analytic process. This may entail a degree of newness in openly discussing some analytic influences in this book compared to many other analytic descriptions.

I subscribe to Gill's new definition of transference, which acknowledges that while the analyst's influence is inevitable, it remains analytically describable and accountable. This influence may or may not result in unanalyzable suggestions. The analyst must recognize that their clarifications, interpretations, and actions always include a component of unconscious suggestion due to their role as active participants and describe these influences in any account of the analysis. However, this inevitable influence must be distinguished from overt, conscious suggestion, manipulation, or boundary violations. So, the analyst's job changed from reporting neutral observations to explaining their contribution to the analysis, including the transference, to the best of their ability.

Contemporary analysts questioned the blank-screen model of neutrality and transference as a patient-only phenomenon. This understanding resulted from the appreciation of the active observer within psychoanalysis, who inevitably contributes to his observations. According to this new view, the unavoidable analyst suggestion must be made explicit from the analyst's or patient's perspective and may need to be subjected to further analysis.

From Abstract Theories to an Experience-Near direction and Patient Involvement in Processing and Working Through analytic Ideas:

Analysts initially employed psychoanalytic metapsychology to describe the human personality, using terms such as forces, energies, and structures derived from natural sciences like physics. This approach assumed that analysts offered objective accounts of their patients and themselves, often referring to themselves in clinical discussions and case reports in the third person as "the analyst."

However, analysts have increasingly developed more appropriate terminology for their discipline, focusing on uncovering meanings within the psychoanalytic dialogue. Patients may agree or disagree with the analyst's interpretations, and they can dispute the analyst's view, as the analyst is not a privileged observer. Influenced by Kohut and others, many contemporary analysts have moved away from abstract metapsychological terms that foster an impersonal aura, instead describing the meanings contained in an analysis in "experience-near" personal terms.

While theories facilitate the production of possible ideas or hypotheses applicable to a particular situation with a patient, it is not enough for an interpretation to conform to theoretical concepts. The interpretation must be tested in the analysis with the patient's view, resulting in some agreement or rejection. Thus, an idea that starts as a theoretical thought can be a successful or rejected interpretation after it is tested in analytic testing with the patient's immediate and long-term reactions.

From the analyst's countertransference contents to the patient's psychological contents: A view of broad countertransference:

Broad countertransference encompasses all the reactions the analyst experiences continuously in their relationship with the patient. According to the definition of a broad countertransference, the patient's experiences and the analyst's countertransference constantly influence each other. This dynamic link allows the analyst to cautiously infer the relationship between the analyst's countertransference and the patient's experiences and psychology. However, because transference and countertransference mutually influence each other, they introduce a degree of uncertainty, making it challenging to infer the precise relationship between the analyst's countertransference and the patient's processes.

The analyst's countertransference may include any combination of perceptions, thoughts, imaginations, emotions, or actions. The broad countertransference provides the analyst with a continuous stream of unconscious or conscious material, functioning as an analytical laboratory. It may highlight a prevailing analyst-patient identification (or objectification), help formulate patient dynamics and aid treatment.

Racker (2007)[54] describes the systematic way in which the analyst and patient structures might be oriented. The analyst's countertransference can be related to the patient's processes and serve as a means to

---

54 Racker, H. (2007). The Meanings and uses of Countertransference. *Psychoanalytic Quarterly* 76:725–777.

understand the patient. The analyst might identify with the patient's id, ego, or superego in a concordant manner (the patient's id relates to the analyst's id, the patient's ego relates to the analyst's ego, or the patient's superego relates to the analyst's superego) or in a complementary fashion (patient's id relates to analyst's superego). Additionally, the analyst might identify with the patient's internalized figures, particular anxieties, themes, or processes. Simplistic inferences cannot be made from countertransference; a thorough and critical analysis is essential to interpret the insights gained from one's countertransference perceptions.

In light of the evolving view in contemporary analysis, the analyst's privilege to unilaterally judge the patient's reality is increasingly limited. Contemporary analysis increasingly recognizes the patient's freedom to contribute to addressing, deciding, commenting, choosing, and accepting-rejecting-modifying the analyst's interpretations. While theory might help the analyst to offer interpretations based on a hunch or a hypothesis, it is only after the patient engages with and tests the interpretation or intervention that its effectiveness can be assessed. If contemporary analysts adopt a privileged attitude towards their interpretations instead of a posture of humility, their increased freedom to draw inferences from their own experiences and link them to the patient's experiences could result in wild analysis.

When benign, inferences from countertransference, subject to uncertainty and patient collaboration, allow the analyst to make reasoned inferences. A small or moderate degree of error can be addressed by the analyst's self-assessment or patient's criticism and occasion fresh evaluations or mid-course corrections of the analyst's theory and practice and offer opportunities for the analyst's self-learning. However, broad malignant countertransference occurs when the analyst's tendencies seriously interfere with therapy. In such cases, the countertransference ceases to serve as a suitable laboratory for understanding the patient.

Malignant countertransference is due to unresolved pathology in the analyst and requires consultation, further analysis, and potentially transferring or terminating the treatment.

The comparison of a narrow and a broad countertransference

In my estimate and the estimates of many others, the change from a narrow to a broad countertransference is a revolutionary shift from classical psychoanalysis to an active observer-based psychoanalysis. Its impact on psychoanalysis cannot be denied, yet its benefits have to be assessed with caution.

In the classical view, relying on observations dealing with the patient's free associations and actions limits the range of information from which the patient can be gauged. However, a broad countertransference view adds to these undeniable elements, hunches from the analyst's own self that may correspond to some aspect of the patient's self. Because psychoanalysis operates in the arena of the unconscious, these hunches add a significant new spectrum of possible information. Nevertheless, compared to the reliability of manifest information from free associations or actions that can be publicly recorded through recording devices or process notes, information from a broad countertransference is speculative and inferential. It requires the additional concurrence of the patient to be counted as information.

The debate on understanding others' minds has engaged philosophers and psychoanalysts. Bertrand Russell (1948)[55] did not rely on empathy

---

55 Bertrand Russell (1948). *Human Knowledge: Its Scope and Limits*. London: George Allen & Unwin.

to prove other minds but aimed to prove the existence of other minds through the argument from analogy and introspection. By analyzing his own thoughts and feelings, he argued that observing similar behaviors in others indicates they also have similar minds. He posited that if a thought (A) causes a behavior (B) in him, then seeing the same behavior (B) in others suggests they share the same thought (A).

Bertrand Russell's argument from analogy for the existence of other minds has faced several criticisms. Critics argue that analogy and introspection have limitations and preclude a logical presumption of the existence of other minds. A fundamental asymmetry between our own minds and others' minds renders analogy an insufficient tool for such a proof. We experience our own consciousness directly but only infer others' consciousness through their behaviors. Introspection is subjective and cannot reliably extend to understanding others' minds. Critics maintain that this method falls short, as similar actions do not necessarily equate to identical mental states, thus underscoring the difficulty of generalizing about others' minds based solely on observed behavior. Many are satisfied by Russell's propositions concerning other minds; the matter is far from resolved.

The ongoing philosophical debate about our ability to truly understand another's thoughts remains unresolved and is likely to persist indefinitely. This debate, which is distinct from the methods of philosophy based on cognition and logic, is a key aspect of contemporary psychoanalysis. Many modern analysts are moving away from the detached objectivity and the "God's eye" perspective assumed by the omniscient perspective of objective observers in traditional classical psychoanalysis, embracing instead the role of an active participant observer who acknowledges some inherent uncertainty on that account. Unlike philosophers who rely predominantly on cognitive and logical methods, analysts draw upon the patient's transference, the analyst's own introspection, empathy, and broad countertransference, as well as the therapeutic relationship, free associations, and an engaged patient who actively accepts or challenges the analyst's contributions in constructing a model of the patient's Self. Analysts must describe the methodologies, terminology, and decision-making processes that underlie their discoveries.

The initial stages of empathy or extensive countertransference may lead to a preliminary concept that the analyst believes is connected to an element of the patient's Self. At this point, it is merely a hypothesis and speculative. The empathic and countertransference constructions gain more credibility when the patient is informed about the analyst's ideas, reflects upon them, and accepts or rejects them.

Arlow and Brenner (1990)[56] emphasize that psychoanalysis is fundamentally a psychology of mental conflict, often rooted in forbidden desires, self-punishing tendencies, irrational fears, and the defenses to manage them. Brenner[57] highlighted the importance of compromise formations. According to Brenner, every perception constitutes a compromise formation, and every emotionally significant aspect of conscious mental life, whether normal or pathological, represents a compromise formation. Successful psychoanalytic work shifts conflicts toward normality, replacing pathological compromises with healthier ones.

Many philosophical arguments can lead to decisive results. In contrast, the compromise formation, a key concept in psychoanalysis, serves as a middle ground, balancing the conflicting demands of the unconscious impulses and the ego's defenses. It is a way for unconscious impulses to express forbidden wishes in a manner acceptable to the conscious mind. This concept reassures us about the effectiveness of our method, as it

---

56 Arlow, J. A. & Brenner, C. (1990). The Psychoanalytic Process. *Psychoanalytic Quarterly* 59:678–692.

57 Brenner, C. (1994). The Mind as Conflict and Compromise Formation. *Journal of Clinical Psychoanalysis* 3:473–488.

represents the best possible adaptation under the circumstances of the patient's life.

Philosophers often demand a higher grade of result than a compromise. Sometimes, a compromise is readily accepted by the analyst but might be resisted by the patient. Alternatively, a patient might settle on a compromise the analyst feels is premature. In an analysis, a patient and analyst might settle on a compromise and decide on a termination date. Unlike the solitary, contemplative method of philosophy, this process highlights the intensely collaborative nature of psychoanalysis, where the patient and analyst actively negotiate and co-create insights to move the analysis forward. Rather than relying solely on individual reflection, psychoanalysis thrives on the dynamic interaction between both participants, making progress through shared exploration and mutual influence.

Grunbaum (1984)[58] is critical of the fundamental method of free association to access unconscious material. He holds that there is an unaccounted or unaccountable suggestion in psychoanalysis exercised by the analyst on the patient. Thus, the evidence's "intraclinical " nature makes scientific tally impossible within psychoanalysis. He suggests that validation can come only from a tally using well-designed extra-clinical studies using "objective" observers. As is apparent, Grunbaum would always suspect the psychoanalytic method and its results.

Philosophers and others have raised significant criticisms of psychoanalysis, often focusing on the need for objectivity and certainty, as emphasized by Grunbaum. However, contemporary analysts approach their understanding as a provisional finding, allowing for uncertainty and future refinement by the patient's and others' feedback. A key element

---

58 Grunbaum, A. (1984). *The Foundations of Psychoanalysis: A Philosophical Critique.* Berkeley: University of California Press.

in this process is the ongoing dialogue, which underscores the dynamic nature of contemporary psychoanalysis. This dialogue ensures that all voices are heard and contributes to the continuous evolution of the field.

This book describes, for example, the inferences and methods of the supervisory process. Sandler illustrates this with an example of countertransference construction in analysis.

Sandler (1976)[59] recounts an experience with a patient who cried during every session. He routinely handed her a box of tissues when she began to cry without fully understanding why. Despite feeling that their progress was somewhat stalled, he did not address that she never brought her own tissues or handkerchief, a practice he would have typically challenged with other patients. One day, he unintentionally failed to offer tissues when she cried, which caused her to accuse him of being callous. She became upset and criticized him for what she saw as a lack of care. Sandler realized that the patient had unconsciously forced him into a role resembling that of a parental figure, and he acknowledged his uncertainty about not offering the tissues. He suggested they explore this reaction together to gain a better understanding. Sandler states, "I believe that this patient had forced me into a role, quite unconsciously on her part and on mine, a role corresponding to that of a parental introject, in which I enacted the part, first of the attentive mother and then suddenly that of the parent who did not clean her up. In the session I was not around to make sure that she was clean, just as she felt that, with the birth of her brother, her mother had not been around to clean her, being busy paying attention to the new baby."

Sandler referred to handing a box of tissues to his patient as countertransference role responsiveness. This could also be described as

---

59 Sandler, J. (1976). Countertransference and role-responsiveness. *International Review of Psycho-Analysis* 3:43–47.

transference-induced countertransference. Regardless of the terminology, it highlights the interconnectedness of the patient's transference and the analyst's countertransference. This interaction demonstrates how the patient's projected feelings and expectations can elicit specific emotional and behavioral responses from the analyst, illustrating their therapeutic relationship's dynamic and reciprocal nature. Through such specific examples, analysts can illustrate how countertransference analysis enables them to make inferences after observing and participating in a distinct series of experiences and actions. By engaging deeply with the patient's behavior and reactions, analysts gather valuable insights that can lead to meaningful interpretations and understanding. This process highlights psychoanalytic work's dynamic participant-observer nature, where both the analyst's observations and the patient's responses contribute to the evolving understanding of the patient's psyche and the analyst's countertransference.

Child analysis and child treatments offer the opportunity to extend the scope of countertransference further than in adult treatments. This session provided such an example. Chi threatened to punish Ching with five hundred math questions in their play.

I said to Ching, "I think both of us agree that Chi was playing the role of the punisher. There may be two options for who unconsciously plays the role of Chi in the game. Option one: She unconsciously assigns Chi's role to the doll that cannot sit still. Option two: She unconsciously assigns the role of Chi to you. You told Chi that she was like a child who gets angry when she cannot do what she wants. Maybe you made her angry, and now she wants to punish you."

While he appreciated both options, Ching said, I do not want to identify with a punished child. I don't want to live the life of a punished child. I don't want to fit into the shoes of a punished child. It is too painful." He was too ashamed to remember his mother slapping and punishing him.

Using the metaphor of the separate, merging, and dividing lanes, I told Ching, "I want to stay in the supervision lane; I do not want to go into your life or analysis lane. The supervision lane contains the job of understanding your countertransference. Your shame could be related to Chi feeling ashamed to tell you that her mother had hit her. Your shame could be related to Chi's mother, who feels ashamed that she lost control and punished Chi. If I deal with such areas, your shame is relevant to supervision."

Ching clapped enthusiastically with his hands and said, "I fully understand you. You are using my shame to understand my countertransference to Chi and the total treatment situation. Every feeling I have is usable to understand my broad countertransference. My shame may be related to Chi, her mother, her invisible father, and even her grandmothers."

Ching's response, in an instant, clarified to me that he understood what I was trying to tell him about the notion of broad countertransference. It made me happy.

In any dynamic treatment, distinguishing between an analyst's broad countertransference and an analyst's view of the patient's transference is crucial. A broad countertransference encompasses the entire therapist's reactions to the patient. These are available through self-perception. In this case, Chi complains of pain and the displeasure of being slapped by her mother. In this case, Ching's countertransference is a reluctance to remember the pain and displeasure of similar experiences in his own childhood.

At its root, when Ching can remember his experiences, they are linked to memories that came into being after his body's nervous system enabled him to feel the sting of experiencing the pain induced by the punishment.

In contrast, while Ching can or may remember his memories of punishments, he never can feel the pain of a slap that Chi experiences, like the way she experiences it herself. He can empathize with her pain from her words, observations of her facial and other expressions, and his memories, but never from his direct sensory experience of her pain.

An analyst's ability to comprehend a patient's suffering is multifaceted, involving their readiness to communicate and articulate their experiences and emotions related to their pain. It also encompasses the analyst's listening, observing, and empathizing skills and proficiency in constructing the patient's perspective. This intricate dynamic suggests that a therapist's awareness of their own countertransference is more immediate than understanding the patient's transference. Acknowledging the nuances of the analytic scenario, it becomes clear that while countertransference presents itself directly, an analyst's insight into the patient's transference is more oblique and not as readily accessible. The traditional model's assumption of an analyst being an objective observer with direct insight into the patient's transference is challenged; instead, the reality is that an analyst's connection to their own countertransference is more pronounced than to the transference.

An analyst's ability to understand a patient's suffering is complex and involves their willingness to communicate their experiences and emotions related to their pain. It also includes the analyst's listening, observing, and empathizing skills and ability to understand the patient's perspective. This complex dynamic suggests that a therapist's awareness of their own countertransference is more immediate than their understanding of the patient's transference. Recognizing the subtleties of the analytic scenario, it becomes clear that while countertransference is directly evident, an analyst's insight into the patient's transference is more indirect and less accessible. The traditional model's assumption of an analyst being an objective observer with direct insight into the patient's transference is challenged; instead, the reality is that an analyst's connection to their own countertransference is more pronounced than to the transference.

The analyst's capacity to understand a patient's pain requires many factors. These include the patient's ability and willingness to converse and express her experiences and feelings about her pain, the analyst's ability to listen, his observational and empathic skills, and his ability to comprehend the patient's viewpoint. This complex interplay means that a therapist's insight into their own countertransference is more direct than their grasp of the patient's transference. Therefore, understanding the analytic situation entails recognizing that while countertransference is immediate, the analyst's access to the patient's transference is indirect and not as immediate.

There is no direct access to the patient's transference as an objective observer, such as a therapist in the traditional model of transference assumes. In the broad view of countertransference, the analyst has more immediate access to the countertransference than the transference.

The approach to countertransference varies significantly between analysts who hold a narrow perspective and those who adopt a broader view. An analyst with a narrow perspective on countertransference may rely solely on the patient's free associations to deduce unconscious processes, transference, and resistance, operating under the presumption of objectivity and the authority to interpret the patient's psyche. In this framework, the analyst's countertransference is typically not acknowledged as influencing their actions. However, should it become evident, it is seen as an indication of the analyst's pathology, necessitating consultation and further personal analysis. Conversely, an analyst with a broad view of countertransference considers a wider range of sources for clarification and interpretation, acknowledging the potential impact of their own emotional responses on the therapeutic process.

In contrast, an analyst with a broad understanding of countertransference considers the full spectrum of their experiences — encompassing all external and internal perceptions, thoughts, creativity, emotions, or actions —potential sources of insights applicable to the patient. This perspective significantly expands the sources from which hypotheses about patient dynamics can be drawn, which must then be validated. Moreover, since transference and countertransference are seen as interconnected, the analyst alone cannot resolve many issues. Instead, the analyst must engage in a dynamic, reciprocal process of confirmation and testing with the patient. Ideas must be tested by sharing them with the patient, who then has the opportunity to affirm or dismiss them. Only ideas that are confirmed can be provisionally adopted, and it must be kept in mind that a patient may later reject an idea they initially accepted. When a patient dismisses an idea, the analyst identifies the error's origin and implements corrections. This process can be a critical source of analytical refinement, introducing concepts of analytical predictions, errors, and corrections contributing to ongoing analysis.

Every interpretation by an analyst must endure the scrutiny of the patient's judgment to be deemed reliable for analytical purposes. Even accurate interpretations may fail this test due to poor timing, intensity, or sensitivity. An analyst alone cannot ascertain the correctness of an interpretation; this necessitates relinquishing personal biases and authority at the office's door. Chi was eager to challenge Ching with five hundred probing questions and thus be a good guide to let him know whether she agreed or disagreed with any idea he may have.

In our discussion, the question arose about Chi's behavior in her play. If Chi resembled her mother in the play, who could Chi be - a misbehaving doll or Ching? I reassured Ching that he did not have to figure everything out alone during the analysis. I suggested that the best way to address this question is to ask Chi directly. Her response may identify the doll, Ching, or both, as Chi or neither as Chi. Alternatively, she might even call Ching an idiot, as she sometimes does. Her answer will provide clarity. I also reminded Ching that he had a reasonable patient in Chi, as she was often willing to answer questions and share her feelings.

Ching had some inclination to run with theories, which are sometimes more interesting than the spade work to everyday practice. Ching clearly understood the concept of broad countertransference. He was willing to listen to Chi and abide by the tests. All these are positive signs for continued progress.

Although somewhat surprised, I appreciated Ching's clapping and applause when he felt I made a good point. It was his way of being. I wanted to clarify that I was doing my job as a supervisor. The case's outcome depended on my guidance but mostly on his treatment of Chi and their ability to gradually work things out, improve her lot, and give her a better shot at life. Her anxiety and difficulties had to be addressed, and hopefully, she would have a less troubled life than her mother.

I felt my supervision of Ching was satisfactory. He seemed less anxious and more settled than when we began. He was a good candidate, learning about starting treatment with a child and understanding broad countertransference. Although not my intention, my supervision in this session dealing with his countertransference merged with exploring the consequences of his personal life on his treatment with Chi. Using the metaphor of a traffic lane, I acknowledged that references to his life were incidental but necessary to explore and understand his countertransference. My primary job remained supervision, and I was not interested in his personal life or analysis (except when Ching spontaneously brought it up in the supervision, or it bears on understanding his countertransference in the context of supervision.) The analysis of the candidate's treatment should remain distinct from their supervision, although occasional intersections concerning broad countertransference may occur. I try to stay in my lane.

Supervision: 20

"I have some observations and a few questions. I can be sure that every Monday will be difficult for Chi. She is disruptive, controlling, and demanding."

When you leave a loaf of bread out, it becomes crusty. The "Monday morning crust" metaphorically belongs to the lore of psychoanalytic bakery! Just as bread left out hardens, the therapeutic process risks growing stale if left unattended. This highlights the necessity for the freshness that comes with the consistent rhythm of regular therapy sessions, often disrupted by the weekend. A "Monday crust" represents the fragile span of a weekend (or vacation) when insights might wane due to a lack of sessions.

"Yesterday, Monday, she brought some books from her home. She barked orders to me to arrange her books in a certain manner. Then, she wanted to play with toys in some boxes. Again, she ordered me in a loud and demanding voice to empty the boxes and put the toys in a row and a particular formation."

"I told Chi, 'You are shouting at me and ordering me. You do this on Mondays. On Tuesdays and other days, you are not so harsh to me.'"

By nodding and approving eye contact, I endorsed Ching's immediate feedback to Chi about her behavior. Immediate feedback is a suitable intervention and gives the patient a clue about how others may perceive her. I had thought of the disruption related to the lack of sessions during the weekend and the ensuing separation. In most clinical situations, the analyst can say something to the patient or act in a particular manner to convey an idea. Often, there are many possible suitable interventions.

"For instance, today, Tuesday, she was different and not so on edge. First, as soon as she walked in, she asked me, 'What shall we play.' I asked her if she had any choice between playing with a book, doll, or ball. She looked at a soft cotton ball in my office and suggested, 'Let us play throwing the ball.' So, we played with her throwing the ball to me, and then I threw the ball back to her. We played like this for a long time, and she was happy to play this repetitive game."

"I read a paper on Child analysis. The patient and analyst play by throwing a paper airplane at each other. The analyst said that this was a good way to express anger playfully. At any rate, we enjoyed playing the game, and I said to her, 'Good game,' She then threw a fastball at me in my face. I cried, 'Ouch.'"

"As I took a moment to recover, I had the idea of adding something to the game. However, I wanted to follow what you said last time: whatever I add must be within the patient's grasp. I read another paper by Gedo. Gedo disagreed with Kohut. In short, I think Kohut appeared to say that understanding, love, or empathy was enough. Gedo's idea was that only love (empathy) was not enough.

An analyst must also lend a helping hand and lead the way to improve the patient's functioning capacity."

"I liked Gedo's idea and tried to implement it. I decided to add some new features to the ball game. I took a deck of cards and only the cards with numbers, excluding the fives and tens. These are very easy numbers for Chi. I mixed the cards for each retrieval. So, when she won, she had to add the new points to her cumulative total. The game helped her keep track of the points.

"Before the session started, Chi was with her mother, trying to teach her to count. For example, Chi's mother gave her a number in the hundreds (180) and a number in the tens (80) and asked Chi to add them up. Chi was too anxious and unable to add them, and her mother became agitated.

"I kept Chi's math difficulty in mind and tried to help her count. Chi has trouble counting beyond twenty. For example, Chi could not count 23 and 8 and said, 'I don't know what to do.'"

"So, I broke up eight into two parts: 5 + 3. I asked her to add 23 and 5. After she finished, I asked her to count 28 + 3. Breaking numbers into smaller numbers helped Chi keep track of the score. We made the game-winner to be the first one to reach 100 points. Chi managed to play without getting too frustrated. Although calculations are still difficult for her, we made calculations part of the game."

I gave Ching two thumbs up.

"I feel the way Chi's mother teaches her math is puzzling and not very helpful to Chi. I think Chi's mother is impatient but calls Chi naughty. So, I sent her mother a message. I told her, 'Chi is difficult. I understand. You are trying to help. We are working together to understand Chi. Disapproval and punishment increase her anxiety and affect her ability to count. Chi becomes needy, oppositional, and bossy.'"

"When she complains to me about you, it does not mean that what Chi says is true. However, Chi needs to be able to express her feelings for the treatment to work."

"Chi's mother responded and confessed, 'Chi's problem is because of me. I imposed my aggression on Chi.'

"So, I came up with a bold hypothesis. Is Chi's mother possibly having a Murder impulse? That is my question to you."

To my ear, Ching spoke in a somewhat unclear manner. I heard both the word "murder" and "mother." I responded, "What you said was unclear to me. Could you please repeat slowly what you said?"

Chang sent me a text: " 'Murder.' Do you have any comments?"

I responded, "Just one minute ago, you said that Chi's mother 'confessed' that she 'imposed aggression' on Chi. Did I hear you correctly?"

"Yes."

"Confession means that she admits to her involvement. Could she be hinting at guilt or shame?"

"That is not how I understood it."

"How did you understand what she said?"

"I thought Chi's mother was telling me, 'I am incapable of stopping my behavior.' She wants my help. What does an uncontrollable impulse require? So, my question to you is, 'How to manage an uncontrollable impulse?'"

I thought of an old-fashioned Freudian formula of Drive/Defense. I said to Ching, "You may be right. The question we must ask is, what are the benefits of focusing on the drive side of the equation compared to focusing on the defense side? However, what do you do if you have a runaway locomotive, car, or bicycle coming down the hill? Change the engine by fitting it with a more powerful murderous engine first or …"

…Ching completed my sentence by squeezing his fingers as though he were engaging in clamping down on the bicycle brakes.

"Engage the brake."
Then Ching laughed, "Murder is a good theory, but brakes are a good treatment."

I said to Ching, "Mother is bringing Chi to treatment. Mother is communicating with you. She confessed she had uncontrollable feelings and that she was the problem. You are communicating with her and showing how useless punishment and disapproval are. All these are different forms of breaks on her impulse. What purpose does calling her a 'murderer at heart' serve?"

"A senior colleague who works with children said, 'The most difficult part of working with children is working with a parent.' Thank you. You cleared up my hesitation. My hesitation in discussing the mother's problems was that I was not the mother's therapist. I am afraid of her pathology. I am afraid that my education or suggestion may not be enough."

I told Ching, "That may be true, and she may need her own therapy. Nevertheless, separate from that, all child therapists and analysts periodically meet with parents to discuss matters of common interest."

"Still, we must also consider how best to understand your idea that Chi's mother might have a murderous impulse. Why is it that the mother does not have psychological brakes in this area? The last time we met, you told me Chi wanted to punish you by giving you five hundred math problems. You told Chi that she was like her mother."

"Yes."

I continued my comments to Ching, "I think both Chi and her mother have poor boundaries, and their personalities overlap in some areas. Chi's mother is, therefore, also a bit like Chi. When Chi fails, the mother feels she is a failure as a mother. The mother wants to slap herself for being a failure, but she slaps Chi instead. So, you could say to the mother, 'You love Chi. You want to be a good mother, so feel very angry and upset at Chi because she makes you feel like a failure.' Of course, this statement is connected to your hypothesis that the mother's anger is murderous.

Saying it might not be the most helpful thing to say to a mother who is already blaming herself. Work on the brakes, not the engine. The mother has a self-blaming engine; giving her a more powerful murderous engine might not be the most useful thing you can do."

> "GOT IT. Another question. Many times in the session, Chi touches her feet or genital area and smells her finger. Recently, she said to me, 'You must have recently had a bath. Your hair smells good.'"

"Many things come up in the session whose meaning we do not know. For example, Mother and Chi could have battles about having a bath and smelling bad."

> "Thank you. What do you think of my math and counting games with Chi."

"Good. No one can tell beforehand how a maneuver will work. Eight can be broken into 5 + 3. Sometimes, you may need to break it down to 5+1+1+1. The main thing is not theory; the main thing is Chi should get it."

Ching clapped and applauded my commonsense statement.

> "I can do this. I can break down numbers. I can play cards. I am good at this because I listen to Chi, I want to understand her, and I want to help her. The main thing I can do is talk to you without fear or shame."

"Be good enough; that's plenty."

My Musings

My attitude towards my musings has evolved. Initially, I viewed the book as a straightforward account of the supervisory process, with an introduction to Essential Psychoanalysis and supervision, and did not consider any musings. Still, the book's essence lies in its supervisory session descriptions. However, as the book's writing progressed, I found myself jotting down immediate thoughts after the supervision, a practice that conveyed my reactions that might be of interest to the reader and understanding of supervision.

Where I once concentrated on insights emerging from the supervisory sessions and secondary accounts of the therapy sessions, I now embrace a broader spectrum of thoughts, linking session insights to wider and sometimes seemingly unrelated topics. This evolution aids in discerning recurring themes, applying the principles of Essential Psychoanalysis, and describing the supervisor's responses or commenting on the analyst's experiences openly and their possible linkages with the ongoing focal issues the patient may have at that time. In addition, the musings help me express myself and help the reader.

In the Essential Psychoanalysis framework, both analyst and patient are seen as engaged observers, moving away from the traditional stance of objectivity, abstinence, neutrality, and the blank screen analyst. I view the analyst's background, upbringing, experiences, and psychoanalytic training as a layered and complex groundwork informing the therapeutic approach and want to describe such influences to the reader. This broad countertransference perspective, which refers to the analyst's emotional reactions and personal experiences that may influence the therapeutic process, enriches the analysis description with the uniqueness of the analyst's Self. As analysts interact and work with patients, each analyst brings their own attitudes, thoughts, emotions, and actions into play.

Many contemporary psychoanalysts acknowledge the significance of the analyst's broad countertransference contributions to understanding the patient. They also recognize the interconnection between the patient's transference and the analyst's countertransference. However, many case reports focus mainly on the patient's transference, with only briefly mentioning the analyst's countertransference. A comprehensive analysis must consider both the patient's transference and the critical aspects of the analyst's countertransference. Here, a distinction must be made between a clinical analysis and the field of psychoanalysis. Details of the analyst's countertransference may be unnecessary, not helpful, burdensome, and even counterproductive if revealed to the patient but may be of substantial value when communicated to peers and readers interested in understanding how psychoanalysis works. The analysis aims to comprehend and alleviate the patient's struggles and distress without allowing excessive focus on the analyst's reactions to overshadow the primary objective.

In Essential Psychoanalysis, the transference-countertransference matrix may seem overwhelmingly complex because there is no privileged, objective, or omniscient perspective. Yet, the profound understanding of the broad countertransference is only accessible through the analyst's introspections. However, in contrast, the analyst's introspections, interpretations, clarifications, questions, comments, behaviors, and office setup are elements in the analytic public domain. However, it's crucial to note that the patient's acceptance or rejection of the analyst's interpretations plays a significant role in the provisional resolutions. This may include progressive exchanges between the patient and the analyst. This interaction fosters mutual recognition, potentially resulting in a shared understanding, a tentative, provisional agreement, or an appreciation of differing viewpoints. This process fosters communications, a sense of connection and mutual empathy, which may be useful in themselves. Despite the complexity, Essential Psychoanalysis acknowledges that while negotiations can be clarified within the therapeutic environment, a degree of indeterminacy, which refers to the inherent uncertainty and subjectivity in the therapeutic process, remains. No perspective is entirely objective or certain; understandings are provisional and open to future revision.

It is crucial for the analyst to continuously differentiate between reactions triggered by the patient's active transference, which are the focus of the analytic process, and personal habitual reactions. This separation often necessitates the analyst's introspection and sometimes testing with the patient. The depth of this introspection is a testament to the complexity and depth of the analytical process.

My reflections, whether they delve into psychoanalytic theory or recount aspects of my life, are meant for the reader's consideration and may not always tie back directly to supervising Chi's treatment.

Today, I begin with Ching's reference to Gedo. This sparked a memory of Gedo and what I felt were his noteworthy characteristics. I will then recap Ching's trait, which we previously discussed. I also found myself reflecting on my own childhood, which is related to my unique manner of reacting to life situations and analysis. Assuming these are key to an analyst's personality, these diverse trends underscore influential patterns in the analyst's unique self and authentic nature that influence the analysis

I want to emphasize that an analyst is better served by trying to understand them and account for their influences rather than assuming a neutral posture, which, in the view of Essential Psychoanalysis, can only be a façade.

First, a few thoughts about this session: Ching is settling down and attending a normal treatment process. He listens to Chi's words, observes her actions as they happen, and provides immediate feedback. I feel this is a helpful practice. For example, Ching discovered a pattern: Chi is edgy on Mondays. He communicated his discovery to her. Ching told Chi that on Mondays, she is loud, orders him around, and is harsh. Compared to Mondays, she is less harsh on Tuesdays and other days. Good job, O thought. This is clear feedback that is expressed in words she can understand.

Ching's role in this psychoanalytic process is not just crucial and significant. His observations and feedback are not just facilitative, they are integral to the process. This is the real business of psychoanalysis: doing what is possible every moment for a particular analyst with a particular patient. Psychoanalysis involves continuously striving to understand and help the patient, expressing that understanding in a language that even a child can understand, and focusing on what may be meaningful to them in each moment.

An analyst attempts to understand the meanings of free association, the spontaneous words patients utter, and their play and actions. The analyst, in this case, Ching, waits for the patient, Chi, to initiate play and plays the role assigned to him by the patient. Ching patiently waited for Chi to choose the game, understanding that both her choosing and the game were. What matters is giving Chi the chance and opportunity to initiate play and act freely. She chose a soft cotton ball to play with. They rolled the ball to each other and enjoyed the exchange. Every word and action of the patient is significant and deserves analytic attention.

There are many soothing songs about a mother or a father and a child rolling a ball back and forth to each other. Parents and preschools use them regularly. However, there was a gentle pattern between Chi and Ching when she suddenly threw a fastball. Again, Ching gave her immediate feedback by exclaiming, "Ouch." Ching had the opportunity to observe that in Chi, there is a tendency to be rough. Much of Chi's problems stem from the roughness of her life, especially her mother's disappointment and punishments when Chi experiences trouble in her life because the mother cannot tolerate Chi's distress. In this context, the game serves as a therapeutic tool, allowing Chi to express herself and for Ching to observe and provide feedback.

Although a game might generally have a gentle tone, it can occasionally acquire a different tone. Ching is trying to address this through his running commentary on Chi's actions, continuous feedback, and occasional feedback to the mother. This commentary and feedback are part of the therapeutic process, helping Chi understand the consequences of her actions and guiding her toward more appropriate behavior.

Memory is a peculiar, fascinating, vivid, or vague glue of our history. Often, and for most of our lives, it works automatically and without much fuss. With aging, just at the point of sharing the accumulated wisdom of experience, memory begins to slide. Ching's recent invocation of Gedo awakened a fragmentary but poignant memory of Gedo. I share this personal memory because it points to the parts of an analyst's core that always shine through.

John Gedo, a renowned analyst in Chicago, frequently hosted gatherings at his home attended by numerous guests. These were primarily analysts or candidates, and often, he invited an out-of-town speaker or frequently held court himself. The atmosphere at these gatherings was always intellectually stimulating, with lively discussions and debates on various psychoanalytic topics. I cannot remember how I first received an invitation, but I attended many of these gatherings.

Gedo delivered his ideas with compelling force and conviction and was commanding. The flow of his thoughts and words was dynamic and precise, like goal-directed, hard-kicked soccer balls or guided missiles launched with a clear objective. His powerful delivery ensured that his intended target received his message and felt its impact.

I remember Gedo sharing his proud memories of his father, who taught him to play soccer as a child. His father was a skilled soccer player.

While Gedo was growing up, he and his dad would often play soccer together. One of their favorite activities was his father teaching him how to be a goalie. Gedo would defend the goal while his father would take shots at the goal. According to Gedo, his father would kick the ball with great force, and Gedo would courageously protect the goal, even as the soccer balls launched by his father came at him with high velocity. Gedo stood his ground and never flinched, even though the ball could have hit him in the head.

However, perhaps in this instance, Gedo's brief recap lasted only a few seconds, and my memory of it is incomplete and indistinct. However, it stands out in my memory because it evoked a vivid and moving recollection of "Casabianca," a poem by the English poet Felicia Dorothea Hemans that we read in school. The narrative of Gedo's early experiences with his father resonated somehow with the emotional depth of Hemans' poem.

The Battle of the Nile, a pivotal naval encounter during the Napoleonic Wars, was a significant event near Alexandria, Egypt. In an attempt to undermine British trade routes, Napoleon Bonaparte launched an invasion of Egypt. The British, aware of a large French naval expedition, dispatched Rear Admiral Sir Horatio Nelson to intercept it. Luc-Julien-Joseph Casabianca, the French flagship L'Orient's ship's commander, asked his young son to remain on deck while a fierce battle commenced between the ship and the British fleet on August 1, 1798.

The poem begins with, "The boy stood on the burning deck, whence all but he had fled." "Casabianca" vividly captures the courage and obedience of a young boy during the Battle of the Nile. The poem opens with a striking image of the boy standing alone on the deck of the L'Orient. Despite the perilous situation and the abandonment of the ship by others, the boy remained dutifully at his post, awaiting further orders from his father, unaware that his father had already died. The boy heroically stayed on board even as flames reached the ammunition in the magazine below the deck. A colossal explosion destroyed the L'Orient. Tragically, the boy and his father perished on that day. This unwavering loyalty amidst the chaos and the impending destruction of the burning ship, a testament to the boy's courage, has become a symbol of ultimate bravery.

During World War II, my dad held the rank of Captain and served as a physician in the British Indian Army stationed in Burma. Occasionally, he talked to me, my siblings, and friends about the war with nostalgia. He may have talked about the Ledo Road, also known as the Stilwell Road, a vital overland route built during World War II. It connected British India with China. The road began in Ledo, Assam, India, and extended to Kunming, China. Along the way, it passed through several Burmese towns. The road was constructed after the Japanese cut off the Burma Road in 1942. This gave the Western Allies an alternative route to deliver war supplies, such as arms, ammunition, food, medical supplies, and fuel, to support China's fight against Japan.

Periodically, he would carefully retrieve and tend to his wartime keepsake collection in an ammunition box. Among these relics was a pair of sturdy black gumboots designed to withstand the relentless monsoon rains and treacherous terrain of Burma's jungles. He taught me how to clean these boots—first the exterior, which was straightforward, and then the interior, which required inverting them to dislodge any unwelcome spiders or scorpions seeking refuge. Following this, using a rag, he taught me to dust the interior of the boots and remove any remaining cobwebs. Initially, putting my hands into the interior of the old dusty boots filled me with apprehensions about any creatures that might still be lurking there. Still, I managed to shape up his boots under his guidance.

On these occasions, my dad occasionally took out his Gurkha knife, another memorabilia from World War II, and applied Vaseline to prevent rust. These moments transitioned into discussions about the end of the war, marked by Emperor Hirohito's surrender and the tragic ritual of Hara-Kiri that some Japanese soldiers chose afterward. Conversations would sometimes turn to marching drills and the topic of malaria and other infectious diseases. He would talk of injuries soldiers endured during the war. Regrettably, these injuries sometimes led to gangrene, making amputations necessary. My curiosity led me to inquire about the amputation process, which brought up the subject of bone saws. Despite my father's warmth and affection, the combined fears of arachnids and scorpions and the grim topics of Hara-Kiri, bone saws, and amputations filled me with a deep sense of anxiety and unease.

In *When Suicide Beckons* (Sripada, 2022), I explore how an analyst's childhood experiences, culture, and training shape their psychoanalytic techniques, particularly in treating a depressed patient. The book delves into how these factors influence countertransference and frame the analytic process, emphasizing that patients and analysts are active participants. I detail the transference-countertransference dynamic, showing how my personal history shaped my responses. While only relevant countertransference insights are transformed into interpretations and interventions, sharing these insights helps readers appreciate the complexity and depth of psychoanalytic treatment, underscoring the importance of the analyst's personal history.

Defining moments of life are preserved as vivid memories or action patterns. They play a pivotal role in shaping an analyst's approach to patient care. For instance, Gedo's bold resoluteness, Ching's shame, and hesitation, and my fearful anxiety are crucial to understanding the personal residues that influence analysis and patient care. These personal attributes—courage, embarrassment, and apprehension—serve as our unique guiding stars, steering us through life's varied climates and seasons, manifesting in our every action and utterance. I am convinced that concealing inherent feelings of pride, shame, or worry behind a veneer of neutrality to maintain an assumption of objectivity robs authenticity from analysis. It does not genuinely enhance analysis. Analysts facilitate healing through sincere engagement; our true selves are a personal characteristic and a vital component of effective patient care. Embracing and acknowledging these personal attributes is crucial for analysts to engage sincerely with patients and account for their contribution to the analysis.

The core problem revealed itself through the tension between Ching's accent and my poor hearing, leaving me uncertain whether Ching said "mother impulse" or "murder impulse."

Chi's mother sought treatment for Chi and has been bringing her to sessions regularly. She has openly admitted her inability to control her thoughts and actions, resulting in her slapping Chi. This has left Chi distraught, leading her to complain about her mother to Ching. Chi's mother feels unfairly portrayed by her daughter and sees herself as a victim. Listening to Chi's mother brought up memories to Ching that he experienced painful punishments from his mother.

For several decades, I worked professionally helping abused and neglected children and mothers involved in domestic violence. My background is quite different from that of my clients. My parents did not physically punish me or my siblings. My wife and I did not physically punish our children.

So, in treating Chi, this diverse group of three individuals, each with unique experiences of the pain of punishment or the lack thereof, highlights that none of us are uniquely equipped to handle aggression and punishment issues. No one is perfectly poised to manage pain and aggression. Nonetheless, the problem of punishment and aggression persists globally. As Ching indicated to Chi's mother, she and he (and me) will try to find the best compromise to address Chi's pain and suffering through our collective efforts and insights. Hopefully, Chi's mother, who has suffered herself and wants the best for Chi, through Ching's ministration or separately through her therapy, could gain some measure of control. Stay tuned.

Supervision: **21**

Before this supervision, Ching sent me a paper by Perelberg ((2017)[60] writing that it helped him understand the "body bond" between Chi and her mother. Ching noted that the paper indicates that because the early body bond is not symbolized, it constitutes a difficult impasse for treatment. He wanted to ask me a question stemming from the paper about this in our subsequent supervision.

> Ching started the session, "The somatic bond between a girl and her mother has the potential to understand melancholia. Change may be impossible because the bond cannot be symbolized. The bond deals with life before language.

"Last week, in my session with Chi, as we approached the end, she asked me if we had enough time to play some game. I asked her to look at the clock. She became ashamed because she could not read the analog clock on the wall. But she asked me to teach her to read the clock. I started with the short needle, and she understood the time was between four and five. The long needle was at eight. I told her that each section of the long needle represented five minutes. She then figured out that if there

---

60 Perelberg, R. J. (2017). Love and melancholia in the analysis of women by women. *International Journal of Psychoanalysis* 98:1533–1549.

were five minutes between digits, and she had to calculate eight dights, the time was 4 40.'"

" 'Yes,' I exclaimed enthusiastically, 'You got it before I could teach you.' She became happy."

"As I told you previously, every Monday, she is down. She does not want to play. She has no interest in dolls, balls, or paper projects. She would ask nonsense questions. Where did you get the carpet? I told her. She asked the same question five times. Then she asked why they didn't give you the carpet as a gift. Slowly, she regained some interest in the hide-and-go-find game. I hid seven dolls. She found three dolls and did not know how many more dolls were left to be found. I tried to get her to subtract three from seven to find out how many more dolls were left to be found. She did not want to think."

"So, I said to Chi, 'Sometimes when you are not in the mood, you don't want to think.' "

"Chi said, 'Sometimes when I am with my mother, and she is trying to teach, my mind shuts off.' "

"I realize that calculation is not an antidote. It turns her off, even if it upsets her mother. I tried to make some games funny, such as calling pairs of dolls with made-up names. For example, when Micky Mouse and a kitty were paired, I called it Micky Kitty. She got tired of the games. It was no good. She finally said, 'I don't want to think. I don't want to calculate. I don't want to play.' "

"So then, I sat on the sofa. She then came and sat next to me. We did nothing; she just sat beside me and seemed to relax. I thought, this is good. She needs to be by my side.

This is the body bond she is missing with her mother. This is what I got from the session. That is all."

I said, "You had said that the Perelberg article helped you. How?"

"I think Chi needed body contact and closeness with her mother. Now, she provokes the contact, although the contact is toxic. She provokes contact even though it compromises her ability to be smart and keep up the bond with her mother."

"I also used the article with an adult female patient. That patient has a good boss who is generally kind and tries to give her reasonable assignments. But the patient remains angry and says, 'I want something more.'"

"I told this patient, 'You are thirty-three years old, but maybe you want to be treated like a three-year-old girl.'"

"My adult female patient said, 'Yes. I want unconditional love.'"

"My question to you and my wish is how to learn from papers like Perelberg and apply it to clinical work."

"Thank you for sending me the Perelberg paper. She is very thoughtful and has many theoretical ideas about melancholia and internalization of the mother's body in development and analyses, in which the patient and analyst are both women. I will focus on one aspect of her treatment method and compare it with yours."

"Perelberg's discussion of the Oedipus complex clarifies its two aspects: Oedipus 1 and 2. In Oedipus 1, common to boys and girls, the mother is the primary object of desire. In Oedipus 2, girls shift their Oedipal object from the mother to the father, while boys maintain the mother as the object of desire but shift their identification from the mother to the father. This segmentation clearly describes the similarities and differences in the developmental trajectory of the Oedipus complex between boys and girls."

"In addition, in this paper, Perelberg discussed the case of Emma, who experiences paralyzing anxiety. Emma describes a lengthy dream where she went to a hairdresser to witness a "horrible" scene of many naked, old people with no skin, a morgue with women with veins emphasizing the pelvic area, a key that would not open a door, but then opened the door. The patient complains that I feel this dream is occupying my head. As reported in the paper, and before any further associations from the patient, Perelberg says, 'A: It was such a horrific dream ... Perhaps this is what you are afraid will happen in the night if you go to sleep; you will have such a horrific dream.'"

I continued, "Now, I am more interested in Perelberg's clinical technique. I want to compare it with yours. I think it is helpful for any analyst to wait for dream associations before offering interpretations or comments. In child work, the analyst should allow the patient to explore herself through play or words.

"A few sessions ago, your patient Chi asked you what you wanted to play. You asked her if she had any choice between playing with a book, doll, or ball. You gave her the choice. She chose the soft cotton ball but threw a fastball at your face after some time. You gave her immediate feedback by crying out, 'Ouch.'"

"I liked it that you waited for the patient to choose. After a dream, I like the analyst to wait for the patient to offer some associations. I liked what you did. Chi was ashamed that she could not read time and asked you to teach her. You followed her lead, and finally, she realized the time was 4 40. I liked what you did."

"From this last session, you said Chi needs to be by your side without calculations. You said this is the body bond she is missing with her mother. I agree with you, especially since there was an eight-month separation from her mother when she was an infant when the mother went off to take care of her sick mother. Yes, the experiences of infancy are beyond language and symbolization and tend to get reenacted. For example, Chi provokes you by throwing a fastball in your face. Chi may be struggling with having missed regular bodily skin contact with her mother during infancy through ordinary child care. She may be downplaying her abilities and skills or not applying herself to math, appearing dependent to provoke her mother unconsciously. This now leads to increased contact, even if it is painful and unhealthy. Ideally, Ching's guidance to the mother or separate treatment for the mother could help her compensate for this loss by exercising more patience. Analysis through play can help Chi understand the potential dangers associated with her provocative behavior."

> "Recently, I was in the bathroom of my office, which is connected to the waiting room. I overheard the mother trying to teach Chi some math. The mother gave Chi the problem of adding $98 + 7$. Then, the mother broke the problem into $98 + 2 + 5$. The mother's tone was more patient and kinder. I had not heard this tone before. I believe it is new. Chi was also paying attention and not being provocative by turning off her mind."

"Good job, Mother and Chi are changing! Continue to follow the psychoanalytic method: First, listen. Then talk."

"You sound like Confucius!"

My musings

While a vast body of literature in developmental psychoanalysis could shed light on Chi's early life, this musing will briefly touch upon a few select contributions that influenced me.

Daniel Stern's (1985)[61] book The Interpersonal World of the Infant is genuinely inspiring. It describes the concept of "fittedness" between mother and infant in understandable terms, a dynamic and reciprocal interaction during early development. This 'fittedness' refers to the seamless coordination of emotional and behavioral responses between the caregiver and child, creating a harmonious relationship. He emphasizes the importance of emotional *attunement* and "matching" behaviors and responses between the caregiver and child. This harmony is evident in the spontaneous and typically unconscious exchange of smiles, movements, and shared looks, where both the mother and her baby instinctively coordinate their actions. According to Stern and colleagues (Stern et al., 1998)[62] , such a "moment of meeting" is "what is happening, now, here, between us." Stern's research suggests that these early interactions are crucial for the child's emotional and social development as they lay the groundwork for the infant's future relationships.

René Spitz's (1965)[63] book, *The First Year of Life: A Psychoanalytic Study*, is a profound exploration of object relations normal and deviant development in the first year of life. It addresses the concept of stranger anxiety, a developmental stage around the eighth month of infancy when

---

61 Stern, D.N. (1985). *The Interpersonal World of the Infant*. New York: Basic Books.

62 Stern, D.N., Sander, L.W., Nahum, J.P., Harrison, A.M., Lyons-Ruth, K., Morgan, A.C., Bruschweiler-Stern, N. & Tronick, E.Z. (1998). Non-interpretive mechanisms in psychoanalytic therapy: The 'something more' than interpretation. *International Journal of Psychoanalysis* 79:903–921.

63 Spitz, R. (1965). *The First Year of Life*. Madison, CT: International Universities Press.

children begin to exhibit distress in the presence of strangers. Spitz coined the term "anaclitic depression" to describe a child's reaction to partial emotional deprivation, characterized by grief, anger, and apathy following the loss of a loved object. He suggested that the child may recover quickly if the loved object is returned within three to five months. However, if the deprivation lasts longer than five months, the child may exhibit signs of worsening deterioration, a condition Spitz referred to as "hospitalism."

Winnicott (1975)[64] Winnicott (1975) introduced the 'good enough mother' concept in his seminal work, 'Playing and Reality.' This idea emphasizes a nurturing approach where a mother initially responds to her infant's needs with an almost complete adaptation to her baby's needs with her utmost abilities. As the child develops, the mother gradually introduces minor, manageable frustrations to foster independence and self-identity. However, the 'holding environment,' where the mother's attunement to her child's needs creates a secure foundation for growth, truly shapes the child's future. He argues that perfection in mothering is neither possible nor necessary; instead, providing consistent, 'good enough' care is essential for the child's healthy maturation and independence. This balanced approach enables the child to face life's challenges while supported by a solid foundation of maternal care. Winnicott's insights have profoundly impacted our understanding of early childhood development and the crucial role of maternal care in shaping a child's future.

Bowlby's (1973)[65] observations on the influence of attachment and loss figures on a child's reaction to potentially frightening situations are genuinely insightful and provide a deep understanding of child

---

64 Winnicott, D.W. (1975). Chapter XXIII. Clinical Varieties of Transference [1955-6]. *Through Paediatrics to Psycho-Analysis*. Brunner/Mazel, pp. 295–299.

65 Bowlby, J. (1973). *Anxious Attachment and the 'Phobias' of Childhood. Attachment and Loss: Volume II: Separation, Anxiety and Anger*. New York: Basic Books, pp. 258–291.

psychology. Bowlby believed that children are naturally driven to form attachments with caregivers for survival, ensuring their needs are met and they are protected from dangers. His theory highlighted the importance of a secure base for a child to explore the world. It emphasized that early relationships with caregivers profoundly influence an individual's emotional life and relationships throughout their lifespan. Along with Mary Ainsworth's further development of the theory, Bowlby's work has significantly impacted psychology by deepening the understanding of the importance of early emotional bonds.

Mary Ainsworth, a developmental psychologist, significantly built upon John Bowlby's Attachment Theory. Her empirical work, particularly the 'Strange Situation' procedure, led to the classification of various attachment styles in infants—secure, ambivalent, avoidant, and disorganized (Ainsworth and Bell,1970)[66]. Ainsworth's work, combined with Bowlby's theoretical framework, established Attachment Theory, a fundamental model for understanding the development of human relationships from infancy to adulthood. Integrating concepts from attachment, internal working models, embodied cognition, language, and brain development has further enriched Attachment Theory (Fonagy and Target, 2007)[67].

During infancy, the brain's lack of myelination makes retrieving memories from this stage of development impossible, meaning that early memories are universally elusive. This applies not only to Chi, who experienced significant trauma due to early childhood separation, but

---

66 Ainsworth, M.D.S., & Bell, S.M. (1970). Attachment, exploration, and separation: Illustrated by the behavior of one-year-olds in a strange situation. *Child Development*, 41(1), 49–67. https://doi.org/10.2307/1127388

67 Fonagy, P. & Target, M. (2007). The Rooting of the Mind in the Body: New Links between Attachment Theory and Psychoanalytic Thought. *Journal of the American Psychoanalytic Association* 55:411–456.

to everyone. Children often learn about their early years through stories told by family members or, in today's world, through visual records like photographs or videos. While these sources do not offer direct memories of childhood emotions and experiences, they provide valuable second-hand insights into personal history, creating a shared understanding of the human experience.

Donald Spence's (1982)[68] concept of "narrative truth" in psychoanalysis emphasizes the distinction between narrative truth and historical truth. He argues that the stories patients create in therapy, while not necessarily historically accurate, are psychologically meaningful and emotionally significant. These narratives are crafted within the therapeutic relationship and are crucial for the patient's understanding and resolution of psychological conflicts. Spence's idea challenges psychoanalysis's traditional focus on objective historical accuracy, underscoring the importance of the patient's subjective experience and the therapeutic narrative.

In child analysis and psychotherapy, memories are reconstructed through transference, play, reenactments, and storytelling, symbolic equivalents of infantile or early experiences without memory residues. These narratives, while not direct memories, help children create a framework to understand their own lives and the lives of their family members. The analyst's role is crucial in shaping a narrative that aids the child's adaptation, even if it is not based on direct recollection. The analyst provides direction and understanding through guidance and support, helping the child make sense of their experiences.

I and many other contemporary analysts believe that formal and non-interpretative elements are crucial in the analytical process.

---

68 Spence, D. (1982). *Narrative Truth and Historical Truth: Meaning and Interpretation in Psychoanalysis.* New York: Norton.

Clarification, interpretation, explanation, confrontation, setting boundaries, and addressing issues related to vacations or illness are part of the analyst's formal operations. They also involve practical aspects such as contractual and billing agreements, confidentiality, safety protocols, and a commitment to ethical and professional conduct. The analyst's demeanor plays a significant role in the process, including routine interactions during sessions, such as greetings, smiles, gestures, postures, tones, exclamations, interjections, and even the use of humor or casual conversation. These subtle behaviors help create a therapeutic environment that fosters connection and trust. Expressions of compassion, concern, empathy, attunement, and the occasional giving of gifts also contribute to this dynamic. Effectively handling and resolving separations, reunions, misunderstandings, and mistakes are crucial to maintaining the therapeutic relationship. These factors underscore the substantial effort required to sustain a successful therapeutic alliance. The analyst's theories are critical aspects of the analyst's training but must be individualized to fit each patient.

Theories provide pathways for analysts to approach and engage with their patients. The metaphor of a neighborhood effectively illustrates how a theory applies to an individual's case. Just as a person encompasses various facets—like a mouth (the point of intake), a heart, a spirit, and a home—a theory parallels community structures such as an airport, train or bus station, postal code, playground, school, or library. These theoretical frameworks guide the analyst's journey to understand the patient. The analyst's theories, critical aspects of the analyst's training, provide a structured approach to understanding and interpreting the patient's experiences and behaviors. However, the unique relationship between the patient and the analyst enables the analyst to move beyond these general frameworks and reach the patient's core—the mouth, heart, hearth, or soul—.

Her mother's absence significantly impacted Chi's early childhood during a crucial developmental period. From 8 to 16 months, while her mother was away caring for her own mother after a severe stroke, Chi was primarily cared for by her father and paternal grandmother. When her mother returned, Chi exhibited signs of disorganization, detachment, and difficulty in adjusting, and these effects continued to linger, manifesting as an anxious attachment to her mother.

Chi's mother works diligently to provide for her, supporting her education and actively engaging in her treatment, although she struggles with certain aspects. She finds it challenging to tolerate parts of the treatment process, mainly when it involves allowing Chi to express herself freely, which she perceives as unfair. The mother's own stress, conflicts with her ex-husband, and difficulties with her mother-in-law compound the challenges in her relationship with Chi. She is also profoundly disappointed in Chi's developmental progress, particularly her struggles with math, difficulty in forming friendships, and excessive dependence, which leaves her feeling embarrassed and frustrated.

The relationship between Chi and her mother is strained, with both contributing to the mismatch. The mother often loses control and resorts to striking Chi when frustrated, especially over math problems or when Chi is bullied, even going as far as calling Chi "stupid." Chi's mother often gives her math problems to solve, which are beyond Chi's reach, and Chi has told Ching that her mind turns off on such occasions.

On the other hand, Chi may provoke her mother unconsciously by not applying herself and seeking excessive help. This provocative behavior extends into her treatment of Ching, where she sometimes acts aggressively, such as hitting him with a ball or threatening him with hundreds of math problems. These dynamics, rooted in the trauma of her mother's absence during a formative period, highlight the lasting impact of early experiences on Chi's psychological development.

Chi finds comfort in Ching's presence, particularly when he is not trying to teach her anything. Ching is not just a therapist but also a significant figure in Chi's life. She enjoys playful and gentle interactions, especially when Ching helps her with math in a creative and non-pressuring way. However, she sometimes expresses frustration through play, taking on the role of the punisher, which mirrors her mother's aggressive behavior. This behavior is evident when Chi throws a ball at Ching's face or attacks him with a water gun. Ching has addressed these dynamics in therapy, recognizing his discomfort in the role of the punished and discussing physical punishment openly with both Chi and her mother. He has also reflected on the parallels between his own countertransference shame and Chi's shame about her math difficulties, as well as the mother's shame when she loses control and physically reprimands Chi. Recently, Ching noticed that Chi's mother is gentler when she gives Chi math problems, and the problems she gives are those that Chi could solve. Chi appears to apply his mind when so engaged with her mother. This analysis moves beyond theoretical constructs and abstract models to understand human behavior to a more profound understanding of Chi's experiences, which involves a deep and empathetic comprehension of her unique situation.

Supervision: 22

Ching and I usually meet on Tuesdays, but due to my travel plans, we rescheduled our supervisory session to Wednesday this week. So, there were more sessions to report during this supervision.

> "Something is going on. Chi has stopped cooperating with me during our games and has reverted to her old behavior, trying to boss me around. Over the weekend, Chi's mother called and told me Chi was getting 'worser.' The Mother said, 'Chi refusing to do her homework and deliberately provoking me to slap her. However, nothing is working. She does not listen to me.' This behavior at home with her mother has now carried over into our sessions with me.
>
> "During our session on Monday, Chi did not want to play with clay, paper games, or dolls. She refused to engage in anything and just sat there with an angry expression. So, I asked her, 'Why are you angry?'
>
> "Chi responded, 'Stop asking questions. I will not answer.'"
>
> "I felt compelled to submit to her. I told Chi, 'You are on an angry tirade. You want to boss over me.'"
>
> "Chi then said, 'Stop talking. I will not talk to you. Just do what I tell you.'"

"Something happened by the time she came on Tuesday. She came and wanted to play with clay, but she looked sad. Usually, she takes out as much clay as she needs. On Tuesday, she went into my storage, took out all my clay, and ripped and destroyed the box in which the clay was stored. Based on the way she was destroying the box, I told Chi, "You seem angry today, too.'"

"Chi smiled at me and said, "You are wrong. I am not angry.'"

"Because she looked sad, I told Chi, 'Maybe you are not angry, but you look sad to me.'"

"Chi said, 'Yes. I am sad. I am sad and angry.'"

In this instance, Ching did not provide contextual information to support his interpretation. Nevertheless, his observation helped Chi acknowledge her own sadness. Ching intuitively grasped that Chi's traumatic experiences had triggered emotional transference, including her identification with the aggressor (A. Freud)[69]. Chi overcame her resistance mainly due to Ching's consistent approach throughout the treatment, which can be called insight, relationship, concern, care, attunement, empathy, or compassion.

"This was the first time Chi mentioned feeling sad. She asked me to get her some magic powder to play with, which is currently popular among many girls in China. It's a colored powder that children can use to imagine various

---

69 Freud, A. (1972). Comments on Aggression. *International Journal of Psycho-Analysis* 53:163–171.

things. Since it's easily available, I promised to get it for her."

"When Chi came in today, she wanted to play with clay and make a swimming pool. She made a huge pool. After making the swimming pool, she wanted to fill it with water. Chi wanted to put the magic powder and have the powder represent water. Chi asked me for the magic powder she had requested several days ago, and I had promised to get it for her. Unfortunately, I forgot to buy the magic powder and told her, 'I forgot.' She became sad and upset."

"Chi them asked me, 'When did you forget? How did you forget?'"

"I felt embarrassed and told her we would order the magic powder from Amazon immediately. So I sat by the computer and ordered the magic powder for Amazon."

"Today, when Chi came to the session, she asked if the magic powder had arrived from Amazon. It has not yet arrived. She did not get too upset. She felt that I ordered it was a sign of good faith."

Although Chi has many reasons to be disappointed in life and is angry and provocative, she still has hope and optimism in magic and can grant that Ching is trying to help her. She is not wholly pessimistic. She trusts Ching and the treatment and is capable of forgiveness.

"Chi was in a good mood; she told me, "Now I have learned how to read the clock," she said proudly, looking directly into my eyes with a sense of accomplishment. Our eyes met briefly, and I could see her pride in herself. We talked about the pool and imaginary houses, and I could not help but think that these might be psychological symbols. The pool could represent a container, with the water acting as an antidote for her life challenges. That is all I have for now. What are your thoughts about this session?"

"There are many good ways to understand any case. This is my view. Transference is a theory, but it is also a felt experience. You started by talking about how Chi had stopped playing last week and said no to your play calculations and that her mother had called you and said she was "worser." Looks like she was treating her mother and you with anger and non-cooperation."

"I felt so and told her, 'You feel angry at too many orders from mom to do the math and from play calculations from me.'"

"She agreed and said, 'I cannot do anything right. I am angry and will not cooperate.'"

"Yes. That is the hostile mother transference. In addition, another transference showed up before and this Monday when you had to submit to her. She identifies with her aggressive mother and treats you like her own Self. For example, she threatens to punish you with hundreds of math questions." You told her, 'You act like your mother and make me feel how you feel.' So, there are two kinds of transferences operating in her.

"You feel how she feels. You understand her. So, you could also see the connection between her anger and sadness. Her sadness in the past was covered up. You could only see anger. Now, she has also acknowledged her sadness. Now, there is a connection established between her anger and sadness."

"Yes."

"You understand how she feels, which allows her to talk about her anger or sadness. You can both discuss a magic powder that can become anything, including water for her pool of imagination in your office. She might have felt sad when you did not remember to buy her the magic dust, but despite her sadness and frustration, she moved past it because you tried to order it online. She can forgive; she trusts your support and feels hopeful even when things fail. That is the true magic of treatment. At any time, there are just a few themes in operation; for example, in one moment, she may treat you like her mother, and in another, she treats you like her own Self. These ideas are experienced in the emotions of the play and best expressed in the patient's language."

"Some key paths to the playground of treatment are found in the big ideas you come across in psychoanalytic books and articles. These theories and constructs can guide you to the doorstep of analysis. However, once you are there, what takes precedence are the perceptions, thoughts, imaginations, emotions, and actions that unfold in the moment between the patient and the analyst. I know you are fascinated by terms like 'containment,' while those concepts are important, they are not as crucial as the 'here and now' of your interactions with Chi. Those ideas belong to the 'there and then' of intellectual psychoanalysis, but what happens between you and Chi is immediate and subtle. In comparison, terms like 'containment' and other technical concepts seem almost gross."

Perhaps because of my pronunciation, Ching's hearing, or the devil on the internet, Ching heard what I said as "growth." Therefore, he told me he did not understand and was looking up the relationship between 'subtle' and 'growth' on his Communicator program.

Just as he was doing so, he had an intriguing look on his face. He told me that a message from Chi's mother had arrived, and he would quickly open her communication. He read its first sentence from Chi's mother.

> "This is the first line from Chi's mother. 'I believe that Chi is revenging me.'"

A snarky comment escaped me, "Revenging happens when you hit someone!"

However, I also believe Chi's mother is beginning to move beyond her usual stereotypes of Chi. Instead of seeing her as a dependent, disobedient, and disruptive child, Chi's mother is starting to empathize with her, trying to see the world from Chi's perspective and understand her motivations. This shift in attitude may indicate a more nurturing approach to parenting. Alternatively, this could indicate that Chi, who was once obedient to her mother out of fear, now rebels against her, resulting in open interpersonal conflict.

> Ching continued to read her mother's communication, which explained how, in her own childhood, her mother and father divorced, and it was hard for her. Ching then said, "This is a long communication. I will read it later and deal with it. We do not have to deal with it now."

I continued my comments about Chi's mother. "Chi's mother is dedicated to Chi. She wants the best for her daughter. Both have experienced the trauma of parental divorce during their childhoods. Mother cares for Chi. Mother spends a great deal of energy trying to help Chi. Chi's mother's love is true but somewhat misguided. Perhaps you could ask Mother, 'Why is Chi revenging?'"

Ching, imagining himself as Chi's mother, said, "Because
I beat her."

It is possible that a child, even without a conscious memory of her
mother's absence between eight and sixteen months, might still harbor
feelings of anger toward fate and a deep-seated desire for retribution.
Chi's frustration could be further intensified during therapy by Ching's
insistence on engaging her in lighthearted math quizzes. It seems that
Chi has recently reached her breaking point.

I asked Ching, "How do you feel about my emphasis on your
experiences with Chi and your treatment, focusing on immediate
interactions in the Chinese language and play while giving less importance
to intellectual constructs like 'containment'?"

Ching replied, "I do not feel undermined by your
emphasis on clinical material experiences over intellectual
constructs. I also believe that treatment experiences are
crucial, aligning with our shared perspective. Perhaps
you suggest I am already applying these principles in
my clinical work without fully realizing it. However, I
appreciate certain theories, as they add value to the top
of clinical practice. Given my lack of experience in child
therapy, it is difficult for me to assess fully. I understand
that terms like 'containment,' 'antidote,' and 'projective
identification' are not part of a child's vocabulary—they
are more suited to adult psychoanalytic discussions."

In Chi's words, actions, and play—whether it is the gleam of
accomplishment in her eyes when she reads a clock or her threats
to punish you with hundreds of math questions—she is offering you

invaluable lessons in psychoanalysis. Through her dolls, paper projects, thoughts about the paper bird in your waiting room, card games, clay pools, and magical powdered water, she reveals fragments of her identity, presenting you with a treasure trove of insights. By deeply engaging with her expressions and challenges and using creative intuition, you will grasp the essence of psychoanalysis and gain a profound understanding of your own experiences. Veering too much toward abstract concepts like 'containment' might dilute your practical grasp of how psychoanalysis works. However, I am happy with your response.

"I am happy that you are happy."

We both smiled. I said, "For now, you are exactly where you need to be— with the anger, sadness, revenge, magic powders, pools of imagination, and the new skill of reading the clock. You do not need to go anywhere else."

"I am not going anywhere. I appreciate what you are saying. For example, after our last session this week, I told Chi, 'I will see you next week.'"

"Chi said to me, 'It will be a long time before I see you again.'"

"I responded, 'You will miss me over the weekend.'"

I thought and said to Ching, "Right on."

My Musings

Ching began the session by indicating that "something is going on," prompting a need to explore what that might be. Ching described the clinical interactions that provided clues: Chi had previously threatened Ching with punishment via math questions, and in this session, she stopped cooperating and began bossing him around, expressing anger and making Ching feel compelled to submit. Chi's mother also reported that Chi's behavior was worsening and that she was "revenging" her. Has an open conflict broken between Chi and her mother? Eventually, Chi admitted to feeling sad and angry.

These observations aided Ching in constructing a preliminary understanding of the situation, deeply rooted in the therapeutic interactions and the unique language, play, and communications among Chi, her Mother, and Ching. This understanding, derived organically from the therapeutic context, holds immense value as it is not based on external intellectual concepts but rather on the intricacies of the situation at hand, underscoring the significance of the psychoanalytic approach.

In a therapeutic setting, exploring multiple perspectives is beneficial and necessary to comprehend the situation optimally. Ching's question invites me to clarify, 'What did I think was going on?'

Although Ching described a set of brief therapeutic encounters, I felt they were significant from the psychoanalytic understanding point of view. Two ideas came to my mind—identification with the aggressor and types of resistance.

The concept of "Identification with the aggressor," a defense mechanism first described by Sándor Ferenczi (1949)[70] and further

---

70 Ferenczi, S. (1949). Confusion of the Tongues Between the Adults and the Child—(The Language of Tenderness and of Passion). *International Journal of Psycho-Analysis* 30:225–230.

expanded by Anna Freud (1972)[71], describes how victims of abuse, often unconsciously, begin to align themselves with the traits of their abuser as a way to manage feelings of passive distress, discomfort, and helplessness. This mechanism is particularly prevalent in cases of prolonged trauma, especially during childhood, where the victim is unable to escape the abusive situation and, therefore, adopts the abuser's characteristics as a means of self-preservation.

When a child or adult is subjected to physical, sexual, or emotional abuse, the abuser typically holds more power, whether due to age, physical strength, or position of authority. The victim, feeling powerless and unable to flee, is forced to endure the abuse, which creates a sense of being trapped in an inescapable situation. The constant fear, anticipation, and uncertainty of when the next episode of abuse will occur leaves the victim in a state of helplessness. Any attempt to resist, seek help, or express discomfort runs the risk of even more severe abuse, further entrenching the victim in their powerless position.

A child who identifies with their abuser might display aggression towards animals or peers, becoming a bully in their own right. In adults, identification with the aggressor can lead to abusive behavior towards children, manifesting as childhood abuse or neglect. This pattern can also occur in adult relationships, resulting in domestic violence, emotional manipulation, or sexual violence. In a workplace, there may be instances where a manager's actions can lead to workplace aggression towards an employee. This could manifest as unjust treatment or unreasonable expectations, contributing to a hostile work atmosphere where an employee might feel undermined or undervalued.

---

71 Freud, A. (1972). Comments on Aggression. *International Journal of Psycho-analysis* 53:163–171.

What does a person gain by identifying with the aggressor? By adopting behaviors or attitudes similar to the aggressor, the victim reduces the perception of conflict between themselves and the abuser. This alignment can create a psychological illusion of safety, as the victim feels less threatened by thinking and acting like the aggressor. A person may experience a sense of power and control over their environment. Instead of feeling helpless and afraid, the victim-turned-aggressor may begin to feel powerful, experiencing a sense of mastery and dominance over others. For example, an abuser may feel a sense of control by being feared by their victims and choosing when and how to inflict harm. This provides a temporary reprieve from their own feelings of helplessness and uncertainty, allowing them to exert power in situations where they once felt vulnerable.

This process is not a deliberate choice; it happens unconsciously, and the victim may not even be aware that they are mimicking the aggressor's behaviors or attitudes. To avoid conflict and potential escalation of the abuse, the victim may unconsciously begin to identify with the aggressor, operating on the premise of "I do not have a conflict with you; I am just like you." This identification allows the victim to align themselves with the abuser in an attempt to prevent further conflict.

What does a person lose by identifying with the aggressor? By identifying with the aggressor, a person loses a genuine connection to their own emotions and experiences. This defense mechanism does not truly resolve the internal conflict or trauma caused by the abuse; instead, it can lead to a profound dissociation from the victim's authentic needs and emotions. By assuming the role of the abuser, they project their denied and displaced feelings onto others, blurring the boundaries between themselves and their victims. This often results in a loss of empathy, compassion, and concern for others, diminishing their sense of humanity. In adopting the aggressor's characteristics, the individual often denies or suppresses awareness of their own feelings of powerlessness, anger, sadness, or fear. This suppression also extends to ignoring similar feelings in their victims. By taking on the traits of the aggressor, the victim avoids confronting and working through their own painful emotions in connection with their victimhood and learning lessons from such experiences.

Unfortunately, this process can perpetuate a cycle of abuse. Individuals who were abused as children and adopted the traits of their aggressors may grow up to become bullies themselves, abusive parents, or adults who continue the cycle of abuse. This transmission of abusive behavior can occur across generations, particularly in cultures or families where strict discipline, often justified by the adage "spare the rod and spoil the child," is accepted or even encouraged. Such cultural or familial norms can make it challenging to recognize these behaviors as harmful, further entrenching the cycle of abuse.

When a victim eventually begins to direct their aggression toward the original abuser, the defense mechanism of identification with the aggressor ceases to function. This shift brings the underlying interpersonal conflict to the surface, allowing the victim to become aware of their anger, frustration, and desire for revenge. However, this awareness also introduces the risk of escalating the situation into open conflict, which can be dangerous and destabilizing.

Understanding this defense mechanism is crucial in therapeutic settings. It helps therapists develop strategies to assist patients in recognizing and breaking free from this subconscious alignment with their aggressors. By helping patients reconnect with their true feelings and needs, therapy can restore their sense of authenticity and emotional connection, enabling them to break the cycle of abuse and heal from their past traumas. Recognizing and addressing the identification with the aggressor is crucial in facilitating this healing process and helping patients regain control over their lives and relationships.

As described in this session, this situation with Chi also brought to my mind Merton Gill's (1979)[72] work in psychoanalytic theory, particularly his insights on transference and resistance. Transference, a key concept in psychoanalysis, refers to the patient's unconscious redirection of feelings from one person to another, often to the therapist. Gill's identification of two critical types of resistance, namely resistance to awareness of the transference and resistance to resolution of the transference, has significantly contributed to our understanding of psychoanalysis.

Resistance to awareness of the transference occurs when patients unconsciously avoid recognizing that they are projecting childhood feelings onto their analyst. Gill believed this should be addressed early in therapy. In this situation, the therapist's responsibility is to subtly assist the patient in recognizing their projections and elucidating the resistance to recognizing how the patient's inner conflicts and life dissatisfactions are linked to the dynamics within the analysis. This process involves a delicate balance of support and insight, helping the patient to see the parallels between their experiences and the therapeutic process.

The lines from Henry Wadsworth Longfellow's (1863)[73] poem that includes "Ships That Pass in the Night" is part of a larger metaphorical narrative. The poem, "The Theologian's Tale," from the collection *Tales of a Wayside Inn*, uses the imagery of ships crossing paths in the night that may symbolize transient and ultimately meaningless human encounters.

---

72 Gill, M.M. (1979). The Analysis of The Transference. *Journal of the American Psychoanalytic Association* 27:263–288.

73 https://en.wikisource.org/wiki/Tales_of_a_Wayside_Inn

"Ships that pass in the night, and speak each other in passing,
Only a signal shown and a distant voice in the darkness;
So on the ocean of life we pass and speak one another,
Only a look and a voice, then darkness again and a silence."

The metaphor of ships crossing paths in the darkness is a poignant representation of the fleeting nature of some human connections. Like vessels that meet only to part ways, individuals often cross paths momentarily, rarely establishing profound ties. Longfellow's poetic imagery accentuates the transient quality of such interactions, which, despite their brief intensity, typically fail to forge enduring relationships. After these encounters, the ensuing 'darkness and silence' reinforce the idea that such lives are a tapestry of transient exchanges, which touch upon our existence but seldom change life's subsequent course.

As Gill clarified, analysts presume that resistance to the transference ultimately rests on the unconscious displacement of attitudes from the past onto the analyst. The resistance is directed at making conscious of any understanding relating to such a displacement.

I (Sripada, 1988)[74] discussed the dynamics during a period when transference seemed absent, yet it was actually at the peak of a mother transference neurosis. In this context, 'transference neurosis' refers to the re-emergence of early neurotic patterns and their associated defense mechanisms within the therapeutic transference. I introduced the term 'generalization' as a broad interpretive approach in analysis aimed at increasing the patient's awareness of common features shared by the analyst, current real-life figures outside the transference (such as a spouse,

---

74 Sripada, B. (1988). Apparent absence of transference: A special instance of transference neurosis. *Annual of Psychoanalysis* 16:155–170.

boss, or friends), as well as genetic features linked to remembered parents and significant others. Generalization can help the patient become aware of feelings like anger or frustration in relationships with others, including the analyst, without intensifying transference resistance. Establishing this common ground can clarify the affect, allowing the patient to explore their emotions while postponing the more complex interpretation of transference displacements.

In psychoanalysis, the genuine nature of transference often allows for revisiting and re-examining early childhood events, providing the patient with an opportunity for a more profound analysis-based resolution. However, when patients are convinced that their transference is a replica of their childhood experiences, it hampers their capacity to dissect and work through these feelings, thus posing a considerable barrier to their resolution. This phenomenon is known as resistance to resolving transference. The patient may feel that the analyst is toxic just as the parent is or was toxic. This concept was exemplified in Chi's situation when Ching observed, 'Something is going on.' These resistances may be fleeting or may endure throughout the analysis. It is crucial to effectively confront these resistances to transference resolution through analytical insight or intuitive understanding to facilitate its resolution and enable further progress in therapy. By effectively confronting these resistances, we can empower our patients and motivate them toward further progress in therapy.

Understanding resistance to awareness of transference versus resistance to the resolution of transference: When resistance involves a lack of awareness of transference, the patient fails to recognize references to it while discussing extra-transference figures, such as a boss or spouse. The problem is realizing that the patient-analyst relationship is reflected in these other relationships. Conversely, when resistance pertains to resolving transference, the patient's strong belief in its reality becomes a barrier. In this case, the patient does not recognize that their feelings for the analyst merely represent their life, providing valuable insights during treatment. This may happen when a patient confuses the transference relationship with a past or a real relationship. While the analyst or treatment situation might introduce certain triggering elements, transference does not precisely replicate past experiences. Here, the patient finds it challenging to differentiate between the emotions directed at significant figures from their childhood and those directed at the analyst in treatment. Thus, the analyst interprets both resistance to awareness of transference and resistance to the resolution of transference to facilitate the analysis.

In analysis, while the objective is to understand a patient accurately, achieving this is far from guaranteed and should not be assumed. A crucial aspect of analytic working through and learning involves identifying and understanding various shortcomings, such as a lack of clarity, a mismatch between the patient's expectations and the analyst's actions, prediction errors, miscommunications, failures of empathy, misunderstandings, misattunements, difficulty in tolerating the other, blunt tactlessness, and failures to resonate. Addressing these analytic shortcomings is essential for refining analytical models, improving future predictions, and enhancing communication. Identifying these shortcomings can help analysts cultivate a deeper sense of self-correcting empathy and better align their mutual expectations.

Like the concept of a 'Goldilocks economy'—where conditions are neither too weak nor too strong—psychoanalysis thrives when there is a balanced transfer of emotions that is appropriately engaged but not overwhelming. This balance creates an environment that is conducive to healing and fosters understanding. These psychoanalytic constructs, containment, identification with the aggressor, resistance to the transferences, and transference to the theory, are crucial in providing the analyst with a sense of direction to endure the psychological turbulence that comes with the pressures and challenges of analytical work but have to be backed up with events in the treatment.

Transference is dynamic and can change gradually or sometimes dramatically, with resistances and transferences occurring in waves. It is essential to differentiate the current wave from previous and potential future ones. In earlier sessions, Ching interpreted Chi's behavior as projecting her feelings toward her mother onto him, which could be understood as an "obedient mother transference." Chi also demonstrated a "self-transference" by identifying with her mother and treating Ching or a doll as if they were her own self. Recently, Chi has shown aggression toward her mother and Ching, reflecting a brief identification with the aggressor. This suggests that the latest iteration of the transference is resistant to resolving the transference.

Ching's therapeutic strategy, emphasizing free associations and therapeutic play, empowers Chi. Chi enjoys the freedom to direct the play scenarios, allowing her to explore her emotions and relationships in a way that is meaningful to her. This approach has already led Chi to recognize the similarities between her interactions with her mother and Ching. Her recent brief worsening indicates that her resistance may be rooted in a reluctance to resolve such similarities.

Ching's support for Chi's math challenges is not just about the problems she endures. It is about the reinforcement of their therapeutic relationship. Ching carefully designs math problems that match Chi's skill level. Although she appreciates their good faith and helpfulness, they remind her mother of forced attempts to teach her. While Chi enjoys solving these problems as they help her make sense of timekeeping, they also evoke painful memories of past struggles with learning to read the clock. As a result, Chi sometimes chooses to engage in quiet companionship with Ching, preferring moments of connection with

Ching that do not involve questioning or problem-solving. These moments reinforce the therapeutic relationship, making Chi feel safe and supported and helping her to process her emotions at her own pace.

Despite these developments, Chi has been able to express her sadness and anger, which is a positive sign. It shows that she still connects to her emotions despite her anger and challenging behavior. Her ability to feel sadness indicates that her fundamental connection to herself is intact, and her stresses and identification with the aggressor have not wholly severed her capacity for hope, imagination, and sorrow. Chi remains in touch with her imaginative world pool and magic powders, crucial for her ongoing healing and growth.

Chi's mother, who has her own history of trauma, struggles with her parenting role but is making a conscious effort to improve. She actively engages with Ching, offering and receiving feedback as she seeks to understand better and support Chi. A significant development is the mother's shift in perspective—she is beginning to see Chi not just as a dependent and disobedient child but as someone who may have her own reasons for acting out, including feelings of "revenge." This new understanding reflects her growing attempts to empathize with her daughter or the outbreak of open conflict between them.

However, some of the mother's parenting methods, though culturally accepted, contribute to Chi's discomfort and unease. Despite the joint efforts of Chi, her mother, and Ching, the situation remains complex and requires continuous, ongoing therapeutic intervention. Given these issues' deep-rooted and severe nature, the treatment outcome is uncertain, but the commitment to addressing them is evident.

Rangell (Rangell 1982; Rangell 2002[75]) proposed the 'transference to theory,' which refers to the emotional attachments that psychoanalysts can form with psychoanalytic theories, like the transference observed in clinical settings. This attachment can significantly impact their clinical practice and theoretical interpretations. Rangell also delves into the implications of this phenomenon in psychoanalytic education and mentorship. He observes that the affective reactions of candidates and analysts, which can range from mild to intense and be both positive and negative, are often transferred from training analysts and institutes to the theories they represent. This can lead to a rigid adherence to specific theories or dismissal of others, including focusing on the analysis of transference and the here and now, sometimes ridiculing the goal of reconstruction and the underlying theory.

In the recent supervisory session, I discussed Ching's tendency to idealize concepts such as "containment." In my opinion, all contemporary psychoanalytic ideas are influenced by personal feelings toward those ideas. I believe that psychoanalysis should not be based on beliefs or assumptions like those in religion or outdated ideas of objectivity, which have been questioned by modern science and the current understanding of broad countertransference. I aimed to help Ching recognize this influence of personal feelings on his understanding of psychoanalytic theories, a challenge that all analysts face. Analysts must know the risks of excessively idealizing or devaluing their attitudes toward theory. I think relying on just one theory to address theoretical questions is a mistake. Theories should be used to create hypotheses for specific cases, but these hypotheses must be tested in each situation. A theoretical proposition is only helpful if it helps a patient; it should be considered provisionally

---

75 Rangell, L. (2002). The Theory of Psychoanalysis: Vicissitudes of its Evolution. *Journal of the American Psychoanalytic Association* 50:1109–1137.

valid only when it is beneficial in practice. I shared this clinical bias with Ching, emphasizing that I do not claim to be unbiased. My goal was to empower Ching and my readers to be critical and reflective about our relationship with theoretical concepts in our work, as this is a crucial aspect of our practice.

Any theoretical framework an analyst uses must resonate with and be comprehensible to the patient. The concepts must be relevant and valuable to the individual's unique situation. However, there may be times when both the patient and analyst find mutual significance in an idea that does not neatly fit within any established theoretical framework. Even if it does not align with a specific theory, it remains clinically relevant, as the analytic relationship and the patient's experience are the ultimate testing grounds for any idea. This underscores the need for flexibility and adaptability in applying psychological theories to individual cases, acknowledging the value of meaningful clinical insights, even if they do not conform to any existing theoretical model. Therefore, the guiding principle I aimed to convey to Ching and the reader was that the patient's response to an interpretation is of the utmost importance, and his role in this process is crucial, while the interpretation's conformity or lack thereof to a theoretical framework is of lesser significance.

Supervision: **23**

"This past weekend has left me feeling exhausted, as it was filled with various situations involving Chi. I will tell you what happened and give you a timeline. At the end of last week, Chi's mother reached a breaking point because she could not care for Chi and suggested that her father take over. Over the weekend, I spoke with both parents and heard different perspectives on the same events."

"Last weekend, Chi's mother lost her temper and temporarily abandoned her. She told Chi to leave the house and not return. Chi gathered some belongings and was out in the rain for an hour. Later, Chi's mother picked her up at the gate of their community and arranged for Chi to stay with her father. Chi's mother then called me and asked me to talk to Chi's father to get his side of the story. I spoke to both parents."

"Chi's father informed me that Chi had been staying with him since the weekend. He believed Chi's problems stemmed from her not having fixed duties and having chaotic routines. His focus now is to bring order and establish routines for Chi with the help of his parents. Although Chi's paternal grandmother has a quick temper, she dearly loves Chi and helps with regular feeding, sleeping, getting her ready for school, and other daily needs. The father believes Chi can finally have a regular life and settle down. He also mentioned that Chi's paternal grandfather is very involved, playing with her and encouraging her to exercise for ninety minutes daily, which the father thinks is vital because Chi is overweight. Her grandfather also spends time helping with her education and arranges playtime with neighborhood friends her age. The father seems committed and eager to do whatever he can to stabilize Chi's life."

"Both parents have mentioned that Chi seems happy living with her father and paternal grandparents, but they express different feelings about it. While they are both trying to find the best way to manage Chi's parenting, the mother, in contrast to the father's description, commented, 'Now Chi has more regular routines, she gets what she wants, but it is a stupid happy.'"

"Using Dr. Sripada's, I tried to comfort the mother by telling her, 'You want to be a good mother. You've done your best, but things have become too difficult right now. Once things settle down, you and the father can share the parenting responsibilities.' The mother has mostly communicated with me through emails, expressing that she feels upset and tends to procrastinate when it comes to speaking with me directly."

"When I saw Chi on Monday, she was out of control. She was utterly restless, jumping on the furniture and running in and out of the office to the waiting room. You may remember that Chi had made a clay pool and wanted to fill it with magical colored powder that she imagined as water. I had not been able to buy it in person, so I ordered it from Amazon. When Chi asked if the order had arrived, and I told her it had, she was thrilled. She immediately filled the clay pool with the colorful magic powder. But then, she wanted to add actual water to it. She went over to my table, where I keep water for making tea, and wanted to pour a cup of water and magic powder into the pool. I told her that it would not be a good idea."

"Chi insisted that I explain why it was not a good idea. I wanted to tell her that adding actual water to the magic powder would be 'messy,' but I could not think of the right word for 'messy' in Chinese."

"After pausing, I spoke to this sentence. Ching spoke in Chinese. He then translated it for me and said he told her that mixing water with the magic powder would make it 'Cibalan,' which means muddy."

"Chi protested, saying it might make things stinky but not muddy."

"I then explained to Chi that the color might stick to her skin, clothes, and the carpet. She accepted this explanation but slumped into her chair and asked, 'What do you want to play?'"

"I responded, 'You do not want to be like water.'"

"She asked, 'What do you mean?'"

"I told her, 'The clay pool is a lovely container for the magic powder. If you add water, it will flow out.'"

"Chi said, 'I do not want to be in a container. I want to flow. I want to be like water—flowing—all over.'"

"You finally got to use the 'container' interpretation! Remember, whether an interpretation fits a theory or not, it has to resonate with the patient. Did the container interpretation work with Chi?'"

> "It seems like the 'container' interpretation did not work." Top of Form
>
> "I want to report on today's session. Chi came into the session by bringing me several flowers as a gift. There were many individual flowers, each wrapped in plastic and tied with a string in a bow. She wanted to present me with a bunch of flowers in her hand, not several individual flowers wrapped in plastic."

I thought Chi had just been through a weekend from hell. She had moved from her mother's house to her father's house. Perhaps she wanted to thank Ching for being the steady person in her life.

> "She became excited and bossy. She wanted to get the flowers out of their plastic wrapping. She started to use scissors to cut the plastic, which was somewhat tough and challenging. I tried to tell her that she could easily untie the string, but she wanted no part of what I was trying to say. I was afraid that she might hurt herself with the scissors. She became unhappy when I told her so. She does not want to be contained. She is somewhat grandiose and feels she is or should be the expert in handling flowers. She wants to be excellent. I thought she was like her mother, who also wanted to be an excellent mother."
>
> "Like her mother, Chi wants to ignore boundaries and be bossy. It seems she wants to treat me the way her

mother treats her. For example, Chi wants to present me with a bunch of flowers. They are individually wrapped and covered with plastic. She wants to cut the plastic coverings using scissors. She is not so good at handling scissors, but she wants to feel like she is the expert in handling flowers. It would be much easier to untie each flower and bunch them. What is your opinion?"

"Excuse me for a minute; I want to use a prop to explain what I mean."

I went to the kitchen, grabbed three small spice jars, and placed them in front of the computer's camera so he could see them. "I think you have several good ideas. Let us use these spice jars to represent them." I arranged two jars vertically, with the third jar placed horizontally on top to form two pillars connected by a bridge. "Let us imagine one pillar represents what is happening between you and Chi, and the other represents what is happening between Chi and her mother. These are the things you need to clarify first. Once done, you can build the interpretative bridge that connects the two clarified ideas."

"When working with a child, take things one step at a time. Start by establishing what is happening between you and Chi. For instance, you may feel that Chi wants to present you with a bunch of flowers. Begin by clarifying that, as it might take some time for both of you to figure out exactly what she wants. Next, shift your focus to what is happening between Chi and her mother, such as Chi's feeling that her mother is bossy. Again, confirm whether this is what Chi has on her mind. Once you and Chi agree about what these pillars represent, you can build your interpretation bridge on top of them. You may feel she wants to boss you. This method helps her grasp how your approach works. Keep in mind that this process often requires patience."

Ching said slowly, "STEP BY STEP. STEP BY STEP. Disassemble my ambition into steps. Nice guidance." He closed his eyes and repeated, "Step by step. Oh, step by step. This is important for me. I feel the pressure. It is hard to slow down and take it step by step. Pressure, no pressure." He took two quick drags from his e-cigarette. "Taking things step by step has always been a challenge for me. I felt this pressure when my daughter was growing up. I will take it up with my analyst. I feel pressured by Chi's mother. I need to connect with my mother inside me."

"Yes, I understand. A lot is happening. I do not comment on your personal life. However, Chi's weekend was filled with pressure because of changes in her living situation and you had to deal with changes in her life. Both Chi's mother and father presented their version of what was happening to Chi. Even in the past, without her explicitly saying anything, you might have felt pressured by Chi's mother to accept her goals for the treatment. You took on the role of a math tutor in your play for Chi. So, you used card games to teach her math, helping her gradually break down problems into smaller steps. You even taught her how to read the clock, and Chi appreciated your efforts. But you also noticed that Chi felt more at ease just sitting quietly by your side, with no words, math, or questions. Maybe although she appreciates who you are, Chi does not want you to be like her mother, constantly pushing her with math puzzles."

"Chi is a girl with poor capacity to regulate her affects. Too much is happening in her life. I need to slow down to control the pace of treatment. I must learn from my inner mother. I need to listen better."

266

When under stress, we may inadvertently overlook or be unable to see the most significant and fundamental aspects of our lives, even when they are right in front of us. As time passes, Ching will realize that caring for Chi was the primary source of his pressure during this period. He will look back and chuckle at his lack of awareness of such an obvious fact.

However, I reassured him at that moment, "You are doing what you can do. You may be the person in Chi's life who most listens to her."

My Musings

Since Ching ended the session pondering the idea of listening, a musing on listening is appropriate. Freud (1913, p.211)[76] emphasized the crucial role of the analyst in maintaining 'evenly suspended attention' during patient sessions. This technique, also known as *gleichschwebende Aufmerksamkeit*, "It consists simply in not directing one's notice to anything in particular and in maintaining the same 'evenly suspended attention' in the face of all that one hears.... If the doctor behaves otherwise, he is throwing away most of the advantage which results from the patient's obeying the 'fundamental rule of psychoanalysis.'"

By then, Freud had already described that by listening to himself, the analyst also becomes attuned to the patient. He expressed this understanding through a formula based on a telephone metaphor, suggesting that the analyst's attention, like a telephone connection, must remain open and receptive to interpret the patient's free associations effectively. For example, Freud (1912, p. 115)[77] stated that the analyst must

---

76 Freud, S. (1913). Recommendations to physicians practicing psycho-analysis. *Standard Edition* 12:109–120.

77 Freud, S. (1912). Recommendations to Physicians Practising psycho-Analysis. *Standard Edition* 2:109–120.

"turn his own unconscious like a receptive organ towards the transmitting unconscious of the patient. He must adjust himself to the patient as a telephone receiver is adjusted to the transmitting microphone. Just as the receiver converts back into sound waves the electric oscillations in the telephone line which were set up by sound waves, so the doctor's unconscious is able, from the derivatives of the unconscious which are communicated to him, to reconstruct that unconscious, which has determined the patient's free associations."

Analysts have commented on the characteristics of the inner world, whether it be the patient or the analyst. For example, Kohut (1959, p.459)[78], stated, "The inner world cannot be observed with the aid of our sensory organs. Our thoughts, wishes, feelings, and fantasies cannot be seen, smelled, heard, or touched. They have no existence in physical space, and yet they are real, and we can observe them as they occur in time: through introspection in ourselves, and through empathy (i.e., vicarious introspection) in others."

Since the mid-20th century, the perspective on countertransference within psychoanalysis and psychodynamic therapy has expanded significantly. It is no longer viewed as a narrow, pathological phenomenon that primarily hinders therapy. Instead, contemporary views on countertransference see it as a valuable diagnostic tool, functioning as a laboratory for the analyst to monitor the mutual interactions between the therapist and the patient. This phenomenon can reveal critical insights about the patient, which the therapist can utilize for deeper understanding and more effective assistance. Countertransference also acts as a delicate gauge of interpersonal dynamics, providing clues to the

---

78 Kohut, H. (1959). Introspection, empathy, and psychoanalysis—An examination of the relationship between mode of observation and theory. *Journal of the American Psychoanalytic Association*, 7:59–483.

therapist about the patient's unspoken thoughts, emotions, and behaviors that may contribute to their suffering and strengths.

However, therapists are tasked with recognizing the spectrum of countertransference, from benign forms that foster empathy and enhance therapeutic alliance to destructive types that may stem from the therapist's unresolved issues. However, pervasive negative countertransference can significantly disrupt treatment, often reflecting the analyst's own unresolved issues. The emergence of countertransference phenomena presents opportunities to reevaluate the analyst's theoretical approach and clinical methods and as a possible moment for the analyst's personal and professional growth, fostering a sense of introspection and self-awareness.

The concept of 'broad countertransference' is crucial in psychoanalysis. It refers to the full range of responses an analyst experiences in ongoing interactions with a patient. This wide-ranging countertransference provides a continuous flow of unconscious and conscious material, serving as a diagnostic tool within the analytical process. It can reveal dominant patterns of identifications, object representations, and constructions by the patient, contributing to the analyst's understanding of the patient's psychological dynamics and facilitating therapeutic intervention.

When an analyst's insights stem from their own broad countertransference-based inferences concerning the patient's identifications, object representations, constructions, or motivations, it is crucial to present these insights as considered opinions. This approach helps the patient understand that these insights are based on the analyst's reactions rather than the patient's own expressions or behaviors.

Opinions, especially those formed from such countertransference about the patient's internal experiences, should be shared with an attitude of openness and with a willingness to allow the patient to propose alternative ideas or reject them easily. Indeed, interpretations stemming primarily from the patient's free associations and actions should also be offered as flexible ideas, subject to patient alterations. This flexibility in interpretation allows for a more dynamic and responsive therapeutic process, fostering an open-minded and adaptable approach in the analyst.

In this instance, Ching reflected somewhat self-consciously on his feeling of pressure and seemed particularly struck by my expression, "Take it step by step." Based on the emotional expression on his face, I felt that Ching's response to the session was primarily influenced by a feeling of "pressure" related to his daughter, his mother, and Chi's mother. Understandably, anyone would first reflect on the implications of their feelings about their own life. In this case, Ching's reactions to pressure seemed primarily related to his daughter and mother. That is as it should be, and he should clarify the implications of such reactions in his personal life through his analysis. However, that is beyond the scope of supervision.

Supervision is primarily concerned with Ching's learning and Chi's treatment. A broad countertransference approach to Ching's pressure experience might have focused more specifically on pressure about Chi's life and secondarily on the pressure related to Chi's mother and father. Perhaps I could have explored how Chi might be experiencing pressure in more detail. As in all situations, time is a passing and limited element, and there is only so much that I could have done as the session ended. I also noticed that while Ching paid attention to Chi's grandiosity and bossiness, despite her poor dexterity with scissors and her desire to bunch flowers as a gift for him, I was more struck by her desire to express her gratitude to him for being in her life by presenting him with flowers.

Overall, Ching is a very compassionate and concerned therapist. I do not doubt that through his words to Chi (which were not reported to me) and his actions toward her, he conveyed that he appreciated her desire to give him a gift. There are many ways to be a good analyst and to help a patient. Ching did this by focusing on specific clinical interactions, which, in the long run, is an excellent way to treat a patient.

Ching felt significant strain while treating Chi soon after her mother asked her to leave the house and not return. This situation brought to his awareness the "pressure" of his experiences with his own daughter, his mother, and Chi's mother. Using his impressions as a countertransference laboratory to understand Chi's feelings, Ching might have explicitly expressed his understanding of the relevance of this "pressure" from Chi's perspective. However, we exist in reality, not in the ideal world we often long for.

Supervision: 24

Ching appeared on Skype from an unfamiliar setting, a new space with an adjoining room devoid of wall hangings or other signs of familiar occupation. The dancing circus bear with heart-shaped balloons, which used to be a fixture in his previous background, was noticeably absent. I asked, "What happened to the dancing bear with heart-shaped balloons?"

"I just moved to this new home. It is much nicer, and I have to set it up. Yes, it is goodbye to the bear in my old apartment. There are several things to cover. Chi is now back to living with her mother. Chi's mother complained about Chi's paternal grandparents, who she felt were too gratifying to Chi. The mother believes Chi's paternal grandparents are bribing Chi to win her love."

"As you know, Chi's mother is giving Chi her math problems to practice at home. Chi never liked such exercises, and now she has become even more oppositional. Chi's mother told me, 'Chi's old pattern of opposing math exercises is back and stronger. Chi protested the math problems and hit me. She took a pencil and attacked the book I was using to ask her questions. She slammed the door.'"

"Chi's mother is seeking my advice about whether she should have Chi repeat the second grade or let her progress to the third grade. She's also discussing this with Chi's father. Chi's mother then added, 'I think Chi's mental and emotional health is the most important. It is more important than her schooling. Chi has met with too many frustrations in life. She needs emotional calmness. She needs to learn to deal with frustrations and learn to regulate her life—sleep, waking, eating, playing, and dealing with school.' I agreed with her."

Ching paused for a few moments.

"Later, Chi's mother sent me an internet message, saying, 'You are the first person who taught me the importance of calmness.' I sent her an email emoji indicating that we are working together to help Chi deal with her anxiety and breakdowns and understand what she needs."

"Chi's mother responded, 'If you think I am not helping Chi but ruining her life, you are wrong. I love her and am trying to help her.'"

Ching then looked at me and spoke.

"Maybe Chi's mother has some unconscious ideas that her ways of parenting may be ruining Chi's life."

"This week, Chi asked me what I wanted to play. I asked her, 'What game did you have in mind?' Chi picked up a soft cotton ball and threw it at me very hard. I was surprised and also felt a flash of anger. I said to Chi, 'Slow down.' Then she quickly lost interest in throwing the ball, said it was boring, and wanted me to suggest a game. I proposed, 'What about 'Jumping House?'"

To demonstrate the game, Ching mimed with his finger jumping around while counting 1, 2, 3, 4, 5, 6, 7, 8.... I asked, "Is it like Hopscotch?"

Ching looked up Hopscotch on the internet and the Chinese equivalent of Wiki and confirmed, "Yes. Something like that. But Chi said it was boring and didn't want to play it. She then suggested that we listen to some stories on her smartwatch. After that, she threw a pillow and piled many pillows on me, resting on them."

"I told Chi, 'You want to be close to me.'"

"Then Chi tried to scratch me and said, 'No. No. No. Every guess you make is wrong.' She stopped scratching me and lay on the pillows for several minutes without talking, but she calmed down. She seemed settled while we spoke no words.

"With so many things happening in the session and Chi's life, it's hard to know what to say or do. But we must choose and focus on what seems emotionally clear and important. At one point, Chi played with the pillows and rested on them, and you interpreted this to mean she wanted to be close to you. Chi responded with, 'No, no, no,' and said that your guesses were wrong."

"More than one dynamic is at play here. She may be reenacting her feelings for her mother with you. After her mother's strict math exercises, Chi hit her and attacked her with a pencil. She also tried to scratch you and threw the ball at you so hard that you felt angry. This could be a reenactment of the hostile mother transference. It's no wonder Chi had a difficult week. Her mother asked her to leave the house and not return. For Chi, it must have been like an earthquake or a hurricane hitting her. She was angry at her mother. She might also be angry at you for not recognizing her anger despite her actions. But you felt angry; maybe your anger was like Chi's. Simultaneously, your anger may be like her mother's anger when Chi attacked her."

"The second dynamic is her wish for calmness without questions or talk, a feeling she experiences only with you. She sat by your side without words in this session and a previous one, seemingly calm. This is her desire for a containment of aloneness. It might be a recognition of how tired she feels from her anger and frustration and a wish for rest from too much math and other demands."

"You can consider a series of dynamics playing out before you. They are lined up like airplanes on a runway. The first dynamic is 'Anger-frustration.' It must be clarified, interpreted, and taken off before the second 'Containment' plane gets the okay to taxi onto the runway. Therefore, the first job is to acknowledge her anger and frustration for having such a tough week. Only then can she tolerate the second 'Containment-calm-closeness' idea. You tried to fly the second plane before the first. So, she said, 'No. No. No.'"

> Ching pensively said, "Learning is a work in progress. I understand. Chi was angry with her mother, and Chi was angry and bossy with me. This is an object-related idea. I thought of a Kohutian supervisor who would have said, 'To be bossy feels good.'"

"You are learning from Chi, your supervisors, and your life experiences. I brought up Chi's anger not because of object relations theory or any other theoretical framework but because you mentioned specific actions:

she hit her mother, threw a hardball at you, and tried to scratch you. These are clear signs that Chi may be upset with you. It's possible that she feels you are behaving similarly to her mother. Even though you approach things tactfully, she might perceive your attempts to help her solve math problems as nagging, just like her mother does, despite your good intentions."

"Clinical facts are the basic information, and theory deepens their understanding by shaping and organizing them. Her words and actions reflect anger; you have personally felt that anger and pressure. What I aim to teach is a bottom-up approach. Start with clinical facts, which form the foundation, and then build towards theory. A top-down approach, in contrast, begins with a fixed theory and tries to fit clinical events into that framework. This risks missing the true essence of what is happening in the therapeutic process."

"There's another way to understand these moments of peaceful silence, which often happen in child therapy but can also occur in adult treatments. Chi seems calm and relaxed when she sits quietly beside you, without speaking or engaging in any activity. During these times, you're not interacting with her or asking her to solve math problems or behave in any particular way. She might appreciate these quiet moments because they give her an experience she hasn't had with her mother. This isn't about transference but rather a new emotional experience and a different relationship. These moments of calm are quite different from her usual anger, which may come from feeling that her mother doesn't accept her intellectual limits. Although her mother's hitting might be culturally accepted, it still causes Chi physical pain."

Ching took two long, deep drags from his e-cigarette.

"I need time to think." He then remained in thoughtful silence for several minutes before saying, "Thank you.

I understand." Ching continued to be quiet for a few moments more.

"Just like you needed a moment of silence in my presence to gather your thoughts, Chi also needs these quiet moments. It is not always necessary to talk during these times. Asking you what you were thinking would have been intrusive. For you, this is a moment of self-reflection; my asking you questions during this time would be an impingement. So, too, for Chi, but for her, it might be a moment of rest from math exercises and external control."

"Thank you. I agree. There is no question that Chi's mother has captured my mind. I feel the pressure to produce a change in Chi that her mother desires. In the next session, Chi started being more verbal and aggressive. She called me 'Poopy.' She wanted to play ball, and she insisted on throwing the ball fast and hard. However, she saw that behind me was a tea area with some breakable China and glass utensils. So Chi asked that we switch sides. Now, behind me was the wall, and she could throw hard without the risk of breaking anything. So she arranged for safe play."

"In today's session, Chi was calm and cooperative. We talked and played. She brought some plastic play teacup toys and a pot to play at a tea party. These are relatively unbreakable toys, and the design does not allow them to play with real water. You could only play with imaginary water."

"In a previous session, you did not want Chi to play with water in the office. I think she wants to compromise and find a way to do what she wants that is also acceptable to you. Such compromises and real-life negotiations are the way forward for Chi. Chi has had a hard life and is trying to maintain hope and build on her connection to you. She is a precious child."

"I agree; she is precious."

"I will summarize the main lessons of today's session. First, acknowledge Chi's feelings; now they are anger and frustration. She needs to feel calm and safe with you, especially since she doesn't often have these peaceful moments with her mother. Chi might see requests to talk, play, behave well, or do math exercises as burdensome. It's helpful for Chi to find compromises—a middle ground that works for her, like playing pretend with water, is a good example."

"Second, Chi's mother means well and wants to prioritize Chi's mental and emotional well-being over her academic performance. As you overheard when you were in the washroom, she is learning to be gentle and soft. However, when frustrated, she tends to become punitive and rejecting."

Third, deciding if Chi should repeat a grade should be a decision made by her parents and teacher, and maybe even with Chi's input. While you can encourage open discussion, it's best not to give definitive advice, as they might blame you if things do not go well. Just like you would not tell someone whether to get married or not, some decisions are best left to the parents or the individual to make.

"Okay, I got it. Three bottom lines. Even without Mother stating it, one of the problems I feel is the pressure from Chi's mother to produce change in Chi. (He pointed to his head with both his hands as if to indicate a vice was squeezing it) Additionally, you are teaching me something important about Chinese culture."

"Oh?"

"Chinese culture is old and has many traditions. I believe it is mostly good, but Chinese culture seldom prioritizes the well-being of children. It is imprinted in us to listen to elders and adults. You are teaching me to prioritize and grasp Chi's mind and emotions"

My Musings

After this session, I organized my thoughts based on the capacity to be alone, fallow, and needing respite and rest from exhaustive parenting.

Winnicott (1958)[79] described the capacity to be alone as the experience of solitude while simultaneously feeling the reassuring presence of another person. This situation enables an infant, still forming a sense of self, to experience solitude while feeling secure and supported by a nurturing, reliable caregiver. He referred to this supportive environment as the "ego-supportive environment." It plays a significant role in the child's ability to learn to be alone.

Understanding the importance of solitude is essential for everyone, as it is an inevitable part of life. At some point, each person will face health challenges, such as illness or injury, and ultimately, everyone must face their own end alone. Embracing solitude can build resilience and

---

79 Winnicott, D.W. (1958). The capacity to be alone. *International Journal of Psycho-Analysis* 39:416–420.

provide a deeper understanding of life's limited nature. Accepting this solitude prepares us for these moments and enriches our experience of life's unique journey, inspiring personal growth and a deeper appreciation for life.

Khan (1983)[80] defined 'being fallow' as a transitional or transient mood experienced or expressed in silence. In the context of child development, this concept underscores the critical need to provide children with moments of quiet and solitude. These moments allow children to process their emotions and thoughts in a peaceful environment, emphasizing the importance of such experiences in their development.

Reflecting on my childhood, I think of my younger sister, who was only a year and a half younger than me. At one stage in my life, our mother had the challenge of caring for four children, juggling the demands of getting two to school while looking after two preschoolers. She had to be efficient and manage both words and actions. I remember a time before my sister and I started school when our household was always bustling. This is the recall of many similar memories telescoped into this brief recall. I recall my mother sitting on the floor, coaxing my sister to eat by offering food on the tip of her thumb. It usually consisted of yogurt rice. During those moments, I would hug my mother's shoulder while she tended to my sister's needs, maintaining a tactile bond with me. My mother might gently encourage my sister with simple words like "come," "eat," "good," "wait," or "nice" while my sister played, often distracted from her meal. Even though her words and actions were focused on my sister, her acceptance of my hug was a comforting acknowledgment of my presence, preserving a non-verbal connection between us. This silent exchange allowed her to care for two siblings simultaneously.

---

80 Khan, M.M.R. (1983). On lying fallow. In *Hidden Selves: Between Theory and Practice in Psychoanalysis*. Madison, CT: International Universities Press, pp. 183–188.

Chi has experienced tranquility with Ching, which might be part of something new for her. In his presence, Chi seems to benefit from periods of silent reflection, which appear to come from a feeling of being nurtured. These moments are necessary to keep hope, dreams and wishes to remain alive. However, Chi's challenge is to grow in an environment filled with tension, where such nurturing experiences are rare. She must learn to adapt to situations marked by stress or strict expectations, where her personal needs are overlooked, and her desire for freedom is not fully recognized or met.

In Chi's case, her task is to learn to grow in the presence of a well-meaning mother. It appears that the mother judged herself by her intentions and not the consequences of her actions. She was skeptical of others, as providing stupid happiness by bribing Chi to win her love. While undoubtedly caring and supportive, this mother is so distracted by Chi's math difficulties that she demeans Chi by calling her "stupid" and striking her when she is too upset. This dynamic presents a common challenge in parenting, where the desire for a child's success can sometimes overshadow Chi's need for essential emotional support and acceptance. Such distraction can lead to a child feeling neglected or unimportant, which can have profound and long-term effects on their self-esteem and emotional well-being.

I believe Chi's life has been overshadowed by her mother's towering expectations, rooted in deep love but narrowly focused on academic success. Intolerant of Chi's struggles with math, her mother has adopted a Tiger-Mom approach, imposing rigorous home tutoring in addition to Chi's already heavy school workload.[81] This intolerance is so severe that her mother echoes the hurtful remarks of Chi's peers, calling her "stupid,"

---

81 Chua, A. (2011). *Battle Hymn of the Tiger Mother*. New York & London: Penguin Books.

further exacerbating Chi's academic stress. Her mother's frustration with Chi's perceived shortcomings sometimes leads to punitive actions, including physical punishment. According to Ching, strict parenting practices are culturally accepted in China, further complicating Chi's emotional landscape.

These relentless pressures have led to deep emotional distress, shaping Chi's perceptions, emotions, and interactions with her mother. As an infant and growing Child, Chi was dependent on her mother, experienced no other option but to passively tolerate such demands for a long time, and comply with her mother's demands for fear of provoking a conflict with her mother. However, when she could no longer tolerate this frustration, she transitioned from passive acceptance to outright defiance, expressing her frustration directly by actively expressing herself through aggressive and sometimes provocative behavior to choose the moment of conflict. Chi felt angry at her mother for such expectations. Chi also experienced a sense of inadequacy due to her difficulty with math comprehension, making such interactions even more difficult to tolerate. It is important to empathize with Chi's feelings of inadequacy, as they play a significant role in her psychological dynamics. However, the awareness of her inadequacy evokes a sense of shame and is well-guarded, so it is not easy for a therapist to convey this empathy.

Ching tried to offer playful academic help during activities like card games or helping Chi learn to read the clock, intending to help her learn. All this was well-intentioned and done from a sense of concern and caring for Chi. However, Chi perceived this as an extension of her mother's oppressive expectations. She may have seen Ching acting as an agent of her mother, leading Chi to a "Tiger Therapist Transference." It is important to note that this transference does not coincide with Ching's behavior or intent, but that is how transference works, and understanding this is crucial in the study of psychological dynamics.

Chi hid her true feelings for a long time, putting up a facade of compliance to meet her mother's demands. However, she has transitioned from passive acceptance to outright defiance, expressing her frustration through increasingly aggressive behavior. This shift, known as "identification with the aggressor," is evident in her playtime with Ching, where she has even threatened to punish him with hundreds of math questions, reflecting this role reversal.

In this dynamic, Chi mirrors her mother's aggression, directing it toward Ching in a 'negative transference' pattern toward maternal figures. Negative transference is a psychological phenomenon where a person's negative feelings or attitudes toward a significant person in their past, often a parent, are transferred onto a current relationship, in this instance, Ching. Despite Chi's antagonistic behavior, Ching has noticed occasional moments of calm when they sit quietly together, providing a brief respite from the emotional turmoil.

As Ching deepens his understanding, he recognizes that Chi's hostility is rooted in her personal history and evolving identity, not a rejection of the therapeutic space he is trying to create. This scenario embodies both hostile maternal transference and identification with the aggressor, highlighting the intricate and challenging emotions at play.

New therapists might initially expect a patient's behavior to match the friendly therapeutic setting. However, experienced therapists understand that each patient responds in ways shaped by their unique personality and past experiences. Additionally, children often display a level of straightforwardness and spontaneity that can try a therapist.

Chi is also aware of Ching's genuine care and concern, when she experiences moments of peace and quietness sitting by Ching's side. These moments serve as welcome breaks from constant engagement and offer a gentle contrast to the more demanding influences in her life. From my perspective, her moments of solitude do not provide the comfort of a supportive presence as described in Winnicott's and Khan's concepts of solitude and 'lying fallow.' In Chi's case, they underscore her desperate need for a break from the constant strain of parental demands. This need for respite and rest due to fatigue is of a different feeling tone. Even if the analysts do not offer any comment or clarification concerning such moments of alone, non-communicative moments, it might be helpful for the analyst to form some explanation for what they might mean.

These moments of calmness and non-communication are welcome experiences. They represent Chi's encounters with Ching, a new object— one of rest, respite, and calmness that offers solace and helps sustain her hopes and dreams for the future. This 'new object' is a psychological concept that refers to a source of comfort and support different from her usual experience with her mother. However, this does not mean Chi has never experienced positive feelings with her mother. Her mother is dedicated and giving but on her terms. Chi's negative attitude makes it difficult for her to recall such moments. Therefore, describing these positive experiences of calmness and non-communication may not be accurate as entirely new object experiences.

Ching increasingly recognizes that a child's spirit is central to the essence of a family and vital for maintaining a nation's heritage and identity. This realization deepens his understanding of the importance of cherishing children's worlds and championing their rights to safety, health, and well-being, recognizing the responsibility of adults to nurture and protect these freedoms. Possibly shaped by psychoanalytic thought, these reflections signify Ching's evolving perspective on the customs and principles of Chinese culture.

Supervision: 25

Ching hesitated as he started the session: "This was a hard week. Chi, her Mother, her Father, and her family are all in turbulence. It is a chaotic period. I spoke to Chi's mother, who wanted to discuss how Chi's father could not care for her. Additionally, she felt that Chi's paternal grandparents did not help much. I could not get a straight answer as to why Chi returned to live with Mother. She said that she could not trust Chi's father and his family, so she took Chi back. I spoke to the father, too. The father said he could not care for Chi and his parents were too old, although his father could still help Chi with his education. I could not get a clear answer from the mother about who decided Chi should return to live with the mother. The Mother seemed evasive and did not tell me the whole truth."

"I spoke to Father and could not get a clear answer about how they decided Chi would return to live with Mother. At any rate, the mother, father, and I decided to meet to discuss Chi's educational plans. Chi wanted to attend the meeting, and I told her that initially, her Mother, Father, and I would meet, and maybe later, she could attend."

"As I told you, Chi was back to staying with her mother and displayed violence. It was hard for me to engage Chi.

Chi threw the ball particularly hard at me. She was angry, and my attempts to acknowledge her anger made her more angry. The more I tried, the more difficult she became. She threw the ball at a lamp. Then she felt guilty and slowed down for a moment and then did something bad, like swearing."

"What did she call you?"

"She called me a 'fucking idiot.' She started to kick the toy box."

"I told her, 'After you do something good, like be careful, you must do something bad, like call me names or kick the toy box.'

"Chi said, 'Yes.' She then started to grab my watch and try to wrench it from my wrist. As she did so, the watch's wristband broke. She then said, 'Sorry.' "

"Maybe you want to see if my watch's wristband will break if you rip it."

"Chi replied, 'Can we be broken?'

"I said, "We must be careful because things can break. If we love what breaks, we feel sad."

"Later, the father arranged for an internet meeting, but the mother came on but did not want to participate through dialog; she was using the text function. The father indicated that his parents were too old to take care of her regularly and that he could not take care of Chi."

"The meeting was somewhat disorganized. The father arranged the call, but the mother did not actively participate via video and typed in messages rather than directly interact. Chi's father felt that Chi's grandfather was best suited to educate Chi, and Chi's mother reluctantly agreed. I effectively took charge and insisted that the paternal grandfather should be in charge of Chi's education and that he should have a free hand in managing the task."

"The Mother appeared angry at me for steering the meeting this way. However, she then insisted that She, the mother, should likewise be in charge of Chi's play. She added that Chi played well together with her and that she should have a free hand in managing Chi's play. Mother also insisted that Chi's paternal grandmother was harsh and that Chi should return to live with her Mother. The bottom line of the meeting was that the grandfather got the responsibility for Chi's education, and Mother got the responsibility for play."

"However, after the meeting, Chi's mother became furious and upset at me and started bombarding me with messages. For example, she said, 'All you males have a bias against women. All of you are idiots. Who gave you the right to understand me? Your understanding is bullshit. You think you understand me. You are projecting your biased opinions toward me."

Ching took a puff from his electronic cigarette.

"I told the Mother, "I am worried if Chi's therapy can continue if you have so much distrust in me."

"The Mother quickly responded, 'Do not worry. Therapy can continue, but I am angry and desperate.

Therapy should continue. However, stop using under-standing; you do not understand me."

"Around 2:00 am, I got a message from the Mother. It said, 'I could not trust you. Maybe we cannot carry on with the therapy.'"

"I responded, 'OK.'"

"At 6:40 am, I got a message from the Mother. 'I want Chi to be decisive. I did not have a decisive father. You are a good influence on Chi, and you can teach Chi to be decisive.'"

"I said, 'OK. Do we have a deal.'"

"Mother said, 'Yes.'"

"So now, we have a common sense agreement. I said to her, 'I will see Chi on Monday.'"

"Mother came with a positive face."

I raised my hand, indicating that I wanted to say something, and Ching immediately waited for me to speak. "I hesitate to bring this up, but I will say it. The last time we met, we ended with three bottom lines."

"I remember."

"What was the bottom line for your role in Chi's education?"

"Leave it for the right people to decide."

"Yes. I said, if you say stay in second grade, you will get blamed. If you say let her continue to go to the third grade, you will get blamed. Chi is fragile. She will continue to have some issues. There is a high risk for therapists to get involved in real-life decisions. In your meeting with parents, who had a decisive role in deciding on Chi's education plan?"

"I pushed it."

"Yes, and you got a double whammy, a bad situation in two different ways. You got Pow Pow from both sides (I mimed a person getting boxed on the jaw with right and left blows.).

"I could not hold. This is not an education issue alone. It is a protection issue. I want genuine care for Chi."

I responded, "What you want for Chi is understandable. Your intentions were good. It is like driving on ice or when the road is slippery. You know where you want to go, but the situation is such that your actions do not take you in that direction; the situation is out of control and unpredictable. Maybe Chi feels that way, too."

"We are on the brink of ending. I distrust the mother because she did not explain the decision to take back Chi. In any case, Chi brought some of her family home toys into the office in this last session. Chi wanted her mother to play with her. So, we opened the door and invited the mother. Mother and Chi became very involved in the play. The play consisted of a little kitty and a little princess."

"As they played, Mother quickly became the main player. Chi became the assistant. Mother said, 'Oh, what a beautiful home.' Chi asked Mother, 'What should the kitty do?' Mother had some ideas about how the kitty and the Princess interact, and Chi followed. Mother was very excited in the play, and both Mother and Chi became very involved in the play, but in the manner I described."

I commented, "In the meeting, when you assigned the education role to grandfather in Chi's life, mother wanted the play's responsibility to herself in Chi's life. Mother claimed that she is good at playing with Chi; it seemed that is true; both get involved, But as you say, Mother becomes overinvolved and takes over the play."

"Yes, I feel Chi must have the main role. The mother should be the assistant, and the play should primarily be Chi's play. Chi is accommodating to the mother. Mother should not insist that she is the main actor in their play."

"I agree with you one hundred percent. The Mother has many unmet childhood needs herself and dominates and takes over the child's life. That is the problem, but Mother cannot change easily, although Mother is currently facilitating treatment by bringing Chi to sessions regularly. Chi and you played in a manner that you feel is correct. So, you do not need to change your playing style with Chi. You continue to assign her the director role and follow her lead."

Ching took several puffs from his electronic cigarette.

"I need your help to prepare for the next session. By playing with her Mother, Chi has become accustomed to being the assistant and the adult in charge. Maybe Chi will get anxious because she wants me to be like her mother."

You have established a pattern of play with Chi. It is based on play therapy. Chi knows how it unfolds. However, you seem concerned that now, with all these changes in her life, Chi has regressed. She may want you to behave like her mother. It is confusing and puts demands on you. That is why psychoanalysis is called the impossible profession."

"I need your help getting ready for the next session. Yes. Regression is the key word to understand Chi at this moment."

Immediately, I knew the principle on which my answer had to be based—"Provide the optimal structure to facilitate analytic work." I tried to find the best combination of words to explain this idea to Ching. I said, "Despite her current situation, Chi brought her own little kitty and a little princess. She is coming prepared with her tools. You know how to play with Chi and must remember and implement it as much as possible."

I reflected on the session and realized that I spoke very little until I brought up the three key points, where I highlighted to Ching the risks of an analyst taking a leading role in life decisions for a patient or their child. Additionally, I noticed that my speech rate had increased after Ching mentioned needing guidance for the upcoming play session. "Let us see how we are responding in this session. How many words did I speak in the first thirty minutes compared to the last ten minutes since you said you needed my help?

Ching anxiously thought for several moments.

"I am myself regressed. I cannot remember the earlier parts of this session."

"As I recall, I barely spoke during the first thirty minutes of the session. However, in the last ten minutes, I said several hundred words. I pointed out the consequences of you taking on a primary role in family decision-making. You know how to conduct play therapy by assigning your assistant role. You have already done that many times. I reinforced your previous correct play technique. Nevertheless, we still need to come up with strategies for addressing Chi's anxiety if it arises in the next session."

The ideas I shared with Ching reflect my approach to handling challenging situations, drawing from my decades of experience with preschoolers and school-age children who exhibit disruptive, aggressive, or anxious behaviors. I stay physically close to the child, allowing me to intervene quickly if needed, and I increase my speech tempo to help the child feel more connected and engaged with me. I said, "Stay close to Chi, communicate with her, and speak to her as it may help her. Most of all, remember that some of what you are feeling, anxiety, breakability, and the brink of ending, may be similar to what Chi is feeling."

Ching seemed revived and said, "What you said about regression was most helpful. I will carry on as best as I can."

My musings

After this session, I have organized my thoughts into two categories: 1) The 'Double Whammy' and 2) The 'Entanglement'.

The 'Double Whammy'

The concept of a 'double whammy' holds significant weight in psychology. It refers to a situation where two adverse events or conditions occur simultaneously or consecutively, intensifying the overall impact. In psychology, a 'double whammy' often describes scenarios where two factors combine to worsen an individual's emotional, cognitive, or behavioral state. For instance, individuals dealing with both depression and anxiety experience a 'double whammy' as each condition amplifies the other. The constant worrying from anxiety can make depressive symptoms feel more overwhelming, and the hopelessness from depression can increase anxiety about everyday activities.

In this instance, the double whammy that Ching suffered was the blows inflicted on him by Chi and Chi's mother.

Ching's efforts were met with increasingly challenging behavior from Chi. She threw a ball toward a lamp, a moment of guilt causing her to pause briefly. However, this respite was short-lived, as Chi soon directed a hurtful insult towards Ching.

Chi called Ching a "fucking idiot."

This was the first whammy.

Chi's mother expressed her displeasure with the direction of the meeting when Ching arranged for the paternal grandfather to be in charge of Chi's education. Post-meeting, the mother's frustration escalated, leading to a barrage of accusatory messages towards him, questioning his understanding and alleging gender bias. Addressing the mother's concerns, Ching conveyed his apprehension about the future of Chi's therapy, given the evident mistrust. Amidst her anger, she maintained that therapy should proceed despite her lack of trust. However, that night, in the early hours of the next day, Ching received a message from the mother casting doubt on the trust and the viability of continuing therapy.

This was the double whammy.

We all know that therapists and analysts are professionals. However, they are humans, too. When an eight-year-old calls the therapist a fucking idiot, even if a transference inspires it, it also conveys an interpersonal sting. The analyst will have some reaction. Although the public may demand the analyst, as a professional, to submit to such behaviors, such behaviors do take a toll on the analyst. Usually, analysts are prepared to deal with one negative transference per patient. In child treatment, as this case shows, the analyst may be subject to two hostile transferences.

In both instances, Ching's response aligned with his belief in containment. Winnicott (2013) emphasized the crucial role of parents and society in adolescent development, likening it to the vital support given to an infant—providing containment without retaliation. This involves creating an environment where adolescents' inherent challenges are met with composure and steadiness, avoiding retaliatory responses, even under provocation. The aim for the parent and analyst is to establish a nurturing and facilitating environment that can assimilate and navigate the complexities of teenage conduct without confrontation.

When Chi provoked him with verbal insults, Ching bore the insult. Subsequently, after breaking his watch strap, she worried and asked, "Can we be broken?"

Ching replied, "We must be careful because things can break, and if we love what breaks, we feel sad."

If Ching had been involved in a pathological countertransference, he could have exploded like Chi's mother and physically retaliated. He could have retaliated by guilt-tripping or shame-tripping her.

Still, if Ching had asked me what I would have done, I might have said to Chi, "You were upset because you wanted to attend the meeting with your mother and father to discuss your schooling. You feel angry because I did not invite you."

Entanglements: How the Analyst's Self-Experience Generates Ideas about the Patient's Self, Communicates Insights, and Negotiates Their Meanings

This section delves into the fascinating possibility of an intuitive connection between one individual's psyche and another's, as well as the dynamic interplay between an analyst's identity and that of their patient. It explores the profound interconnectedness of our inner worlds, particularly within psychoanalytic relationships, and the possibility of greater exploitation of the broad countertransference.

While Freud's (1919)[82] unconscious mind's mode of thinking found telepathy intriguing, he maintained a cautious stance on it. He aimed to establish psychoanalysis as a concrete science and thus was wary of telepathy, partly due to its links to other mystical phenomena. Freud proposed that telepathy could be understood as a mental bridge between individuals, allowing them to share knowledge, emotions, and experiences.

Previously, we discussed how Freud (1912, p. 115)[83] indicated that by listening to himself, the analyst also becomes attuned to the patient. He expressed this understanding through a formula based on a telephone metaphor, suggesting that the analyst's attention, like a telephone connection, must remain open and receptive to interpret the patient's free associations effectively. Nevertheless, can connections exist that do not involve free associations outside of sensory channels?

---

82 Freud, S. (1919). The 'uncanny'. *Standard Edition* 17:217–256.

83 Freud, S. (1912). Recommendations to physicians practising Psycho-Analysis. *Standard Edition* 12:109–120.

Jacobs (2019)[84] explored the role of unconscious communication based on the patient seeing his analyst in an old family car, sparking an unconscious recollection of a distressing time that symbolizes his strained relationship with his father. As the patient and analyst engage in this subconscious exchange, their connection to the present moment softens, allowing for daydreams and musings and the emergence of deeply buried memories, fantasies, and suppressed secrets that often lie at the heart of our patients' psychological issues. Unconscious communication is crucial in uncovering and revisiting these impactful memories from childhood and adolescence, playing a vital role in the therapeutic process of psychoanalysis.

Quantum entanglement describes a situation in quantum physics where two or more particles become interconnected so that their states depend on each other, even when separated by vast distances. This means that measuring or knowing the state of one particle instantly reveals the state of the other, defying classical ideas about space and time.

Imagine two magically connected coins: if you flip one and it lands on heads, the other coin, no matter how far away, will also land on heads at the exact moment. This occurs even though no signal or information seems to travel between them.

Quantum entanglement, while central to quantum mechanics, was met with skepticism by classical physicists like Albert Einstein. Einstein (1947) [85] famously referred to it as "spooky action at a distance," or involving as it violated the principle that nothing, including information,

---

84 Jacobs, T.J. (2019). Now streaming: On unconscious communications in the analytic process. *Psychoanalytic Inquiry* 39:184–188.

85 Letter from Einstein to Max Born, 3 March 1947; *The Born-Einstein Letters; Correspondence between Albert Einstein and Max and Hedwig Born from 1916 to 1955*, Walker, New York, 1971.

can travel faster than the speed of light. This "spooky" connection remains one of quantum theory's most fascinating and puzzling aspects.

Gargulio (2013)[86] defines mind in the context of a psychoanalytically based notion of consciousness as, "Mind, then, is best thought of as a bridge, not just a personal possession or an exclusive subjective experience. Mind is a statement about our entanglement with community. It cannot be appreciated as if it were solely an internal possibility. Consciousness makes mind possible, and makes meaning and therefore culture possible as well."

Robust vs. Weak (Qualified) Entanglement in Psychoanalysis

Feelings of love or hate are often experienced in an entangled manner. However, in psychoanalysis, entanglements or connections between the analyst and patient can be conceptualized as either strong or weak (qualified). A strong entanglement theory posits a deep connection between the identities of the analyst and the patient's Selves. This is reminiscent of Kohut's (1971)[87] concept of *alter-ego twinship transference*, where the patient and analyst form a narcissistic connection grounded in a perceived sense of sameness. In this dynamic, the patient seeks an experience of shared identity with the analyst, looking to feel understood through a mirror-like relationship that reflects their own sense of self.

In this robust entanglement model, the analyst constructs the state of the patient's experience based on the conviction of a shared identity or

---

86 Gargiulo, G.J. (2013). Some Thoughts about Consciousness: From a Quantum Mechanics Perspective. *Psychoanalytic Review* 100:543–558.

87 Kohut, H. (1971). *The Analysis of the Self*. Madison, CT: International Universities Press.

experience. This strong entanglement view suggests a direct link between the analyst and patient, where the analyst might feel justified in bypassing testing stages and verifying the idea based on the patient's response. Based on such a view, an analyst can make a bold claim regarding a patient's self-state.

The strong entanglement approach might be appropriate for some patients. However, this approach can sometimes resonate with patients who idealize their analyst and may come with significant risks. The analyst may dominate the therapeutic process, shaping it without adequate checks or validation from the patient. This increases the potential for mistakes and reinforces possible misunderstandings, as the patient might accept the analyst's interpretation prematurely or without critical reflection. It is crucial to be cautious and aware of these risks in a robust entanglement approach.

Essential Psychoanalysis: A Qualified Entanglement Approach

Essential Psychoanalysis offers a qualified approach to entanglement, drawing from the abovementioned sources and philosophical arguments, such as Bertrand Russell's. The debate on understanding others' minds has long intrigued philosophers and psychoanalysts. Russell, in his work Human Knowledge: Its Scope and Limits (1948)[88], did not depend on empathy to argue for the existence of other minds. Instead, he relied on the "Argument from Analogy" combined with introspection. This argument posits that since we have direct access to our own minds and

---

88 Bertrand Russell (1948). *Human Knowledge: Its Scope and Limits*. London: George Allen & Unwin.

see similar behaviors in others, we infer that others must also have minds, even without direct empathetic access.

In Essential Psychoanalysis, this philosophical stance on the nature of the other's mind provides a theoretical backbone for entanglement. Rather than assuming empathy provides privileged knowledge of another's emotions, entanglement suggests a more uncertain, inferential approach. The analyst's own emotional responses and subjective experiences become provisional hypotheses about the patient's emotional state, aligned with Russell's view that understanding another's mind requires inference rather than vicarious experience of the other.

Furthermore, the ability to accurately appreciate another person—and, just as importantly, to learn from mistaken assumptions—matters more than the specific terminology used to describe this process. Whether we frame it as empathy, entanglement, or another theoretical construct, the value lies in refining our understanding of the other through ongoing engagement and correction of errors. In psychoanalysis, this emphasis on learning from misapprehensions reinforces the collaborative nature of therapy, where both the analyst and the patient contribute to shaping a deeper, evolving awareness of the patient's inner world. Adjusting and refining these interpretations allows for growth and greater therapeutic insight.

Essential Psychoanalysis, therefore, does not endorse a strong entanglement theory. Instead, it advocates for a qualified approach to entanglement, emphasizing a connection between the analyst's Self-constructions and the analyst's construction of the patient's Self. In the qualified entanglement theory of Essential Psychoanalysis, this connection serves as an initial hypothesis about the patient's inner state held by the analyst. It is subject to testing, verification, and modification that may include refinement or rejection by the patient. By its very nature, this approach offers the potential for a more collaborative, dynamic therapeutic relationship between the analyst and the patient.

Rather than assuming a direct identity between analyst and patient, the analyst in this model acknowledges that the analyst's interpretation of the need for careful testing, processing, and judgments about its usefulness can be made only after patient-analyst collaboration and negotiation. Whether they accept, reject, or modify the analyst's interpretations, the patient's responses are crucial in shaping the therapeutic process. By maintaining a more nuanced and collaborative stance, the analyst avoids the pitfalls of over-identification and premature conclusions, allowing for a more dynamic and flexible therapeutic relationship where the patient's role is significant and empowering.

This qualified entanglement approach mitigates the risks of overstepping identity boundaries and fostering a therapeutic process that respects the patient's autonomy and capacity for self-exploration.

Entanglement in Essential Psychoanalysis

In Essential Psychoanalysis, the term "entanglement" is used metaphorically, departing from its origins in quantum physics. Whereas the entangled entities in quantum physics are liked by identical properties, in qualified entanglement theory of essential psychoanalysis, they are linked and similar but not identical. The modest theory of entanglement in Essential Psychoanalysis refers to the immediate connection between the analyst's self-construct and the constructs of others within the analyst's psychological framework. For example, the analyst's own emotional experience—whether it is anxiety, anger, or the sense that therapy is at risk of suddenly ending—can be directly linked to the patient's similar emotions, according to the analyst's construction of the patient. In theory, it is not just the analyst's emotions connected to the analyst's construction of the patient but the entire spectrum of the analyst's experience, including perception, thought, imagination, feeling, and action. These facets of the analyst's entangled internal associated with the constructions of the patient may or may not parallel the patient's experience. Furthermore, the qualified theory recognizes limits between the analyst and patient and between any two living entities whose unique bodies and nervous systems prevent identical properties. The analyst, being more aware of concerns within the patient's unconscious or preconscious, can clarify and heighten the patient's conscious awareness. How best an analyst should communicate ideas arising from these analytic entanglements is not apparent or universally accepted. They rely on the analyst's theoretical framework. Essential Psychoanalysis advises that these ideas should align with the analyst's theory and be communicated timely and tactfully in language the patient can understand without undermining the patient's autonomy through the analyst's implicit authority.

Entanglement is an Idea-generator and not a proof.

During a session, an analyst may encounter a variety of internal experiences—perceptions, thoughts, fantasies, beliefs, emotions, conflicts, defenses, compromises, inhibitions, predictions, or risk assessments. These experiences are not in response to empathy for the patient; they are experiences relevant to the analyst. However, these experiences reflect the analyst's personal life and resonate with the patient's potential emotional states. When the analyst tests and confirms that such internal responses are relevant to the patient, it establishes a shared reality, intertwining the analyst's consciousness with the patient's. This dynamic can be a powerful way to understand patients beyond what they express through free associations or behaviors.

A kaleidoscope or transformer allows a single set of elements to be reconfigured to different patterns with a shift in perspective. Similarly, an analyst's experience can be reconfigured into patterns specific to the patient; this shifting perspective lets the analyst view the patient's situation from a fresh angle.

A kaleidoscope captivates with a fusion of art, geometry, and illusion, offering a stunning visual feast. This cylindrical tube houses angled mirrors that multiply and transform reflections, creating a symmetrical and enthralling pattern. Vibrant glass fragments, beads, and other materials fill the tube, shimmering between transparent discs. Rotating or shaking the tube causes these pieces to shift, reflecting off the mirrors into ever-changing geometric patterns, each as fleeting as unique. The magic of a kaleidoscope lies in its infinite variety, ensuring that each turn brings a new, breathtaking view where colors and shapes perform an ever-evolving dance.

Hasbro and the Japanese toy company Takara Tomy collaborated to create transformer toys, which soon became a global sensation. The slogan "More Than Meets the Eye" captures their allure. They are not mere toys; they are robots in disguise. Imagine a stylish car or a rugged truck in your grasp. Then, with twists and flips, a magical transformation occurs, and the vehicle becomes a formidable robot. Transformers are akin to undercover agents, masquerading as ordinary items until they unveil their different but linked identities. Throw in a few young guns and pretty babes; you have a billion-dollar business!

The kaleidoscope or transformer metaphor beautifully captures the dynamic and adaptive nature of the analytic process. Just as elements shift and reorganize in these devices, an analyst's experience, when reworked into interpretations or dialogue, can mirror and connect with a patient's experience, helping to catalyze growth and self-awareness. The analyst's experience may be more readily conscious, while the patient's may reside in the preconscious or unconscious. Through this interaction, the previously hidden aspects of the patient's inner world can be brought into awareness, facilitating their therapeutic progress.

The analyst's flexibility, rooted in their own experiences, allows them to adapt and attune to the patient's needs. This constant reconfiguration fosters deeper understanding, opening new perspectives that enrich the therapeutic relationship.

By recognizing these parallels, the analyst can initiate ideas that enhance attunement and collaboration, guiding the therapeutic process with the patient. This deepened connection improves understanding of the patient's conflicts and emotional landscape, strengthening the therapeutic bond.

These subjective experiences enable the analyst to hypothesize about potential parallels or related processes in the patient. Qualified entanglement thus allows for the spontaneous generation of ideas rooted in the analyst's own experiences. However, these ideas require further exploration and testing by the patient, as the theory focuses on hypothesis generation rather than verifying or proving interpretations. As a result, qualified entanglement provides ideas rather than definitive conclusions.

Limits to identical identities between the Self and the others or other Selves

The qualified view of entanglement acknowledges the inherent limitations when considering the construction of our bodies, Selves, and our perceptions of others from a biological and neurological perspective. Each person's bodily and self-experiences are uniquely shaped by their own sensory inputs—such as pain, pleasure, perception, emotions, and memories—exclusively tied to their nervous system. In contrast, our understanding of others is constructed through inference, empathy, and attunement, but never through direct access to their sensory system. For instance, while an analyst may directly experience the sensory input of a toothache, their understanding of a patient's toothache relies on the patient's expressions, emotional cues, and the analyst's own prior experiences. Though both may have toothaches, their experiences are distinct and individualized. Only an aspect of the analyst's experience may be entangled with some aspect of the patient. This point of reference may be easy for the analyst to detect or, like Waldo, may require searching before it is discovered.

Within this "qualified entanglement" framework in Essential Psychoanalysis, the analyst may perceive the patient as either an object-entity in an interpersonal context or a self-entity within an intersubjective sphere. Regardless of the perspective, the analyst and patient do not share the same nervous system, establishing natural limits on the depth of their entanglement. Because genuine entanglement of identical entities is impossible when separate nervous systems are involved, the qualified entanglement theory seems a reasonable basis for psychoanalytic work.

The Interpretive Process in Qualified Entanglement Theory

The patient's response—whether it is surprise, recognition, acceptance, or rejection—serves as a gauge for the relevance of the interpretation. A tepid response may signal that the timing was premature, while outright rejection may suggest that the interpretation lacks significance in the present moment. The analyst accepts such a fate and the patient's judgment of it. On the other hand, when the patient strongly resonates with the interpretation, it indicates a meaningful alignment between the analyst's and the patient's experiences, reinforcing the intervention's patient relevance.

Collaborative Engagement

After presenting the interpretation, the analyst engages with the patient on equal terms, remaining open to acceptance, rejection, or deferral of the interpretation. The analyst does not insist on or emphasize the importance of interpretation or assume its accuracy. Whether in agreement or opposition, the patient's response reflects their autonomy and freedom to navigate the therapeutic process.

Initial Empathy and subsequent corrections of mistakes

The analyst's understanding of the patient's psyche and interpretations are shaped by the patient's free associations, behaviors like play, and the analyst's psychological state. This involves a complex interplay of perceptions, thoughts, beliefs, creativity, emotions, and actions that may subtly mirror the patient's mental state. The analyst's initial insights emerge from the dynamic interaction between their relationship with the patient, their empathy, and their theoretical orientation. Analyzing sources of understanding theoretically is possible, but not in practice.

Drawing from their prior understanding and appreciation of the patient's Self, the analyst offers this interpretation to align with the patient's internal experience. As the patient responds—through verbal or nonverbal cues—the analyst can assess the degree of impingement, misattunement, empathic inaccuracy, predictive error, intrusions, or distortions within the interpretation.

The patient's feedback, combined with the analyst's reflective introspection, enables the analyst to reassess and potentially revise the interpretation based on new insights. This continuous cycle of offering interpretations, receiving responses, and adjusting accordingly forms the backbone of both analytic progress and the overall analytic process. The analyst's capacity for adaptability depends on their ability to initially empathize with the patient's experience and refine their approach by acknowledging and addressing any empathic errors or misattunements. In doing so, the analyst strengthens the therapeutic connection, progressively closing the gap between their initial perceptions of the patient and their evolving lived reality, fostering deeper empathic resonance and alignment.

When both the analyst and patient have experienced trauma, the analyst may re-experience their own traumatic memories during the treatment. Such a situation may reflect some current trauma in the analyst's life or provide insight into the patient's suffering through their entanglement. This shared emotional landscape can foster empathy and support the patient's healing process.

Psychoanalysts use various methods to understand their patients, including free associations, behavioral observations (such as body language, tone of voice, and other non-verbal cues like therapeutic play), and transferences. Empathy and entanglement offer additional tools by focusing on the analyst's internal experience to gather insights about the patient.

In Kohutian Self-Psychology, empathy is viewed as a profound process of *vicarious introspection*. Through transitory trial identifications with the patient, empathy allows the analyst to step into the patient's emotional world, experiencing their feelings without losing their own Self-consciousness. For example, this unique ability to sense the patient's emotions, such as shame, while maintaining their own emotional state, like pride, is a powerful tool. It enables the analyst to understand the patient's inner world without confusing it with their own, a crucial aspect of psychoanalysis.

Empathy, in this context, allows the analyst to grasp key elements of the patient's *Self*, including their needs for *mirroring, idealization*, and *twinship*. It plays a central role in addressing narcissistic injuries, which are wounds to the patient's self-esteem caused by early empathic failures from caregivers. In mirroring transference, a patient with grandiose needs may look to the therapist for validation, seeking the kind of admiration they expected from caregivers but may not have received. Through idealizing transference, the therapist becomes an esteemed figure with qualities that help calm the patient and feel secure. Twinship transference involves the patient seeking recognition of a shared identity or mutual qualities from the therapist. When the therapist cannot meet these roles as a mirror, ideal, or twin, the patient might experience self-fragmentation, which often leads to self-esteem issues and rageful emotional outbursts. However, the therapist's consistent empathy and responsiveness within analysis allow the patient to process and repair these ruptures. Over time, this therapeutic process helps address deep-seated vulnerabilities, restoring the patient's cohesive sense of Self and reducing tendencies toward narcissistic injury.

In Self Psychology, the "leading edge," sometimes called the "forward edge," represents the individual's innate tendency toward growth, self-cohesion, and positive change, contrasting with the "trailing edge," which reflects past vulnerabilities and repetitive defensive patterns rooted in unmet developmental needs (Zimmermann and Paul[89] and Tolpin, 2002[90]). The leading edge embodies emergent possibilities for adaptive functioning, striving for meaningful connections, self-esteem regulation, and achieving aspirations. The therapist's role is to recognize and nurture this growth-oriented potential by providing attuned selfobject experiences, such as empathic mirroring or idealizing responses. This support strengthens the patient's self-cohesion, fosters resilience, and integrates fragmented aspects of the self, allowing for healing and the emergence of healthier, more adaptive ways of being.

Self-psychology views narcissism as the overarching framework for understanding human development and psychological difficulties.

---

89 Zimmermann, P. & Paul, H. (2021). The Origins of the Leading Edge in Kohut's Work. *Psychoanalytic Review* 108:169–196.

90 Tolpin, M. (2002). Chapter 11 Doing Psychoanalysis of Normal Development: Forward Edge Transferences. *Progress in Self-Psychology* 18:167–190.

Accordingly, it views instinctual conflicts (e.g., Oedipal struggles), ego-structural id-ego-superego, and relational conflicts as fragmentation products secondary to Narcissistic injuries.

Entanglement uses different assumptions concerning the analyst's Self to understand the patient. *Entanglement* begins with recognizing that every individual inhabits a realm of unique lived *qualia,* vivid interlinked shapes, sounds, thoughts, imaginations, and emotions that form our experiences. Complete immersion in another person's reality is impossible, as those of others can be understood only within the framework of names, grammar, communications, constructs, interpretations, and relational constraints. While language helps bridge the gap between individuals and remains communication-bound, uncertain, and requiring periodic validation, it is not comparable to the first-person experience of any person. For example, when we feel love or hatred toward someone, we can only infer that they feel similarly based on a model of their mind, which is always tinged with uncertainty. Any relationship, however intimate and close, has elements of significant surprise. Only some aspects of the analyst's experience are entangled with the patient's, and the interpretative process and patient's feedback are required to discover if the inference of entanglement is accurate.

According to Self-psychology, empathy offers a privileged insight into the patient's emotional world in therapy, allowing the analyst to step into the patient's experience momentarily. Entanglement is based on the analyst's self-perception, linked to the patient's experience through inferential processes. The analyst's first-person experiences are provisionally transposed to the patient's experiences. However, whether through empathy or entanglement, both approaches must acknowledge the fundamental reality that the analyst and patient are distinct individuals with separate nervous systems and life histories. For example, an analyst's own toothache, directly sensed through their pain fibers, is experienced distinctly from the vicarious discomfort they might feel when a patient describes tooth pain. The latter sensation is shaped by the analyst's memories, associations, and personal interpretations rather than the immediate physical experience of pain.

Entanglement, unlike empathy, is not a privileged mode of understanding. Entanglement claims a coincidental similarity to the patient's internal state. The analyst's emotions serve as a speculative starting point, requiring further exploration and validation within the therapeutic process.

Self-psychology offers a superordinate framework of narcissism as a central lens for understanding human development and pathology. It views narcissistic dynamics—how individuals establish and maintain a cohesive sense of Self—as the foundation of psychological functioning. Heinz Kohut, the founder of Self-Psychology, posited that early empathic failures by caregivers disrupt the formation of a stable Self, leading to what he termed "narcissistic injuries." These injuries, in turn, contribute to a range of psychological issues, including instinctual conflicts (like the Oedipal struggle), ego-structural conflicts, and relational difficulties. According to Kohut, these psychological disturbances are secondary manifestations of deeper issues tied to narcissistic fragmentation.

In contrast, the concept of entanglement rejects any single superordinate framework, including the centrality of narcissism. Entanglement recognizes the complexity of the therapeutic process and the diverse nature of human experience. It allows for applying various approaches—instinctual, ego-structural, relational, Self, developmental, or neurodynamic—depending on what is most clinically appropriate for the patient and the situation. This flexibility emphasizes that no one framework holds ultimate authority. Instead, the therapeutic method is adapted to the specific needs of the patient, which may shift over time.

An analyst's technique in therapy is shaped by multiple factors, including the coherence of the underlying theory, the evidence supporting it, and personal experiences with both the theory and the teacher who conveyed it. These personal experiences, along with the idealization or devaluation of a mentor, can significantly influence how a theory is applied in practice. Both empathy and entanglement serve as valuable pathways to connect the analyst's self with the patient, offering different lenses through which the patient's emotional world can be understood.

However, the effectiveness of any technique is ultimately determined by the patient's understanding and response to interpretations, not by theory. The patient's feedback—whether they accept, reject, or question an interpretation—along with post-interpretative negotiations, plays a crucial role in shaping the utility of a particular method in a specific therapeutic context. This dynamic process of patient engagement and validation is not just important but essential to refining the technique for that individual.

No matter the theory attached, any superordinate theory will limit the variations and flexibility available to the analyst. In contrast, an approach that allows the analyst to select the most suitable theory or method based on the patient's needs fosters adaptability and responsiveness in treatment. Maintaining a balanced, patient-centered approach that emphasizes the patient's input, feedback, and validation is crucial. This approach ensures that the patient feels honestly heard and understood. It mitigates the risks of over-reliance on any single interpretive technique, keeping the patient's experience central to the therapeutic process and their well-being at the forefront.

Entanglement theory, Chi, her mother, and Ching

During treatment, an analyst can select from various approaches to comment on a patient's condition. These choices are shaped by both conscious and preconscious decision-making processes, often influenced by their theoretical framework. Analysts strictly adhering to a particular theory may feel an internal pressure to interpret every opportunity, experiencing regret if they miss one or a sense of loss if they see it as a missed chance. They may also view interpretations based on alternative theories as somewhat flawed.

Conversely, Essential Psychoanalysis empowers patients by allowing them to shape their therapy. It emphasizes the flexibility in integrating various psychoanalytic theories and using them judiciously for the patient's benefit. It acknowledges that multiple valid interpretations exist. However, every choice has consequences. Essential Psychoanalysis gives the analyst significant freedom to present their insights within a dialogical framework. This framework allows the patient to process the interpretation and decide whether to accept, modify, or reject it. A vital aspect of this method is the patient's ability to reshape interpretations and provide feedback, fostering a collaborative therapeutic environment where critique is welcomed.

Essential Psychoanalysis fosters an egalitarian, active participant-observer relationship between the analyst and the patient. This relationship is grounded in the analyst's ability to provide value through meaningful interpretations. It rejects interpretative techniques that rely on the analyst's power, privilege, or an assumption of an objective, omniscient "God's eye" view of the patient's psyche. Essential Psychoanalysis promotes a shared exploration in which the analyst's interpretations are subject to discussion and co-construction with the patient, encouraging mutual engagement and collaboration.

During sessions # 23 and #24, Ching stated he felt "pressure" when treating Chi. His nonverbal gestures—pressing his hands against his head as if caught in a vice—and his anguished facial expression said it all. He attributed it to unspoken expectations from Chi's mother to bring about change in Chi. During session # 24, Chi expressed frustration by throwing and piling pillows on Ching and resting briefly on them. When Ching suggested Chi wanted to be close to him, she resisted this explanation, scratching him and rejecting his interpretation, insisting, "Every guess you make is wrong."

Ching tailors his technique by closely observing and responding to the patient's behaviors. This is an essential skill for any analyst to develop and maintain. At this moment, Ching attributes the pressure to Chi's mother's expectations. This, too, is an essential aspect of self-awareness, which seeks to find the source of a feeling. However, Ching is still unaware of the dynamic that Chi might herself be experiencing a pressure that she cannot become aware of or express and articulate. Ching is still learning to recognize and respond to the more profound commonalities between the analyst and the patient that emerge from their entanglement. A nuanced understanding of broad countertransference is necessary to fully engage with and explore the patient's experience. Once learned, the analyst can use broad countertransference (namely, the feelings and experiences of the analyst) as a laboratory to test the patient's self, which can be applied to many other situations.

Here, I summarize sessions 23 and 24. In session #23, Chi's mother, in a moment of frustration, temporarily abandoned Chi, telling her to leave the house and not return. Chi gathered some belongings and spent an hour outside in the rain. Eventually, her mother retrieved her from the gate of their community and arranged for Chi to stay with her father.

In session #24, Chi's mother gave her math exercises to practice at home. Chi, who has always disliked such tasks, became even more oppositional. According to her mother, Chi protested the exercises, hit her, attacked the book with a pencil, and slammed the door in frustration.

Like professionals in other fields, psychoanalysts must distinguish between individual elements (the trees) and the broader context (the forest). While details are crucial, there are times when the larger picture demands priority. In Chi's case, the broader perspective involves recognizing her emotional crisis after being put out of the house by her mother. This event likely felt overwhelming for an eight-year-old, akin to experiencing a natural disaster—a complete emotional upheaval. This sense of catastrophe was compounded by her father's admission in session 25 that he could not care for her.

Analysts must be attuned to a patient's significant distress during such crises, acknowledging the anxiety, fear, and sense of doom accompanying them. In these moments, the analyst's role is to manage the immediate emotional fallout and provide clarity. By articulating the experience, they help the patient make sense of the situation and recognize that it is not their fault. This is especially important for children, who often internalize parental conflict and feel guilty or responsible for the chaos around them. The analyst guides the child through the emotional storm by offering reassurance and helping the child relinquish misplaced blame.

So, what is the meaning of Chi's "Every guess you make is wrong."

Chi wants Ching not to dwell on the particulars of what she says; she wants him to acknowledge her terror, a pressure he feels on his own. Ching could have relied on his own Self-state—his experience of pressure—and interpreted it as a reflection of Chi's response to her mother's extreme actions. This approach would align with the entanglement theory, using the analyst's Self-state as a lens for interpretation.

For Chi, it must have been like an earthquake or a hurricane hitting her. She was angry at her mother for treating her thus, but she was afraid to get into a conflict with her mother. She is angry with Ching for behaving like an agent of her mother rather than recognizing that his feelings mirror her own.

In contrast to the missed opportunities regarding Ching's feeling of "pressure" from an entanglement perspective, Ching's processing of the risk of treatment ending prematurely demonstrates a more profound engagement with the entanglement of this idea. The sudden end of treatment concerns Ching, Chi, and her mother. The entanglement here highlights how anxiety about potential disruption in treatment is felt across all three, reflecting a shared emotional current. Recognizing this commonality enables a more attuned and meaningful exploration of their collective fears, creating an opportunity to address these anxieties within the therapeutic space.

After the meeting, during which Ching assigned Chi's education to the grandfather and play to the mother, Chi's mother expressed her anger and frustration in a series of messages. She accused Ching of gender bias, questioning his understanding and blaming him for the situation. Concerned about how her distrust might affect Chi's therapy, Ching shared his worries with her. In response, Chi's mother acknowledged her frustration and feelings of desperation but insisted that the treatment should continue, asking him to avoid claiming that he understood her. Ching is exploring Chi's mother's desperation and how it might affect the treatment.

In the early hours of the morning, she messaged again, expressing her lack of trust and casting doubt on whether therapy could move forward. This is an example of the entanglement between Ching and Chi's mother. Later that morning, however, she reached out again, emphasizing her wish for Chi to develop decisiveness—a trait she felt her father lacked. She recognized Ching's positive influence on Chi and believed he could help her toward this goal. Between 2 a.m. and that morning, Ching faced the uncertainty that the therapy might have come to an end and also his own mistrust of Chi's mother, whom he felt was not forthcoming with the reasons why Chi had returned to living with her. Ching felt, "We are on the brink of ending."

Readers will recall that Ching told Chi that after doing something good, she often followed it with something bad, like name-calling or kicking the toy box. Chi agreed and then grabbed Ching's watch, breaking its wristband. She apologized, and Ching suggested that perhaps she wanted to see if the watch would break. Chi asked Ching, "Can we be broken?"

Ching replied, "We must be careful because things can break, and if we love what breaks, we feel sad."

Ching sensed intuitively that the therapy was on the verge of ending, influenced by the emotional undercurrents from both Chi and her mother. They had expressed concerns about the fragile trust between them, creating a precarious situation that felt ready to unravel. These shifting perspectives, like the changing patterns of a kaleidoscope, revealed different interpretations of the same complex scenario. Ching is in the process of recognizing the interconnected flow of information, suggesting that his feelings mirror Chi's. His thought, "We are on the verge of ending," likely reflected not only his own emotions but also Chi's and her mother's viewpoints.

This process of entanglement draws information from Chi's free associations and play, as well as from her mother's communications. Still, it also operates through the analyst's own memory, perceptions, thoughts, imagination, emotions, creativity, gut instincts, and actions. Whether labeled as entanglement, ego diffusion, relationship, attunement, fit between patient and analyst, or empathic understanding, the core idea is recognizing a direct emotional link between analyst and patient. An analyst can trace his links to the patient through free associations, actions including play, or the analyst himself. Entanglement is a way to explore this connection through a profound reflection on the analyst's broad countertransference.

Readers may recall that Ching recently pointed out to Chi that her polite play was often followed by hostile actions, such as insults or aggression, to which Chi agreed. She then impulsively damaged Ching's watch and apologized. Ching suggested that perhaps she was testing if it could be broken.

This led Chi to ask, "Can we be broken?" Chi, thus, communicated her concern about the fragility of their relationship verbally. Ching responded, noting that things can break and that we feel sad when we love what breaks. Ching sensed an approaching end to their therapeutic journey, as both Chi and her mother expressed concerns about their fragile situation. However, Ching had yet to grasp how his emotions intertwined with Chi's. Such entangled connections shared among Ching, Chi, and her mother could be explored further if therapy continues.

Analysts must remember that broad countertransference and empathic inferences should be treated as hypotheses, not definitive conclusions. Analysts must remain flexible, continually adjusting to the evolving dynamics of the therapeutic relationship. However, asserting or imposing these untested notions onto the patient would be inappropriate due to the inherent power imbalance between analyst and patient. Patients, especially those who idealize the analyst, may unconsciously conform to the analyst's expectations. This can heighten the risk of relying too heavily on unverified empathic connections, potentially leading to distorted interpretations or reinforcing unexamined assumptions.

Supervision: 26

"It works. Today, more progress was made. I also have a different enigma. I bitterly failed an adult patient who reminds me of Chi. I started with her when she was nineteen years old; now she is twenty-eight years old. When the treatment started, she felt it was helpful, then she felt frustrated, and then she became aggressive towards me. I felt controlled by her aggressiveness. I am annoyed because I do not understand such serious, unprovoked aggression. The treatment was interrupted after nine years because we could not solve this. She still communicates with me through email messages. Chi and this patient are similar. I spoke to my analyst, Jorge, and he and you have no answer to such aggressiveness."

"I do not have an answer, but I have a response."

"What is it?"

"It is the difference between social reality and transference. It is the difference between your intentions and what Chi feels. Chi feels bad because she has a problem with math."

"Yes."

"Chi's mother loves her deeply but hits her to help her but is unsuccessful. Chi feels pressure to perform for her mother and get the correct answer."

"Yes."

"You approach Chi with a good heart and try to help her with math by using simple examples with cards, as well as helping her with reading the clock."

"Yes."

"Chi is grateful to you for helping her to some extent. However, Chi feels you are also acting like her mother by using opportunities to drill her with easy math questions but still math exercises. Maybe you should remind her of her mother's methods, which she hates. Is she happy about math questions also in her treatment?"

"Probably not."

"The evidence is that she quickly gets angry at you and has tried to scratch you. You expect a reality response because you are kind, listen to her, and try to help her with math. She gives you a transference response, you remind her of her mother, and she treats you like her mother with anger and aggression."

"This view makes sense. About three years ago, the adult patient I mentioned adopted an internet pseudonym to safeguard her real identity in our communications. Coincidentally, she chose the name Chi. She said, 'You have to bear my anger. Everywhere else, I must control myself or risk destroying my life if I express what I truly feel. Only with you can I speak from my heart.'"

"It is unfair to me, but that is what she said and attacked me every time."

Ching fell silent for a while.

"I feel there is a discrepancy between this view that Chi feels towards me like she feels towards her mother and the view you expressed a few weeks ago, that Chi treats me the way her mother treats her."

Before I could respond, Ching quickly continued to speak.

"Now Chi's play has resumed, but it is wild. We played a game of throwing a ball into a basket to see who wins. She shaded the rules so that she always won.

"I told Chi, 'You do not like my suggestions to make the game fair; you want me to follow your rules. You want to dominate and win.'"

"Chi replied, 'Yes.'"

"After that, Chi wanted to play a different game. She wanted to play one of us pretending to be dead and the other pretending to be a monster. I asked her for the rules for playing the monster game, and she explained them to me. The first time, she wanted to play dead and wanted me to play the monster."

"So, she played dead, and I made 'ROOAARRR!!!!!', a spooky monster noise."

"Chi woke up from her dead pose and said, 'Don't make too scary monster noises. Make only somewhat too scary monster noises.'"

"So I made a less scary noise, like 'Roooaaaaarrrr!!!!!' "

"Chi then brought a toy sofa and said it had magical protective properties. She was protected from the monster when she held the sofa in her hands and near her head. Then she said her whole body was protected by the sofa, not just her head."

"I told Chi, 'Yiu would like the power to control the monster so you are not scared."

"Chi said, 'Yes.' "

"I said, 'You like your rules; you do not like other people's rules' "

"Chi said, 'Yes.' "

"I think this play was significant. It is useful to be specific. For example, which specific 'other' person are you talking about? You told me Chi's teacher is generally kind and not scary. Is that true?"

"Yes."

"In real life, Chi dislikes her mother's math rules when her mother becomes upset and angry."

"Yes."

"But Chi's mother is a complex person. Chi's mother loves her daughter and wants the best for Chi. When relaxed, Chi and her mother can play and have fun playing Little Kitty and Little Princess, although mother dominates that game."

"Yes."

"Chi is scared of her mother when she is the Math Monster."

"Yes. Chi hates Mother's education rules. Mother's education rules are the scary Monster rules. Yes. I have to learn to be specific when it is possible."

"But when it was my turn to play dead, Chi became aggressive and mean. She started to spit on me. It was hard for me to tolerate it. I could no longer play dead. So, I woke up and said to her, 'You are trying to see how much I can tolerate.'"

"Chi continued to spit on me and began kicking as well. She grabbed the curtain, threatening to destroy my furniture, saying she would tear the curtain off the rod and break it."

"I told Chi, 'This is too much,'"

"Chi disagreed and said, 'We are playing the attack game. You attack me, and I attack you.'"

"I told Chi, 'This is not good. We need a win-win game where both of us can win. In the game you have going, one of us must suffer.'"

"Chi insisted, 'The game is attack, and one of us must lose.'"

I remarked, "'No win-win, one must suffer.' This captures the heart of this analysis. You are observing a fundamental truth about psychoanalysis. Without transference, analysis is cold, and progress halts. With too much transference, the process overheats, and treatment stalls."

"The analyst's role is similar to that of a thermostat, finding a balance where both patient and analyst can make sense of the treatment and the patient's progress. It does not have to be perfect, but it cannot be dead; it has to be alive and working."

"It is your job not only to appreciate the attack game inside your treatment but to see how it is connected to Chi's life."

Ching looked astonished and relieved.

"I understand." Chi's no-win attacks with me are only the preliminary explanation; I need to explain how her life with her mother is similar."

"Yes, Chi is too scared to face that monster alone; she needs your help. In a few sentences, say how would you explain that to Chi."

Ching paused and took a deep drag from his e-cigarette.

Ching thought for several moments and then said, "I have to return to an old trick."

"Oh."

"Yes. Baby tone voice."

"OK"

Ching coughed and prepared himself to speak, speaking in a baby-toned voice.

"Today, you attacked me, but your home is where the attacks are happening. When your mother teaches you, she hits you; now, you are hitting her back. Is that right (baby tone)?"

"Right on."

"Baby tone. I used it while babysitting my cousin. It is easier for a child to hear that tone. It is less scary."

"Yes. Mother put the pressure on your head; Chi put the squeeze on your heart? You could not contain them, but with those few sentences, you explained to Chi the connection between play with you and her life with her mother."

"Thank you. I spoke to my analyst about this, and he said, Life is full of challenges; enjoy it."
     "That is old man's wisdom speaking!"
     "Now I am preparing to speak those sentences!"

My Musings

Ernst Kris (1956)[91] coined the term "Regression in the service of the ego," which refers to a deliberate and beneficial retreat from typical, advanced ego processes to engage in primary process thought patterns or actions. This psychological mechanism is linked to artistic or inventive endeavors, allowing one to delve into novel concepts and profound feelings. This form of regression is constructive, unlike its pathological counterpart, as it promotes creative thinking and problem-solving by temporarily setting aside logical limitations.

---

91 Kris, E. (1956). On Some Vicissitudes of Insight in Psycho-Analysis. *International Journal of Psycho-Analysis* 37:445–455.

Using a baby tone within the analytic setting is a prime example of "Regression in the service of the ego," as demonstrated by Ching. His playful tone allowed him to draw on his previous babysitting experience, tailoring his approach to communicate with the child in a way that was both engaging and accessible. While the effectiveness of this technique remains a separate issue, Ching was able to address the intense pressure he felt as a therapist, which stemmed from the combined transference of the child and her mother. By employing this approach, Ching formulated a strategy to redirect the overheated transference dynamics back to the source of the conflict.

It might be appropriate to recall the story of *The Nightingale* by Hans Christian Anderson (2006)[92]. In the tale, the Emperor of China is initially captivated by the beautiful song of a plain-looking nightingale, who is later confined to a cage despite her pleas. Over time, a mechanical bird, with its impressive appearance and predictable song, replaces the nightingale, gaining the court's favor. However, when the Emperor falls gravely ill, the nightingale returns to heal him with her authentic, heartfelt music. Her song revives the Emperor and even moves Death to spare his life.

Similarly, when Chi struggles to find her voice, Ching uses understanding and a playful, baby-like tone to connect with her. Just as the nightingale's genuine expression proves invaluable, Ching's approach is designed to navigate the complexities of working with Chi. Like the nightingale's song, we hope Ching's efforts will help Chi find her voice and experience a meaningful blossoming of her true self. This way, psychoanalysis alleviates human suffering by fostering authentic self-expression and healing by pursuing freedom.

---

92 Andersen, H.C. (Hans Christian), (1835-1873). *The Complete Hans Christian Andersen Fairy Tales.* New York: Gramercy Books, 2006.

A child's desire for change often carries a sense of fantasy, much like the magical effects of a potion, with aspirations resembling the heroic feats of Wonder Woman or Superman. In Chi's case, it was a magic powder. However, an analyst recognizes that real change occurs after working through conflicts, repairing deficits, and addressing misunderstandings, and often a gradual process involving insights, change, compromise, and adaptation. Even small transformations demand a complex interaction of factors, often facing resistance, e.g., the force of habit and inertia. The nature of change is inherently unpredictable, with unexpected elements frequently accompanying its arrival, making the journey toward transformation more nuanced and challenging than the child might initially envision.

Supervision: 27

"It works. I am trying a playful method to communicate with Chi."

"For example, I playfully say in a baby voice, 'You come here to do whatever you want.'"

"Chi yelled, 'Yes.' She then said, 'I decide. I decide.'"

"You may remember when I spoke about an adult patient who also referred to herself as Chi. This was her assumed name for Internet purposes. Chi had been intensely angry with me, often lashing out. During one session, she asked how I felt, and I told her that her anger had become intolerable, which led to our decision to stop. Though we no longer meet, she occasionally reaches out. Recently, she messaged me, expressing her shock at how abruptly things ended. However, she also shared her gratitude for the treatment, explaining that a profound change occurred after we stopped.

"Chi described her journey from her 'old me' to her 'New me.' She explained, 'My old me always wondered why my parents beat me and were violent toward me. I concluded that I must have done something wrong and was bad.' She shared that when she was in analysis with me, she was in her 'old me' state, feeling compelled to express her anger toward her parents through me because no one else would tolerate it. At the time, she believed she was evil and angry."

"However, after we stopped the sessions, she realized she was no longer angry and no longer saw herself as a bad person. She now sees herself as a good person—this is her 'New me.' She feels thankful and is learning to accept and grow into this 'New me,' finding herself less consumed by anger. Interestingly, she mentioned that she could not discover this 'New me' while still seeing me."

"For the past few days, I have been reflecting on that Chi's concept of the 'Old me' and the 'New me.' I feel deeply grateful to my twenty-eight-year-old patient, Chi, for communicating with me and sharing her experience of change. Her insights also apply to the younger Chi, the patient you supervise. I sense similar dynamics may be at play. When Chi first saw me, she was polite and nice, but now she is disruptive, angry, and even violent."

"This leads me to a new question for you: What is the benefit for Chi in this identification?"

"Which identification? The old or the new?"

"The 'Old' identification. Chi used to be obedient. Chi attacks her mother and destroys books in the' New' identification. Her mother is shocked. What is the benefit of 'Old' identification for Chi?"

"OK. "Let us take a closer look at the history between Chi and her mother, especially regarding when her mother became upset over Chi's academic performance. For a while, when Chi struggled with math, her mother would call her an 'idiot' and hit her.

"Yes."

"How did Chi feel when she behaved obediently but when her mother hit her?"

"She suffered, felt bad, and was angry."

"So, Chi suffered and felt bad. Who was she angry at?"

"Her mother and herself."

"Let us begin with Chi's anger towards her mother. Despite this anger, Chi's obedience was a protective mechanism, helping her avoid conflict with her mother. However, she could not express her anger."

"Yes."

"Chi's 'New' identifications enable her to openly express her anger and aggression towards both her mother and you as part of the mother transference. In this dynamic, Chi's anger and aggression are no longer suppressed; they are expressed freely, leading to open conflict rather than obedience."

"Yes."

"Now let us go back to the point you raised earlier; what if her anger was anger at herself."

"OK"

"Chi's anger at herself could likely represent anger originally directed towards others, particularly her mother, which has been turned inward to avoid conflict. By internalizing this anger, Chi may have sought to protect herself from the emotional and physical consequences of confronting her mother directly."

> "Yes. It is starting to be clear to me. Chi's policy change is a new development. Chi forced the environment to adjust to her. She will no longer sacrifice herself. She is clearly saying, " 'No' to others."
>
> "The situation is making my duty clear to me. I should never let her feel bad about herself and revert the bade onto herself."

"What is bade."

> "Blade, knife, I should not let her turn the blade back on herself."

I thought Ching did not control Chi's defenses, but I chose not to express this to him. Instead, I said, "You understand 'turning aggression against the Self,' as it applies to Chi now and not as a theoretical abstraction."

> "With your help. I need to figure out how the personal art of treatment works. It is not theory."

"Last time, you mentioned the idea of using a baby tone as part of a personal approach in treatment. You wanted to softly say, 'You attacked me, but the real attacks are happening at home. When your mother teaches you, she hits you; now, you are hitting her back. Is that right?'"

"Yes. I remember. I practiced the lines. Then, I decided that the message was too much to convey. I should break it into smaller pieces. Chi's anger to Me. Chi's anger at her mother."

"However, things did not work out the way I planned. She was not so much into attacking me this last time. She tickled me and wanted me to tickle her. She became angry when I would not tickle her. She angrily shouted that I should tickle her. She insisted that even if she resisted, I should tickle her forcibly."

"My twenty-eight-year-old female patient, before she stopped seeing me, said that she had a fantasy of rape. She said that she had similar fantasies from when she was a girl. I was shocked. I felt now I was witnessing something similar with Chi, who wanted me to tickle her forcibly. I felt maybe there was some erotic element in both of them. I felt that the tickling, which could be related to anger, was slipping into something else. Maybe the taste of being forced was related to some sexualization."

"Fortunately, our time was up, and I told Chi, 'It is time for us to stop.'"

"Chi refused to go, and I had to ask her mother to come in and take her."

"What do you think of her insisting I tickle her by force at some point in the session."

"I am thinking of an idea called an active attempt at mastery, where Chi picks the moment of conflict or particular encounter with you. Rather than speculate too much, I will try to explain the concept of Chi's own history to you. What time does Chi get back from school?"

"Maybe 3:30 pm."

"Roughly when does she go to sleep?"

"Maybe 9:00 p.m."

"So, when her mother is in a 'math mood,' Chi has to wonder when she will be hit constantly. It is uncertain. Maybe 3:30, maybe 4:00 p.m., maybe 5:00, 6:00, 7:00, or even 8:00 p.m. It is radically unknown, and Chi has to tolerate the anxiety of not knowing when her mother will get upset enough to hit her. Now, when did she insist that you forcibly tickle her?"

"Around 5:00 p.m."

"So, similarly, if Chi attacks her mother at 5:00 p.m., she forces the conflict to happen at a time of her choosing instead of passively waiting for it to occur. By initiating it, she actively chooses the moment of conflict rather than being left in suspense. That is called active mastery!"

"I do not know about Chi, but I know what you are talking about. As a child, when it became dark, I started to wonder when my mother might hit me. I know the dread of waiting and not knowing when something will happen. Active mastery takes out the mystery."

Ching recalled a childhood incident that illustrates the concept of active mastery. A boy accidentally pushed him on the playground, and Ching instinctively responded by pushing back. The simple accident escalated into a spontaneous push exchange between the two boys. This chain of reactions exemplifies active mastery, where each child responds to regain control over the situation. The initial push triggered a sequence of actions, showing how individuals, even in seemingly casual interactions, may actively engage to assert agency and navigate unpredictable circumstances.

Ching's memory brought to mind a classic example from Freud's work. Freud (1920)[93] observed his grandson playing a simple game with a wooden reel tied to a string. The child would throw the reel away, exclaiming "fort!" (meaning "gone"), and then pull it back, joyfully shouting "da!" ("there"). Freud interpreted this game as a symbolic reenactment of the child's experience of separation from his mother, who would leave him for short periods. By reenacting the mother's absence and return through play, the child gained a sense of control over a distressing situation. Freud saw this game as a quintessential example of active mastery, where the child transforms a passive, anxiety-inducing event (his mother's departure) into an active one he can manage and influence.

> "Before we stop, I wish you would comment on the sexualization and eroticization I mentioned when Chi said forcibly tickle me."

Recalling my experiences many years ago as a consult liaison psychiatrist at Cook County Hospital, I had a thought. Initially, I hesitated to bring it up because its relevance to Chi seemed highly improbable. However,

---

93 Freud, S. (1920). Beyond the Pleasure Principle. *Standard Edition* 18:1–64.

for the sake of straightforward communication and the psychoanalytic associational method, I decided to share it with Ching and let him determine whether it was relevant.

Early onset or precocious puberty is a health condition characterized by the body entering puberty sooner than the typical age range—before eight years in girls and nine years in boys. Specialists in gynecology and endocrinology often manage this condition due to its association with the premature development of secondary sexual traits, which are triggered by hormonal shifts. While precocious puberty can be idiopathic—meaning no clear cause is identified—known causes may include brain tumors, genetic conditions, or other underlying health issues that influence hormone production. Children with this condition typically grow and mature despite the premature start. Nonetheless, pediatricians might consult child psychiatrists if they come across cases of early puberty without a clear medical explanation.

A mother of an eight-year-old girl asked, "Doctor, she just started to have her periods. How do I talk to her about it? What should I say?"

"Puberty is never easy for a parent, regardless of the child's age. At thirteen, when a child starts blushing at the thought of boys and fantasizing about interpersonal relationships, the discussions around these issues shift naturally. However, when a child's mind is still immersed in fantastical creatures such as a Little Princess, Monsters, or Wonder Woman at age eight, it becomes much more complicated for a parent to navigate. Cognitive development also has a bearing on what a child can integrate. So, while Chi's primary concerns still seem to revolve around math problems, punishments, anger with the mother, and the anger being expressed in treatment with you, there may also be early signs of adolescent issues emerging beneath the surface."

"I overheard a conversation between Chi and her mother a few weeks ago, where they mentioned that Chi just had her first period. Her mother was making arrangements to take her to the doctor, but neither of them brought this up with me."

"What a coincidence. I almost did not mention the case of early puberty I encountered. We must trust our associative method. In Chi's case, the tickling might represent some interpersonal excitement, symbolize her anger with her mother being reenacted with you in the transference, or relate to an early awareness of pubertal concerns. I still believe the issues with her anger toward her mother, and you have not been adequately addressed. There is more work needed in that area."

"I agree."

Before the session commenced, Ching planned to understand Chi's resentment towards him as an extension of her unresolved issues with her mother and to approach this with a gentle, childlike tone. The session began positively, with Ching expressing that this tone worked. However, as the session progressed, tickling preoccupied Chi, and Ching did not have the opportunity to interpret her underlying anger further. It seemed to me that Ching believed he had not fully expressed the meaning of her anger in the caring way he had intended.

My Musings

My reflections began with a comment about the falling age of menarche in girls, which I made with considerable hesitation. After the supervision,

I decided to verify what I had mentioned about the declining age of menarche, as I thought it might be relevant to Chi's case. In China, the average age at menarche decreased from 13.41 to 12.47 years between 1985 and 2010 (Song et al., 2014). This decline in the age of menarche could potentially have implications for Chi's case, as it may influence the psychological and emotional development of girls at a younger age[94], which reassured me that the information I provided to Ching was not inaccurate.

My thoughts drifted back to memories of Rosita Pildes, Peter Barglow, and the time I met T. Berry Brazelton. For a brief period, I served as a consult liaison psychiatrist at Chicago's Cook County Hospital. Part of my responsibilities included providing psychiatric consultations in the Neonatal Intensive Care Unit (NICU), where Dr. Rosita Pildes was the chief of neonatology. Many infants in the unit had low birth weight, and at that time, advances in neonatal care had just begun, allowing even tiny babies to survive. Historically, 2 pounds (1 kilogram) had been considered the threshold of viability, but new techniques were improving outcomes for infants born at even lower weights.

Incubators played a critical role in maintaining the fragile balance of body temperature, humidity, and oxygen levels for these newborns, while tube feeding ensured they received adequate nutrition. Continuous monitoring of vital signs, such as heart rate and breathing, was essential. However, a concern raised by the staff was that many mothers and parents, having been discharged while their infants remained hospitalized, often did not return regularly to visit their newborns. This absence raised bonding and emotional support issues for the infants and their parents, highlighting the need for empathetic and supportive care for all involved.

---

94 Song Y, Ma J, Wang H.J., Wang, Z., Hu, P., Zhang, B, et al. (2014). Trends of age at menarche and association with body mass index in Chinese school-aged girls, 1985–2010. *Journal of Pediatrics* 165:1172–1177.

Around the time I worked in the Neonatal Intensive Care Unit at Chicago's Cook County Hospital, Klaus and Kennell's (1976) [95] research on maternal-infant bonding was gaining attention. Their work emphasized the importance of early postpartum contact between mothers and newborns, such as skin-to-skin interaction, for fostering secure attachment. They argued that these initial moments could lay the foundation for the infant's psychological and emotional development, promoting essential maternal behaviors like attentiveness and caregiving. Conversely, separation due to premature birth or medical complications could hinder the bonding process.

This was a central concern for Dr. Rosita Pildes, the neonatology team, and myself. We often discussed ways to encourage mothers, many of whom were afraid to touch their fragile infants, to engage physically with their babies. Many mothers were tentative, fearing they might harm their newborns, especially in cases of extreme prematurity or congenital conditions. Even as an infant was close to discharge, some mothers said, "The baby looks so frail; I am afraid I may hurt the baby by accident." A mother gingerly touched her infant near discharge, remarking that the baby felt as delicate as foam or cotton. We were aware that bonding could feel risky to these mothers, mainly because the child's survival was not always assured. Encouraging parents to look at, touch, and bond with their infants remained a critical focus of our work.

During one of my rounds, I witnessed a case of Sirenomelia, also known as mermaid syndrome. This rare and severe congenital anomaly, marked by the fusion of the lower extremities, was accompanied by severe malformations of the spine, limbs, and vital internal organs. Peering through the incubator's window, I glimpsed a tiny infant whose lower body seemed fused in a way that defied description. The sight was so

---

95 Klaus, M.H., & Kennell, J.H. (1976). *Maternal-Infant Bonding*. St. Louis: C.V. Mosby.

unsettling that my mind instinctively recoiled, unable to fully grasp the strangeness before me. It was an image profoundly foreign to anything I had ever encountered, a stark contrast to what I thought possible, leaving me momentarily disoriented by its unfamiliarity.

In this particular case, Dr. Pildes explained that the fetus had survived in utero by relying on the mother's kidneys for renal function. Tragically, the newborn was born without kidneys and was not compatible with life. Dr. Pildes conducted her medical rounds. She informed the team that a fetus relies on the maternal renal system to filter waste during gestation. Regrettably, the newborn in question was born without kidneys. Dr. Pildes conveyed, "Without essential organs, the infant cannot survive long. We must prepare the mother for the inevitability that her child's life will be brief, allowing her time with the infant to bid farewell and providing her an opportunity to work through her feelings with our team." It was a poignant reminder of life's fragility.

The application of the Brazelton Neonatal Behavioral Assessment Scale (1978)[96] represents significant contributions to the field of neonatology and developmental psychology. It is a comprehensive tool to assess a newborn's behavioral patterns and capabilities, providing insights into their neurological development, temperament, and the early relationship between infants and their caregivers. One of my mentors was Peter Barglow, M.D., a psychoanalyst with diverse interests. He began using the Brazelton Neonatal Behavior Assessment Scale to explore this area at the Neonatal Intensive Care Unit at Reese Hospital, particularly studying infant irritability and soothability. I had the opportunity to practice BNBAS assessments on newborns alongside Barglow.

---

96 Brazelton TB. (1978). The Brazelton Neonatal Behavior Assessment Scale: introduction. *Monographs of the Society for Research in Child Development* 1;43(5–6):1–13. [PUBMED: 752799]

On one occasion, Pildes invited T. Berry Brazelton to Cook County Hospital, where he demonstrated the examination of a newborn in the mother's presence. Dr. Brazelton, a pioneering American pediatrician, significantly advanced newborn behavioral research, most notably by developing the Neonatal Behavioral Assessment Scale (NBAS). This tool transformed our understanding of newborns by evaluating their physical and neurological responses, emotional states, and individual differences. Insights from the NBAS revealed that even vulnerable newborns exhibit remarkable capabilities from birth, communicate their needs through behavior, and act as social beings capable of influencing their caregiving environment. Brazelton's work challenged the notion of infants as passive and highlighted the importance of early interactions between infants and caregivers. He also served as president of the Society for Research in Child Development and authored influential books on infant development and parenting.

The Brazelton Neonatal Behavior Assessment Scale (BNBAS), established in 1973, assesses a newborn's neurological and behavioral functioning. The assessment begins with the infant at rest and records their responses to the examiner's stimulating and soothing actions across different states of arousal. The BNBAS evaluates 1) the infant's ability to maintain sleep and filter out unpleasant stimuli (habituation), 2) responsiveness to visual and auditory stimuli while awake, 3) soothability, 4) motor functioning, and 5) reflexes. A critical aspect of the BNBAS is assessing the infant's level of arousal or state of consciousness, which can be influenced by factors such as hunger, nutrition, hydration, and their position in the sleep-wake cycle. The states of consciousness measured include: 1) deep sleep, 2) light sleep, 3) drowsy, 4) alert (where the infant can focus attention with minimal movement), 5) alert and active (reactive to stimuli with high activity), and 6) crying. Each state reflects a level of arousal that determines awareness, possible contents, and access to motor actions.

Brazelton's method of assessing visual and auditory responsiveness when the infant is awake is particularly relevant for psychoanalysts. In this part of the assessment, a red ball is presented about a foot from the infant's eyes and moved horizontally to gauge the infant's ability to focus on it. The ball is also moved vertically to assess vertical attention.

Importantly, this assessment is an empirical measure where the examiner plays an active role rather than remaining an objective or neutral observer. The examiner is encouraged to engage the infant directly, ensuring that the infant sees the ball before it is moved. Instead of recording a single observation, the examiner employs various strategies to capture the infant's best performance by actively drawing their attention. This method focuses on documenting the infant's highest capabilities, requiring the examiner's involvement, which contrasts with the traditional notion of objective or neutral observation. The examiner's deliberate efforts to stimulate and engage the infant emphasize that this widely accepted scientific method is not purely objective but designed to elicit optimal responses.

In front of the mother, Dr. Brazelton gently awakened the infant, encouraging the baby to focus on the red ball and follow it with their eyes. The mother was captivated by how many capacities her child already possessed and how efficiently Dr. Brazelton could engage her baby. Dr. Brazelton cooed softly when testing the infant's hearing, prompting the infant to turn its head toward the sound. Soon, he invited the mother to join in by calling the baby's name. Immediately, the infant recognized her voice, turning energetically toward her. Compared to the degree of head turning when Dr. Brazelton called her name, the infant responded more vigorously to the mother. Dr. Brazelton remarked that the baby was clearly attuned to her and responded readily. The mother was delighted to witness this interaction and felt glad she had attended the demonstration, as it filled her with joy and pride in her baby's responsiveness.

Dr. Brazelton's joy in his profession was unmistakable to observers of his work. His fondness for infants was apparent. He listened attentively to the mothers, acknowledging their innate skill in engaging their infants' focus. He was actively involved and did not attempt to preserve a neutral or impassive demeanor. This underscores the notion that a scientific observer can be engaged, involved, and empathetic. The examiner can express care, concern, and compassion as a good doctor. Similarly, many contemporary analysts recognize that the analyst actively co-creates the transference. This process of co-creation requires a thorough description. In the same way, the genesis of an interpretation should be transparent to the psychoanalytic community. The extent to which an analyst reveals how they arrived at an idea is also a crucial part of the technique, and those therapeutically effective elements should be communicated to the patient. However, the analyst's contributions should never become a burden for the patient, nor should they manipulate the transference. In addition, patients undergo psychoanalysis to change their lives and not merely to have themselves objectively observed.

In Ching's case, he prepared to deliver an interpretation using a baby-like tone during the last two sessions. This can be compared to an analyst striving to offer a meaningful and credible interpretation in the most optimal manner possible. Such approaches are not neutral or objective but align with the contemporary analytic view that both the analyst and patient are active co-participants and observers in the unfolding analytic process.

Admittedly, Ching's best-laid plans did not come to fruition, as the opportunity to deliver his interpretation never materialized. Chi's anger quickly shifted to a demand for a tickle, leaving no space for Ching to offer the interpretation he had prepared. This highlights the inherent uncertainties in both psychoanalysis and life. However, Ching's planned interpretation still offers valuable insight into the genesis of an interpretation, even one that remains unspoken. To that extent, it illustrates the analyst's role as a participant-observer, actively engaged in the unfolding therapeutic process, even when outcomes are unpredictable.

Consider Ching and his ideas before he started to work with Chi. He bought a rug with a global map for the office. He imagined engaging his patients with imaginary scenarios using the rug. In this scenario, Ching imagined a peaceful exchange between a patient and himself. However, his experience featured an enraged, confrontational, and wild Chi who insisted on targeting him with a water pistol, a gesture of defiance. He was bewildered, believing that he had fostered a space for mindful play and honesty, and struggled to grasp the intensity of Chi's anger and antagonism towards him. Clarity emerged as he identified the difference between societal expectations and Chi's psychological transference towards him. He came to realize that she was grappling with her mother's inexplicable fury, hostility, and physical outbursts, which were as incomprehensible and unacceptable to her as they were to him. In time, he wanted to find a way to convey his understanding of Chi's rage to her using a baby voice. However, her anger evolved into a continuous plea for tickles.

The idea that the patient and the analyst actively participate in co-creating transference and countertransference without being privileged observers is a common theme in contemporary psychoanalysis. This hypothesis evolved after the contrasting concept of an abstinent, neutral, privileged observer who presents a blank screen for the patient's transference. These are not fixed truths but theories that can be examined and better understood as more transparent data is gathered from various analysts treating different patients.

Supervision: 28

"Psychoanalytic work is too difficult. Chi threw all my toys onto me. Then she said, 'I don't want treatment. Stop it. Can you stop it? Can I stop it?' Then she began to attack me and said, I want to bite off your nose.' "

"I became angry and scared. I know that the jaw muscles are one of the strongest muscles in the body. I held her and stopped her."

"Chi said, 'I just want it to stop.' "

"I said to Chi, 'Oh. I see. This is how you feel when you are beaten; you want it to stop.'"

"We previously discussed that Chi's transference to you is too strong and difficult for you to tolerate. When transference is too weak or too intense, the analyst lacks sufficient leverage to engage in effective analytic work. Ideally, transference should fall within a middle range—neither too much nor too little—to facilitate the process. To tone down the intensity of the transference, you decided to link it to her real-life experiences. You considered speaking in a baby voice and connecting her anger with you to the anger she feels toward her mother. You applied the same idea when interpreting her desire to stop treatment, likening it to her wish for the beatings to stop."

"Correct. I said that Chi wanted the beating to stop the way she wanted therapy to stop. Curiously, her face, which was contorted with anger, relaxed. I suddenly felt that I could understand her moods. So, I said to Chi, 'You are now a little less angry than you were a minute ago.'"

"Then her face immediately looked angry. 'Now you are suddenly again angry.'"

"Then she smiled. I told her, 'Now you are smiling and playing with your moods.'"

"Chi said gruffly, "I must be angry, so I do not spill my secrets to you.""

"I also realized that she had been careful to throw only soft toys at me and had not thrown hard metallic or wooden toys at me. So, I told her, "So secrets are why you must be angry.""

Talking to me, Ching continued, "It looks like we have some kind of relationship, but it is hard. Do you have any comments before I get to another session?"

"Two sessions ago, you considered speaking to her in a baby voice to explore the connection between her anger in the session and her anger toward her mother. However, since she shifted to tickling, you were not able to deliver the interpretation of her anger. In this session, using a similar approach, you linked her desire to stop the interaction with you to her wish for the beatings to stop. You are beginning to see the connections between your feelings and Chi's. You do not have to be entirely correct, but you offer the most thoughtful interpretation possible at that time, presenting it in good faith."

"Yes."

"Let us consider what happened during this session after your intervention about stopping. You have begun connecting therapy to her home situation. There was a momentary smile on her face. You noticed that Chi hit you only with soft toys. It looks like your interpretations are resulting in momentary micro improvements."

"I understand."

"Now, I go to the next session. Although she stopped throwing things at me, her resistance was still there. On this day, Chi and her mother arrived early, came before me, and were seated in the waiting room when I arrived. I overheard a loud conversation between them. Chi told her mom, 'I want to stop; I won't go into the session.' Chi's mother tried to persuade Chi to go into the session."

"I opened the door and greeted Chi in my usual polite and welcoming manner. Chi said, 'I am not going in.'"

"I told Chi, "I will keep the door open if you change your mind."

"In a hateful tone, Chi said, "I will not go in" and closed the door."

"Then Chi's mother stood up and said to Chi, "I will leave so both of you can sort it out."

"Chi insisted to her mother that Chi would go out with her. Chi's mother disagreed, and they finally decided to compromise that Chi would stay and attend the session. After the session, they would go together to McDonald's, and the mother would buy Chi a Happy Meal with a toy. Her mother left to see if Chi's favorite toy of the chosen color was available."

"After Chi entered the office, she wore a deeply contemptuous expression and said, 'You are wasting my time.' She then grabbed some toys and clay from my office and walked towards the waiting area. On her path, she purposefully stepped on my toes."

"After a while, Chi returned with clay and took an expensive incense stick box from my mantle, which was not part of the play equipment. She broke each stick before me and filled the box with clay."

"I was angry. I got up and stood by her side and said, 'Do you think the incense sticks belong to you?'"

"Leave me alone. I do what I want."

"I said sternly, 'The incense sticks and box are mine.'"

"No. They are mine."

"I told her, 'Taking other people's things is theft. Take out the clay from the box.'"

"She started to clean the box of clay but said, 'If you push me, I will not clean the box.'"

"Because the clay was sticky, she had trouble taking out the clay from the box. Then, she gave me the box and said, 'Help me.'"

"I showed her how to remove the clay by being patient and told her, 'You have to be patient. Clay is sticky. Trying harder makes it stick to the box more. Maybe, after you broke the incense sticks, you felt bad—like your mother might feel after she hits you.'"

"She did not respond. Chi discovered that she could make a ball with the clay, which was surprisingly bouncy. She started a game of throwing the ball gently at me, and

I threw it back to her. So, we played a friendly game of throw the ball."

"Although the game was good, being with Chi is very hard."

Ching paused, taking a puff from his electronic cigarette.

After exhaling, he said, "That is it. What do you have to say?"

"Today, you connected some happening in the session and her life. You said that she felt bad after breaking your incense sticks and when she could not clean the clay from the incense box, and that may be how her mother feels after she hits Chi. You made a connection."

"Yes, also, I felt Chi's frustration."

"First, you felt your frustration, anger, and pain in your head, heart, and toes when she stepped on them. Then you felt her frustration."

"I understand. I recalled another aspect of her expression when Chi said, 'The incense box is mine. I can do whatever I want with it.' Through her facial expression, Chi conveyed, 'I do not pay attention to you. I do not care how you feel.'"

"I felt provoked and said to Chi, 'You are provoking me.'"

"With the most contemptuous look I have ever seen on a child, Chi muttered, 'Fuck off.' Then she added a phrase in Chinese that is difficult to translate directly, but it was something along the lines of, 'Shut your mouth,' or 'Close your mouth.'"

"What is it they say? Psychoanalysis is impossible work—no, they call it an 'impossible profession.'"

"I told Chi, 'You want to make me angry and then be quiet; maybe that is what your mother does to you. She makes you angry and then wants you to be quiet.'"

"That is all that I have. I want to hear what you have to say."

"Excuse me for a moment. I am looking for something to show you."

I looked around the room for a coin. Coming from the previous millennium, I was accustomed to having simple things like coins that were always within reach. Alas, I could not find a coin.

"I was looking for a coin and could not find it. We are in a digital age. You know what a coin is?"

"Yes."

"Just as a coin has two distinct sides, heads and tails, both integral to its whole, we can liken the head side to the analyst's personal experiences. Everything the analyst undergoes reflects their own life. In your work with Chi, you have experienced a wide range of emotions, from the joy of playful engagement and moments of reciprocal interaction to intense frustration and anger when confronted with her hostility and disruptive actions, like calling you 'stupid' or spitting on you. Chi's emotional volatility, including her threat to bite off your nose, left you alarmed, struggling to comprehend why she reacted to kindness and civility with such hostility."

"Her actions often seem designed to provoke you while expecting you to remain silent and compliant, much like her demand to 'shut your mouth.' Despite offering her a safe space for expression, her aggressive resistance becomes puzzling and sometimes unbearable. Her play, words, and actions challenge your ability to stay composure and engaged. You want to offer her understanding, but her provocations push you to the edge, forcing you to respond with 'stop it,' testing your tolerance as a therapist."

"However, you have recently realized that your feelings are deeply entangled with Chi's. Your relationship with Chi mirrors Chi's relationship with her mother. Your anger at Chi is similar to the anger Chi feels toward her mother. Just as you struggle to understand Chi's hostility despite your efforts to provide kindness, Chi too cannot comprehend why, when she offers her love and obedience, her mother calls her 'stupid' and punishes her. Chi wants to be herself, not what her mother wants her to be. Chi cannot passively take it anymore, and just as she provokes you, she is now provoking her mother. Chi fears her mother. Chi was shocked and helpless when her mother asked her to pack her belongings and leave the home. Chi is turning the tables with you—stepping on your toes, leaving your office defiantly as if to say she has the power to walk away."

"In short, you realize that the same feelings you experience on the 'head' side of the coin are mirrored by Chi's experiences on the 'tail' side in her relationship with her mother. The mirror is just a metaphor; they are linked, and you are deciphering how they are linked with Chi's cooperation. Your emotions may offer clues to her emotions. This is the intimate link between your relationship with Chi and her relationship with her mother—something Chi tries to keep hidden, and you are now beginning to expose."

"I applaud you. You gave me an understanding of the possible relationship between my feelings and Chi's feelings. Our work can happen when the transference is not too hot or too cold. It must somewhere be in the middle." I realize that my situation is like a spontaneous drama play, but the meaning of my role can only be understood afterward."

"Yes, we often uncover the true meanings of our actions only after they have borne fruit. Recently, you reflected on the importance of recognizing and understanding Chi's anger, suggesting that by doing so, she might avoid turning that aggression inward. However, when she claimed the incense sticks box as hers today, you found yourself asserting that it was yours."

"At that moment, you realized the tension between your desire to help her express feelings like anger or an illusory sense of ownership and your own need to maintain boundaries. This tension echoes a broader, long-standing dilemma in psychoanalysis. On one side, we have Kohut's emphasis on empathy and understanding or Winnicott's call for containment—creating a safe space for self-expression without retaliation. On the other side stands Kernberg, advocating for limit-setting and firm boundary maintenance to protect the therapeutic process and the patient's reality testing by addressing pathological defenses."

"Navigating these opposing approaches is challenging. Some analysts believe that analysts must always strive for empathy and containment, while others insist that strict limit-setting and boundaries are essential. Both perspectives involve rigidly adhering to a technical principle."

"Alternatively, the opportunistic approach offers a more flexible strategy that relies on the clinical situation and the analyst's sense and is less theoretically bound. Here, the challenge lies in discerning when to lean toward deeper understanding and when to hold firm on boundaries. This method acknowledges that both empathetic tolerance and clear boundaries are crucial, aiming to balance them according to the patient's needs and the therapeutic context. Instead of rigidly applying one principle, this approach tailors the response to the unique and evolving dynamics of the therapeutic relationship, navigating the tension between understanding and limits with sensitivity and adaptability."

"I understand. It might not be wise to be completely uniform with empathy, containment, or limit setting. My tolerance has limits."

"I believe you should remain true to yourself and be authentic. Everyone has limits to their tolerance, and within those limits, you can choose when to be empathic or when to set boundaries. When you reach that limit, you are forced to set limits. However, what truly matters is not just the intervention itself but how you follow up on how the patient reacts. The patient's response is key. An analyst must consider the patient's perception and response, not just their own self-assessment. What the analyst intends or believes to be empathetic and tolerant may be experienced differently by the patient, who may feel misunderstood or dismissed. Therefore, engaging with the patient's interpretation of events is critical, rather than relying solely on the analyst's judgment."

"A case in point is Chi's relationship with you. You see yourself as patient, empathetic, and generously offering space and time for play and understanding. So, it may be hard to grasp why Chi responds with such anger, hostility, disruption, provocations, and threats. However, Chi perceives it differently. Only now are you beginning to realize how deeply your emotions may be intertwined with hers. You have compared this experience to being part of her drama, where the significance of your role only becomes clear in hindsight. Chi has pulled you into a whirlwind of emotions far more moving than any Disney film or the layered complexity of *Crouching Tiger, Hidden Dragon*. Furthermore, like any movie, admission is at a cost. In your case, today, it was the price of a box of expensive incense sticks."

> "Yes, Chi's interactions with me have made me experience feelings through my eyes, ears, and mind, with hidden meanings still gradually revealing themselves."

"Before we stop, a question for you. Today, you said applaud me. Why?"

> "I applaud the insight you brought to me in the session. For example, Chi was forced to remain silent in her pain, and now she wants to silence me. The damaged incense box symbolizes Chi's body, which belongs to her. My frustrations mirror Chi's frustrations. You are also helping me learn to handle situations in the moment. Through several intense sessions over the past week, I have somehow found myself in a state where I can scrutinize my feelings and use them in the treatment. It is difficult but not impossible."

"It is unnecessary to applaud a supervisor trying to do his job. You are generous, and I appreciate it."

Supervision: **29**

Ching missed our supervision session and did not call at the appointed time. After waiting a while, I reached out to him, but he did not answer the phone. I left a message saying, "I hope you are okay. I was expecting you to call. Please confirm that you are all right when you get this message." The following day, I received an email from Ching.

> The email said, "Oh! I totally forgot today. It completely slipped my mind. Monday started the National Day vacation, a Golden Week, a full week of public holidays."

Ching asked if I had time to meet the next day. We arranged a Skype call.

> When we connected, Ching apologized, saying, "I became disorganized because of the Chinese National Day. I know this is not the scheduled time, but I wanted to talk to you briefly. I think there has been a change, and I'd like to discuss it."

Ching explained that before his last session with Chi, he had received a message from Chi's mother, who mentioned that Chi gets along better with boys than with girls. Chi's mother explained that Chi had bumped into a girl to express her fondness, but the girl had been upset by the gesture. According to her mother, Chi often feels frustrated when girls reject her.

"I noticed a shift in Chi's attitude and behavior during this recent session. Chi entered the room happily and calmly, carrying a tennis ball from home. I thought she came prepared for the session. Once there, Chi wanted to compare the bounciness of the tennis ball with the clay ball they had used in the last session."

"Chi suggested playing catch with the tennis ball, bouncing it off the wall. We played together in a friendly manner. We passed the ball back and forth without much talking. I thought this was similar to how two boys may play. The ball bounced almost outside my reach at one point, but I quickly caught it."

"Chi admired the catch and asked, 'Where did you learn to catch the ball like that?'"

"I responded, 'When I was a boy, I played ball and learned naturally by playing.' We continued playing, and I told Chi, "Looks like you're having fun just playing catch today.""

"Chi responded, 'Yes, today I feel like a boy when I play catch with you with a tennis ball. Last week, it was different when we played with the clay ball.'"

"After a while, Chi began humming a well-known Chinese song by a female artist as she lay on the couch. She asked me to sing along. Initially, I could, but soon I could not. Chi was creatively altering the song's lyrics while maintaining the tune. As I listened, I realized that Chi was not merely singing the song but making up creative lyrics. So, I asked her, 'What song is this and whose song is this?' "

"Chi replied, 'This is my song, I am making up the words.' "

"But Chi was willing for me to listen to her song from which her imagination and fantasy came out. I remarked, 'Now you're making up your own girl song.' "

Chi responded thoughtfully, "Yes. Depending on my wish, sometimes I play being a girl, sometimes a boy. Sometimes I play being small, sometimes being big."

My Musings

The latency phase, typically occurring from ages six to twelve, typically features a child who is well-behaved, pliable, educable, and receptive to learning (Sarnoff, 1971)[97]. According to Sarnoff, this stage is characterized by psychological operations like repression and displacement, indicating the presence of somewhat quiescent drives. This phase also sees the emergence of symbolism and fantasy. Symbols safely relieve feelings towards primary objects and their substitutes. Interests in collecting dolls, stamps, coins, and rocks and playing by rules of games bind anxiety. Fantasy becomes a means to resolve conflicts internally, circumventing real-world confrontations and lessening the impact of primal urges, thus aiding in maturation and sublimation. Such fantasies are the typical products of the latency structure that help the child deal with unbearable wishes concerning the parental figures. In prelatency, that is, before the

---

97 Sarnoff, C.A. (1971). Ego structure in latency. *Psychoanalytic Quarterly* 40:387–414.

age of six, conflicting wishes are expressed directly and result in direct sexual or aggressive actions of the growing child.

Blos (1968)[98], clarified that sexual identity boundaries remain fluid before physical sexual maturity. A shifting or ambiguous sexual identity is more the norm than the exception within limits. This is more apparent in the girl than in the boy. This phenomenon tends to be more observable in females than males, exemplified by the widespread social and personal acceptance of the "tomboy" phase in girls before adolescence.

Human experiences can be interpreted through multiple lenses. For instance, genetics explores our biological foundations, linking aspects like sex to DNA, whereas our feelings, life experiences, and social interactions shape our understanding of gender and self-identity. While these factors often intersect, each has its specific domain of influence. Classification systems such as the ICD-10 and DSM-5 offer structured frameworks for categorizing genetic conditions, sexual health, gender, and personal identity. These tools have standardized the diagnosis and discussion of such conditions, enabling a deeper understanding of how biological, psychological, and social constructs interact to shape our experiences.

Early psychoanalysis, though progressive for its time, was rooted in traditional views of sexual development and prioritized the analyst's perspective. For example, Freud (1938)[99] promoted the idea of penis envy. Modern psychoanalysis acknowledges these historical limitations today, embracing a broader understanding of human experience. Contemporary analysts view LGBTQ+ identities as natural variations, with gender identity considered essential to personal development.

---

98 Blos, P. (1968). Character formation in adolescence. *Psychoanalytic Study of the Child* 23:245–263.

99 Freud, S. (1938). An outline of psycho-analysis. *Standard Edition* 23:139–208.

In the contemporary psychoanalytic model, the role of the unconscious mind and the transferential dialogue between patient and analyst are paramount. Therapy centers on understanding the individual's unique journey, promoting self-acceptance, and addressing internalized and societal biases. It also delves into the psychological impact of social discrimination, particularly in the context of gender and sexuality. Furthermore, psychoanalysis is continually evolving, with diverse perspectives among analysts reflecting the field's ongoing sensitivity to the complexities of human identity.

The contemporary psychoanalytic model marks a significant shift from the pathologization of gender identities to a more inclusive and understanding approach. This emphasis on self-acceptance reassures individuals about the field's progress, moving away from authoritative interpretations. It underscores the importance of the unconscious, patient, and analyst's dialogue. Therapeutic practices are geared towards understanding and accepting the individual's relationship with their gender and challenging societal or internalized prejudices. The patient and analyst may own concurring or diverging perspectives on such matters. There is also a diversity of perspectives among analysts, reflecting the field's dynamic and evolving nature and responsiveness to the individual experiences of both the analyst and the patient.

Chi was not well-behaved or compliant and struggled with math, which added to the difficulties shaped by her anxiety and trauma. In short, Chi had not consistently achieved latency. Her mother had been absent for several months during her infancy, and later, her parents divorced. When Chi faced challenges with math at school, her mother's disappointment escalated to the point where she began calling Chi an idiot and sometimes even hit her. As a result, Chi was constantly on guard, defending herself from the chaos around her and her anger.

Despite having an active imagination filled with princesses and monsters, she had not entered a stable latency period.

In this session, however, Chi was starting to explore a new world of shared imagination, particularly around her sexual identity. She fantasized about being a girl or a boy, big or small, signaling her gradual entry into latency, a stage where imagination could offer her refuge. This imaginative space allowed Chi to address some of her challenges indirectly or within the context of the therapeutic transference without triggering interpersonal conflicts or outbursts.

For many months, the focus of Chi's mother's transference with Ching revolved around anger and aggression. Now, in this session, there was a shift in the theme—from trauma to a developmental exploration of age-appropriate fluid sexual identity. Through play and fantasy and the extent to which she could sustain her latency, Chi was starting to work through some of her traumas. She was also discovering ways to build a future with less anxiety, exploring her sexual identity, and finding joy in activities like games and singing. These served as therapeutic outlets for addressing her inner conflicts.

The reader will notice that Ching missed his supervisory appointment with me. However, despite this forgetfulness, the session opened up new opportunities for Ching to help Chi work through her traumas and conflicts, primarily through fantasy. Fantasy functions as an age-appropriate defense mechanism, allowing Chi to navigate conflicts vicariously without triggering unmanageable interpersonal tensions, especially in her exploration of aggression and the fluidity of her sexual identity.

Decision-making is central to any therapeutic or learning choice, whether for a patient, an analyst, or a supervisor. Should a supervisor prioritize a trainee's clinical management or focus on a memory lapse? Not every symptomatic unconscious action automatically becomes the focal point of supervision. Only when an action obstructs learning, or signals resistance does it rise to such a priority. In this case, the clinical treatment seemed to have arrived at a playful fantasy; despite Ching's unconscious oversight, I saw no significant signs of resistance impacting the supervision. For this reason, I chose not to dwell on his forgetfulness, leaving it to his introspection or personal analysis. Nevertheless, readers may wish to speculate on the underlying dynamics of his lapse or my decision not to address it.

When a therapeutic dialogue reaches a natural pause in any session, the contours of agreements, disagreements, and uncertainty between the patient's and analyst's perspectives become apparent for that moment. These differences can then be revisited and explored further in future sessions. Exploring these processes is never-ending; in contrast, it is possible to say when a session or book ends!

Postscript

Psychoanalysts face the challenge of summarizing complex treatment experiences with patients into reasonable and meaningful narratives. After thousands of hours with patients, they must decide how to present their work concisely yet meaningfully. Two primary approaches can be taken: the "forest" approach or the "tree" approach.

The "forest" approach, with its selection of vital therapeutic moments—such as dreams or critical vignettes—while considering the patient's history, resistances, transference, and unconscious motivations, is akin to 'stringing pearls on a necklace.' Each pearl, a clear and cohesive example, is carefully selected to present the overall narrative of the treatment. Just as a necklace is carefully assembled, each pearl chosen for its unique beauty, the "forest" approach selects key moments that best represent the patient's journey. By focusing on these select moments, the analyst creates a polished, coherent presentation of the treatment process, organizing complex observations into an understandable and logical framework.

However, because the "forest" approach prioritizes cohesion and clarity, it often omits extraneous details, smoothing over therapy's more intricate and disorderly aspects. This 'varnished' presentation might lead some critical readers to question whether specific nuances or complexities are overlooked or overly simplified. The necessary omissions in crafting a more digestible narrative could give the impression that the true unpredictability and complexity of the therapeutic process are being understated. This could raise concerns about the potential loss of the "warts" of the therapeutic process, which a critical reader may ask: "Where are the warts?"[100]

On the other hand, the "tree" approach offers a more detailed account of therapy. Instead of summarizing the entire treatment, it focuses on a specific period, recounting every supervisory session in detail, including relevant and seemingly irrelevant information. This approach captures therapy's unfiltered, sometimes chaotic nature, providing a raw but authentic view of the supervisory and therapeutic processes and fostering a sense of connection with the lived experience.

This view is like visiting a city park on a particular day —a green haven amidst urban chaos. Tall pines, spruces, and fir trees line the walkways. The trees sway gently in the breeze while the vibrant red cardinals flit from branch to branch, chirping alongside sparrows and warblers. However, as one walks across the park, the idyllic scene is disrupted by overflowing garbage cans, their contents spilling out, filling the air with the unpleasant odor of rotting food and discarded waste. Seagulls peck through the trash, breaking the park's tranquility. The park is a testament to nature's persistence amidst the city and its urban waste and refuse.

I adopted the tree approach in my book, documenting twenty-nine supervisory sessions with Ching and Chi. These raw, real-time sessions were not summarized but described in detail, capturing the perspectives of the supervisor, candidate, and patient without much

---

100 The phrase "warts and all" is a metaphor for authenticity, meaning that no flaws or imperfections should be hidden when presenting someone or something. This idiom dates back to the 17th century, when Oliver Cromwell, the Lord Protector of England, famously insisted on being painted with all his imperfections by artist Samuel Cooper. Cromwell's demand to be portrayed truthfully, without idealization, gave rise to the expression. Over time, "warts and all" has come to symbolize a commitment to presenting unvarnished truth, whether in art, storytelling, or self-representation, embracing both strengths and shortcomings alike.

benefit of hindsight. The outcome of Chi's treatment is unknown, leaving the narrative incomplete and open-ended. This unfiltered and open approach also includes my personal reflections, which were not shared contemporaneously with Ching as a candidate, but are offered to the reader as additional context, making the reader part of the narrative process. The meanings attributed to any given event are never fixed; each attempt at interpretation may generate a new and distinct pattern of meaning.

This type of detailed, real-time reporting is uncommon, especially in psychoanalysis. It highlights the supervisor's role as an active contributor, along with the patient and analyst, who are viewed as co-participant observers in the therapeutic process. The narrative, by necessity, is less cohesive and explanatory, emphasizing the complexity and uncertainty inherent in human psychology.

The portrayal of Chi as the "Little Princess" encapsulates her innocence and vulnerability as she grapples with her monsters and struggles. This metaphor, akin to the park's blend of beauty and chaos, reflects the layered and nuanced nature of human experience. The "Little Princess" represents the innocence and vulnerability of the patient, while her ongoing journey mirrors the continuing nature of psychoanalysis itself.

It recalls the words of Keats from "Ode on a Grecian Urn":
"Beauty is truth, truth beauty,—that is all
Ye know on earth, and all ye need to know."

I do not mean that only the tree view represents truth. Instead, the forest and tree perspectives offer their truths, serving distinct yet complementary purposes. It reminds us that both views capture different facets of the therapeutic journey, neither providing a singular or definitive truth. The inherent limitations of time-bound descriptions, especially in supervision, reflect the transient nature of the process.

Keats' concept of *Negative Capability* refers to embracing uncertainty, doubt, and ambiguity without needing clarity or resolution. He admired this quality in great artists, particularly Shakespeare, whose creative genius thrived in the presence of mysteries and contradictions. In a letter to his brothers, John Keats (1817, p. 261)[101] introduced the concept of *Negative Capability*: "That is when a man is capable of being in uncertainties, mysteries, doubts, without any irritable reaching after fact and reason." This idea reflects Keats' belief that embracing ambiguity and uncertainty without the compulsive need for clarity or resolution is essential to creativity. This capacity for holding doubt and ambiguity is not only relevant to poetry.

Negative Capability reflects the role of the analyst as envisioned in Essential Psychoanalysis by emphasizing transparency regarding the analyst's uncertainties and doubts. Instead of falling into the trap of exerting the traditional power or privilege associated with the analyst's position, both the patient and the analyst engage collaboratively in exploring the therapeutic process. They must navigate the inherent ambiguities together, valuing the contributions from both perspectives. This co-creative process highlights the importance of remaining open to uncertainty, embracing the unknown as a space where insights and transformation can naturally unfold, and allowing these developments to be transparently articulated.

Supervising from 10,000 miles away in an unfamiliar culture and language was a unique challenge. My role was to guide Ching through the psychoanalytic process of treating Chi. Still, the real work rested on

---

101 Keats, J. (1817). *John Keats: Selected Poems and Letters*, ed. D. Bush. Boston: Houghton Mifflin, 1959.

him—he adapted, improvised, and met Chi, where she was emotionally and developmentally. Like all children, Chi needed deep understanding and support. Throughout this collaborative effort, Ching remained dedicated, doing his best to attune to Chi's needs while navigating the complexities of psychoanalytic treatment in a different cultural context.

During supervision, Ching openly discussed the pressures of treating Chi and managing her mother's expectations. He also shared personal aspects of his life, which were critical in exploring his broader countertransference and deepening his insight into Chi. While he sometimes idealized me, Ching valued my guidance, and I found great fulfillment in supervising him.

Psychoanalytic supervision guides candidates in their therapeutic work, showing that progress and healing are achievable, even in complex and unfamiliar situations. This narrative offers the most authentic reflection of the supervisory and psychoanalytic process I could provide. Although this book concludes here, my supervision of Ching's work with Chi continues. In the future, I may share further developments in their story as it unfolds. Thus, there may be more to come.

Essential Psychoanalysis Appendix to some psychoanalytic terms

Psychoanalysis encompasses many theoretical perspectives, including Instinct, Ego, Object Relations, Self-psychology, Intersubjective, Developmental, and Neuropsychoanalytic schools. Each school has developed its specialized terminology to articulate its distinct ideas. While these terms are carefully crafted, their full significance often emerges through application in diverse clinical settings and patient interactions. Freud's concept of the "narcissism of minor differences" (1930)[102] illustrates how minor theoretical variations can lead to significant debates over definitions. Contentious debates and demarcation conflicts frequently emerge at the intersection of theoretical models or when distinguishing between psychoanalysis and psychotherapy, whether among theorists or followers. However, in the realm of practical ideas, where the well-being of patients is of utmost importance, or for a clinician who prioritizes tangible outcomes over theoretical disagreements, the broader commonalities rather than magnified differences become apparent. This segment explores psychoanalytic terminology, emphasizing

---

102 Freud, S. (1930). Civilization and its Discontents. *Standard Edition* 21:57–146.

that the practical application of these theories transcends academic contention, highlighting their value in enhancing patient care.

The potential for broader applications may sometimes emerge beyond a term's original context. This appendix is not an exhaustive academic reference but a practical guide and adaptable toolkit for both practicing psychoanalysts and students. Its primary goal is to foster interdisciplinary dialogue by integrating classical and modern psychoanalytic theories, encouraging a more pluralistic and flexible understanding informed by various psychoanalytic insights and traditions. By stressing the interdisciplinary nature of psychoanalysis, this text aims to make the audience feel part of a diverse and inclusive community.

Unconscious

Definition of the Unconscious: The unconscious consists of mental contents or processes that individuals are unaware of, yet these contents significantly influence conscious experiences and behaviors. It is a hypothetical mind region where thoughts and feelings are kept from awareness due to repression.

Dynamic Unconscious: This concept encompasses thoughts and feelings that are actively repressed due to motivational forces and is a crucial focus of psychoanalysis. The field's primary aim is to uncover these contents through their disguised effects on conscious life, shedding light on the hidden aspects of our minds.

Topographic Model: Freud's early model divides the mind into three systems: conscious (awareness), preconscious (easily accessible), and unconscious (actively repressed). The unconscious, where unacceptable wishes and drive derivatives are stored, plays a fascinating role in shaping our experiences, often finding expression in disguised forms like neurotic symptoms or dreams.

Primary and Secondary Processes: The unconscious operates according to primary processes, characterized by the pleasure principle, absence of negation, and lacking logical coherence, while conscious thought operates according to secondary processes, guided by the reality principle.

Repression and Symptoms: Repressed thoughts do not disappear; instead, they exert influence through symptoms, inhibitions, and anxieties. Freud suggested that neuroses are manifestations of repressed, unacceptable wishes returning in disguised forms.

Therapeutic Aim: Psychoanalysis, focusing on the unconscious, aims to make the unconscious conscious. This process enables patients to confront and work through repressed memories and conflicts, facilitating healing. Freud's evolving models highlighted the complexities of the unconscious, incorporating defensive processes and moral imperatives, providing a roadmap for understanding and healing.

Further developments: While Freud laid the groundwork, later psychoanalysts expanded on his ideas, introducing concepts like the dynamic unconscious, unconscious conflict, and the influence of internalized object relations. Contemporary perspectives also emphasize relational dynamics and the intersubjectivity of the analytic process, keeping the field of psychoanalysis dynamic and ever-evolving. This ongoing evolution ensures that psychoanalysts remain engaged and part of a field constantly adapting to new insights and understandings.

Unconscious content can be understood through object-relational, Self, or intersubjective contexts. Some theorists posit nonconscious or non-dynamically unconscious implicit relational knowing. This knowing consists of interactions with caregivers encoded in procedural rather than declarative memory and, therefore, cannot be verbalized. Procedural memory is a subset of long-term memory responsible for knowing how to perform certain tasks without conscious awareness. This memory allows us to execute various actions and skills, such as riding a bicycle, playing a musical instrument, or engaging in daily routines like brushing our teeth. is Declarative memory is typically referenced in common parlance when discussing 'memory.' It encompasses the ability to recall everyday facts and events. Such memories can be consciously retrieved and reflected upon, forming an essential component of daily cognitive processes.

The analyst's participation in the intersubjectivity of the analytic situation, where both the analyst and the patient contribute to understanding and interpreting the patient's experiences, enables the patient to investigate, articulate, validate, and reorganize his unconscious experience collaboratively.

Cognitive Science and the Unconscious: The rise of cognitive science has led to a renewed interest in unconscious processes, incorporating concepts like tacit knowledge and implicit memory. Some cognitive theories align more closely with the dynamic unconscious concept from psychoanalysis, reflecting a convergence in understanding unconscious influences on behavior.

Neuroconscious model[103]: The Neuroconscious model, my synthesis of neuroscience and psychoanalysis, is centered on the organization of the brain, differentiating between arousal states, primarily governed by subcortical mechanisms, and awareness contents, which depend on subcortical and cortical integration. Arousal states of consciousness are classified as normal or pathological based on an individual's responsiveness to external and internal stimuli. These states range from full consciousness to unconsciousness and encompass conditions such as conscious resting, confusion, delirium, somnolence, obtundation, stupor, minimally conscious state, vegetative state, locked-in syndrome, REM sleep, NREM deep sleep, general anesthesia, and coma. These arousal states are regulated by subcortical mechanisms, with each state exhibiting varying degrees of awareness, experience, and voluntary action capacity. A state of arousal refers to the overall level of wakefulness or alertness without addressing the specific contents of awareness. For example, stating that a person is dreaming refers to their state of consciousness, whereas considering the dream's content involves analyzing the specific images, thoughts, or emotions in the dream. The two are distinct, as the arousal condition is about the state of being, while the content of awareness involves the particular mental experiences occurring within that state.

The Neuroconscious model posits that the brain utilizes past experiences and learned behaviors to predict sensory input, influencing perception, thought, imagination, emotion, and action. The ongoing interaction between these predictions, actual sensory input, and the "surprises" that arise when sensory input deviates from expectations

---

103 The Neuroconscious model is my integration of neuroscience and psychoanalysis, currently being developed for publication. Drawing on my understanding of contemporary neuroscience, I differentiate between arousal states of consciousness and the awareness contents explored in psychoanalysis.

shapes our understanding of the Self, others, and the environment. Depending on the degree of surprise, the brain's activity can be categorized into unconscious, preconscious, and conscious levels. Unconscious processes occur when predictions are accurate and surprises are minimal, while significant prediction errors bring information into preconscious or conscious awareness. This segmentation reflects varying levels of awareness, illustrating the brain's continuous balancing act between predictive functions and conscious experiences. Unconscious processes require fewer metabolic resources, whereas conscious processes involving attention, decision-making, and risk assessment are more metabolically demanding.

In contrast, Solms' Neuropsychoanalysis challenges the division between arousal and awareness consciousness.[104] Solms contends that the brainstem controls both arousal and awareness, with awareness being secondary to arousal. Despite these differences, both models emphasize the brain's role in managing predictions, sensory input, and surprise to conserve metabolic resources.

The Neuroconscious model offers an alternative perspective by separating arousal states from the contents of consciousness and highlighting the involvement of whole-brain functioning. In contrast, Solms' model prioritizes a hierarchical structure driven predominantly by brainstem (subcortical) functions. This distinction enriches our understanding of brain organization, balancing regulating arousal mechanisms with the complexity of awareness content processing across various levels of consciousness.

In psychoanalysis, the unconscious contents are not within conscious awareness; they significantly influence thinking, emotions, and behavior. Just as a slip of the tongue can reveal an unknown force that escapes

---

104 Solms, M. (2013). The Conscious Id. *Neuropsychoanalysis* 15:5–19.

immediate understanding, the presence and impact of unconscious contents are often recognized only in retrospect. This is because the unconscious, by its very nature, keeps its contents hidden until they rise into conscious awareness. The contents of the unconscious can be categorized into several key areas:

1. **Instinctual Drives**: Fundamental urges related to survival, reproduction, and aggression, often associated with Freud's concept of the id. These drives may not always be accessible to conscious thought but can manifest in behaviors and emotions.

2. **Desires and Fantasies**: Unconscious desires and fantasies that may not align with societal norms or personal morals, including sexual fantasies, wishes for power, or desires for unattainable goals.

3. **Dream Content**: Dreams are a window into the unconscious, where repressed thoughts and desires can surface in disguised or symbolic forms.

4. **Unconscious Emotions**: Repressed feelings outside awareness, such as guilt, anger, jealousy, or sadness, can significantly impact behavior and relationships.

5. **Defense Mechanisms**: Strategies employed by the ego to protect against anxiety or uncomfortable thoughts, such as denial, repression, projection, and rationalization, which operate unconsciously to manage internal conflicts.

6. **Unconscious Conflicts**: Internal struggles between different parts of the psyche, such as the id, ego, and superego, which can lead to anxiety and manifest in various psychological symptoms.

7. **Repressed Memories**: Traumatic or distressing experiences are pushed out of conscious awareness and can influence behavior and emotions without the individual's knowledge.

8. **Implicit Beliefs and Attitudes**: Unconscious biases, attitudes, and beliefs that influence behavior and perception, shaped by early experiences, cultural context, and social conditioning.

9. **Unconscious Relational Contexts**: Patterns and dynamics in relationships outside conscious awareness affect interactions and emotional responses.

10. **Unconscious Aspects of the Self**: Parts of the self that are not fully acknowledged or integrated into a conscious identity can influence self-perception and behavior.

11. **Automatic Actions**: Procedural memory is a type of long-term memory that is responsible for knowing how to do things, i.e., memory of motor skills. It enables individuals to carry out tasks without conscious awareness, operating under the domain of implicit memory, which functions automatically and without conscious input. This memory includes actions and behaviors that people can perform instinctively, like cycling, without active contemplation or deliberate thought.

These unconscious contents are crucial in shaping an individual's personality, behavior, and mental health. Psychoanalytic therapy seeks to bring these unconscious elements into conscious awareness to facilitate insight, healing, and personal growth.

Transference

Definition:

Transference is an unconscious, preconscious, or conscious process in which a conflict, wish, fear, emotion, or anticipation from one person, time, place, thing, or experience is linked to another. Often forgotten during the initial part of the treatment, the original source can often be rediscovered and reconstructed through free association, interpretation and introspection. Psychoanalysis recognizes transference as a universal phenomenon, and its understanding is essential to the cure process.

Transference arises when a patient, unconsciously or consciously, projects, redirects, or displaces thoughts, feelings, fantasies, beliefs, and attitudes from past or present relationships onto the analyst. It results from a complex interplay of unconscious, preconscious, and conscious processes, influenced by the patient's psychological defenses and their state of wakefulness or dreaming. Transference reflects a nuanced fusion of reactivated memories and present sensory inputs. During dreaming, experiences are predominantly shaped by internal sources, drawing heavily on memories linked to day residues. Similarly, in wakefulness, much of what feels like immediate experience—particularly in the background with diminished attention —is constructed through subtle modifications of reactivated memories, seamlessly integrated with current sensory input. This dynamic interaction between memory and perception forms the foundation of ongoing experience.

In psychoanalysis, transference manifests through free associations, play, actions, symptoms, anxieties, behavioral patterns, emotions, and stresses. The study and understanding of transference provide valuable insights into unresolved conflicts, unmet needs, and opportunities for change, growth, and development.

Background: Earlier psychoanalytic theories considered transference to be primarily a patient phenomenon. It consisted of the inappropriate displacement of past feelings into the present context and the unobjectionable appropriate feelings of the patient towards the analyst. Over time, however, many analysts have come to acknowledge the influence of the therapist's attitudes, behaviors, and the structured routines of the analytic setting in shaping the transference. Additionally, some analysts now view transference as a cocreation arising through the interplay between patient and analyst within the analytic process.

These projections are deeply shaped by the patient's early experiences and personal beliefs. Analysts hold varying perspectives on the scope of transference: some view it as limited to inappropriate or exaggerated responses, others see it as encompassing all patient reactions toward the analyst, and still others regard it as a mutually co-created phenomenon. The unique setting of psychoanalysis, which encourages the patient to freely associate, express thoughts, and experience or reexperience emotions, offers a space where the analyst's interpretations, actions, and the therapeutic relationship illuminate the origins of the patient's thoughts, fantasies, emotions, personality traits, and behaviors— especially those tied to unresolved conflicts and deficits.

Through this process, the patient can explore a broader range of choices, assess risks and rewards, make decisions (whether deliberate or automatic), and enhance their coping strategies. It facilitates the development of healthier defenses, more adaptive compromises, and more satisfying relationships, ultimately supporting growth in areas like love and work. Transference can profoundly reshape the patient's psyche as a therapeutic tool, influencing their personality, self-perception, interpersonal connections, memory processes, and habitual behaviors.

Transference is a core element of psychoanalytic treatment, acting as a mechanism through which unconscious and conscious wishes, conflicts, and unresolved intrapsychic and relational issues emerge for exploration and understanding. Rooted in the unique relationship between patient and analyst, transference creates a space where past and present experiences can reemerge and be reexamined, facilitating the reshaping of memories, habits, and relational patterns. It often revives infantile prototypes—representations of early relationships or significant current connections—charged with immediacy and deep emotional resonance. The dynamics of transference are integral to the analytic process, shaping the therapeutic alliance and informing the analyst's interpretations, interventions, and capacity to provide containment and holding. By engaging with and interpreting transference, patients gain insight into their intrapsychic and interpersonal strengths and vulnerabilities, enabling therapeutic change and fostering emotional growth. This process defines the psychoanalytic cure by facilitating transformation, as patients experience the analyst as a transference object, a new object, and a potential source of identification, solidifying transference and its interpretation as foundational to psychoanalytic healing.

The assessment of transferences is inherently layered with uncertainty and complexity, as it involves nuanced, detailed, and non-reductive self-assessments by analysts navigating intricate human relationships. Modern psychoanalysis increasingly recognizes the analyst's role as a professional participant observer, understanding that interaction between two autonomous individuals inevitably involves mutual influence. As a result, many analysts now emphasize exploring their contributions to the analysis from their own assessments and the patient's perspective. Many analysts have abandoned the view that the analyst is neutral or objective and that the analyst is merely a "blank screen." However, the possibility of manipulation or unethical behavior by the analyst cannot be overlooked. This highlights the need for analysts to rigorously test and validate their interpretations of transference, ensuring they do not misuse their professional authority by imposing their views on the patient or engaging in inappropriate relationships, thus maintaining the highest ethical standards in psychoanalysis.

A thoughtful interpretation of transference requires the analyst to remain attuned to the patient's perspective, especially when disagreements or differing opinions arise. Processing the patient's views of the analyst's errors, misunderstandings, or miscues can provide valuable insights and enrich the analytic process. The analyst's role is not just about making interpretations but about actively participating in the therapeutic relationship, acknowledging and learning from mistakes, and adding depth to the therapeutic relationship. This collaborative approach not only aids the patient in understanding their emotional world but also fosters personal insight, emotional growth, and overall development.

Instincts and transference

Instincts, or drives, in psychoanalysis, are not simple forces but intricate biological and psychological phenomena that propel behavior and mental activity. Rooted in physiological needs and psychological desires, the sexual instinct is linked to survival, reproduction, and pleasure, while the aggressive instinct manifests as outward aggression and hostility toward others, as well as inward self-destructive behaviors. The concept of instinct is an inferred construct, and within the framework of instinct theory, transference encompasses the manifestations of sexual and aggressive drives as they surface in analytic treatment. These transferences reflect the patient's unconscious desires, internal conflicts, and relational patterns rooted in instinctual impulses, offering a pathway for exploration and understanding within the therapeutic process.

According to instinct theory, development is driven by instinctual energy, or libido, which represents the life force fueling the sexual instinct. This energy becomes focused on specific body parts and activities during different developmental stages (e.g., oral, anal, genital), shaping psychological growth. Instincts, as powerful unconscious forces, influence human behavior and personality formation.

In instinct theory, transference primarily concerns the expression of pleasure, reproduction, survival, aggression, hostility, and self-destruction. Psychological emotions and desires, initially associated with one person or situation, are unconsciously redirected to another person or situation, often interpreted through the lens of instincts. This analytic phenomenon can be explored in terms of sexual or aggressive drives. A patient's free associations and responses to treatment routines reveal feelings from early relationships, including affectionate, sexual, hostile, and aggressive emotions projected onto the analyst through transference. Initially, these feelings may be displaced or split off onto current objects or dream elements. Contemporary analysts recognize that countertransference offers valuable insights into a patient's wishes and transference dynamics.

Id-Ego-Superego and transference

In the ego theory of psychoanalysis, transference is viewed as a crucial mechanism in which patients project unconscious feelings, desires, defenses, and compromises onto their therapists, stemming from past relationships, especially those in childhood. These projections are not random but are deeply tied to the patient's ego functions, framed by the interplay of the Id, Ego, and Superego. Transference in ego theory involves the unconscious reenactment of past relationships within the present therapeutic relationship, revealing underlying defenses and compromises. This process offers valuable insights into the dynamic aspects of the personality, providing an opportunity to develop more adaptive defenses and healthier compromises, promoting healing and growth.

Transference provides a window into the patient's internal world, enabling the therapist to understand how early relational experiences and conflicts shape current behavior and emotional states. By engaging with these projections, the therapist helps the patient recognize and analyze these unconscious patterns, fostering self-awareness and more adaptive ways of relating to others. A key mechanism of change and growth occurs through the emergence of signal anxiety, which is a form of anxiety that serves as a warning, offering the patient time and space to create healthier defenses and prevent overwhelming or toxic anxiety from manifesting.

The Oedipus complex and transference

The Oedipus complex involves a child's unconscious desires for the opposite-sex parent and rivalry with the same-sex parent. These early experiences, including relationships with siblings and others, significantly influence an individual's personality and adult relationships.

Transference in the Oedipal context refers to the unconscious process by which unresolved Oedipal conflicts are transferred onto the therapist during psychoanalysis. The analyst's reality and role are crucial here. For example, a patient might develop affection, rivalry, or hostility toward the therapist, reflecting unresolved childhood emotions toward their parents. By observing and interpreting these transferred emotions, the therapist plays a pivotal role in helping the patient gain insight into their Oedipal conflicts, providing a space for working through them. This therapeutic process allows for greater self-understanding, resolving internal conflicts, and developing healthier relationships.

The Oedipus complex marks a crucial developmental point in a child's life, signaling an increase in the complexity of their personality. Before this stage, an infant's main concerns are rooted in basic dependency needs (hunger, thirst, comfort, etc.), usually met by a primary caregiver. This dependency creates passive dyadic relationships, where satisfaction arises from the timely and appropriate responses of others, while dissatisfaction stems from unfulfilled desires or frustration.

As the Oedipus complex emerges, it introduces the complexities of triadic relationships. These relationships involve the child, the parent of the same sex, and the parent of the opposite sex. The child's love for one parent is interfered with by jealousy and competition, leading to inevitable conflicts and fears. Emotions such as guilt, desire, castration anxiety, jealousy, and inhibition arise, alongside struggles with sexual orientation and object choice. Triadic transference becomes more complex and elusive as the presence of a third figure—imagined or real (such as another patient, the analyst's spouse, or even fantasies of the analyst's personal life)—becomes integrated into the transference process. This third presence shapes free associations and emotions, complicating the therapeutic dynamic and further enriching the analysis.

The Oedipus complex involves a child's unconscious desires for the opposite-sex parent and rivalry with the same-sex parent. These early experiences, including relationships with siblings and others, significantly and profoundly influence an individual's personality and adult relationships.

Transference in the Oedipal context refers to the unconscious process by which unresolved Oedipal conflicts are transferred onto the therapist during psychoanalysis. For example, a patient might develop affection, rivalry, or hostility toward the therapist, reflecting unresolved childhood emotions toward their parents. By observing and interpreting these transferred emotions, the therapist helps the patient gain insight into their Oedipal conflicts, providing a space for working through them. This therapeutic process allows for greater self-understanding, resolving internal conflicts, and developing healthier relationships.

The Oedipus complex marks a crucial developmental point in a child's life, signaling an increase in the complexity of their personality. Before this stage, an infant's main concerns are rooted in basic dependency needs (hunger, thirst, comfort, etc.), usually met by a primary caregiver. This dependency creates passive dyadic relationships, where satisfaction arises from the timely and appropriate responses of others, while dissatisfaction stems from unfulfilled desires or frustration.

As the Oedipus complex emerges, it introduces the complexities of triadic relationships. The child's love for one parent is interfered with by jealousy and competition, leading to inevitable conflicts and fears. Emotions such as guilt, desire, castration anxiety, jealousy, and inhibition arise, alongside struggles with sexual orientation and object choice. Triadic transference becomes more complex and elusive as the presence of a third figure—imagined or real (such as another patient, the analyst's spouse, or even fantasies of the analyst's personal life)—becomes integrated into the transference process. The triadic perspective shapes free associations and emotions, complicating the therapeutic dynamic and further enriching the analysis.

Relational Perspectives: Object Relations Theory emphasizes that our early relationships, especially with primary caregivers, significantly shape our emotional growth. Rather than relying solely on instincts, these relationships play a crucial role. A maternal transference and a paternal transference, which recaptures the essence of such relationships, is an exemplar of a relational perspective. In this theory:

- **Objects** refer to significant figures in our lives (like parents or caregivers), not lifeless things. These interactions form the basis for our self-esteem, attachment patterns, and social bonds.
- **Unconscious Phantasy** involves an infant's inner world of drives from birth. These "phantasies" are not deliberate daydreams but expressions of unconscious drives. They transfer innate anxieties

onto tangible items (like toys) or symbolic partial objects (such as the breast or penis) during play.

- **Infants initially experience the Paranoid-Schizoid Position**, where the world is divided into extreme "good" and "bad" aspects. This leads to anxiety and defensive projection.
- **As they grow**, they transition to the **Depressive Position**, recognizing the blend of positive and negative aspects of life. This fosters guilt and empathy, marking emotional complexity.
- **Transference**, according to object-relational analysts, involves the patient's shifting feelings about their relationship with the analyst. These feelings manifest in verbal and nonverbal ways, including projective identification.
- **Splitting**, where patients separate good and bad objects and emotions, is relevant in transference. Analysts learn about patient anxieties and defenses by paying attention to their subjective experiences and how patients respond to their words.

Self-Psychology Perspective: Self-psychologists focus on transferences organized by the patient's needs mirroring from a selfobject rather than by wishes and fears related to instincts or internalized object relationships. A selfobject is another person experienced as part of the self, serving essential functions for the self. Self-psychologists define mirroring as a fundamental selfobject function that involves reflecting on the individual aspects of their self and identity, affirming their feelings, and validating their experiences. This process is crucial for the development of a cohesive sense of self. When childhood needs for selfobject functions are unmet, individuals may seek fulfillment with others or defend against feelings of deficit and longing. Self-psychologists interpret defenses against the emergence of these transferences, and when mobilized, the analyst empathizes with the selfobject longings expressed. Selfobject Transferences include:

- **Mirroring:** Seeking validation and affirmation from others, akin to seeing ourselves reflected positively.
- **Twinship:** Desiring connection and similarity with others, as if we share a common identity.
- **Idealizing:** Looking up to someone as an ideal figure to make oneself feel cohesive.

Self Psychology distinguishes between the "leading edge" and the "trailing edge" within the transference. The "leading edge" embodies the individual's inherent drive toward growth, self-cohesion, and positive transformation. In contrast, the "trailing edge" reflects the pull of unresolved maladaptive patterns, particularly around the unmet needs for idealization and mirroring. By attuning to both edges within the therapeutic relationship, the therapist gains a deeper understanding of the patient's ambitions and goals, enabling a process that fosters healing and restoring a cohesive self.

Intersubjective Perspective:

In intersubjective psychoanalysis, transference is viewed as a dynamic, mutual process emerging from the real-time interaction between patient and therapist. Unlike traditional views of transference as one-sided, this approach highlights the interdependent nature of the therapeutic relationship, where both participants bring their subjective experiences to shape and influence the interaction. The therapist's responses, informed by their own unconscious and subjective processes, become integral, blurring the lines between transference and countertransference.

Transference meanings are co-constructed through the evolving interplay between patient and therapist rather than being fixed or solely patient-derived. Exploring differing perspectives often reveals multiple meanings that may align, overlap, or even conflict, adding richness and complexity to the therapeutic process.

Instead of seeking a singular, shared interpretation, intersubjective psychoanalysis prioritizes collaboratively developing the most meaningful and adaptable understanding suited to the patient's unique circumstances. This approach requires the therapist to balance their own perspective with the patient's interpretation of transference, navigating this dynamic interplay to deepen insight, foster understanding, and support the patient's growth. The process emphasizes the transformative potential of the patient-therapist relationship in promoting emotional healing and psychological development.

Intersubjective Dynamics: Intersubjective psychoanalysis emphasizes the interdependent nature of the patient-analyst interaction, likening their relationship to a dance in which both contribute to movement, rhythm, and emotional resonance. This perspective views analytic transformation not as the simple recovery of repressed unconscious content but as the recognition of unconscious, mutually influencing interactions that foster change. These dynamic exchanges are central to the process of therapeutic transformation.

Personal Histories and Unconscious Motivations: The patient and analyst bring their unique personal histories and unconscious motivations into the therapeutic encounter. These past experiences inevitably shape their interactions. Effective psychoanalysis, therefore, prioritizes the implications of these interactions rather than focusing exclusively on the content of the analyst's interpretations. The therapeutic relationship becomes a site where both participants' subjectivities intersect and inform the work.

Empathic Insight: Rooted in self-psychology, the intersubjective approach highlights the reciprocal impact of conscious and unconscious elements on both patient and analyst. This dynamic interaction allows the therapist to access a deeper empathic understanding of the patient's inner world. By attuning to the subconscious interplay, the therapist gains insight into the patient's mental framework and therapeutic needs, creating a more resonant and responsive analytic process.

Constructing Significance: Intersubjectivity transcends verbal exchanges, engaging the co-construction of meaning within a dynamic and evolving system. This collaborative process involves dialogue, emotional resonance, and the shared comprehension that arises between two individuals. Sometimes, in agreement and sometimes in disagreement, the patient and analyst create a meaningful framework that reflects the unique circumstances of the therapeutic relationship.

Neuroconscious perspective: From a neuropsychoanalytic viewpoint, transference involves the brain's endeavor to streamline existence by reducing surprise and unpredictability. The initial predictions reflect transference anticipations. When they match with sensory input, subsequent actions remain unconscious and not registered. Preconscious and conscious processing comes into the picture only when there is a surprise. Drawing from previous experiences, learning, and memories, the brain is in a perpetual state of hypothesizing and proposing actions. When its forecasts are precise, the brain experiences minimal surprise and unconsciously fine-tunes those actions that have proven effective in comparable past scenarios. Conversely, unexpected sensory experiences contrary to predictions compel the brain to assess the situation and take actions consciously. Conscious actions demand more excellent cognitive resources. During psychoanalysis, the patient's anticipations about the analyst are shaped by the patient's past experiences, learning, and memories. These expectations evolve as the patient encounters surprises, leading to the formation and ongoing refinement of a mental model of the analyst. This model is rooted in the neurological foundations of transference, which include past experiences, learning, and memory. By examining the patient's conjectures, the analyst can deduce the patient's inner conflicts and stressors, providing insights that enable the patient to formulate more accurate predictions within the therapeutic context. This iterative learning process equips the patient to make more effective predictions in various life scenarios, gradually adopting more adaptive behaviors.

Meanings and transference

In psychoanalysis, language and enacted actions are essential tools for uncovering the meanings embedded in transference. Through verbal expression and behavior, patients communicate emotions, thoughts, and past experiences that reflect unconscious conflicts and relational patterns projected onto the therapist. Therapists reveal the dynamics of transference by exploring the symbolic, displaced, and layered meanings—unconscious, preconscious, and conscious—within the patient's language and actions.

This process deepens insight, enabling the patient to address unresolved issues, foster self-awareness, and develop healthier relational patterns. The interplay of language and transference serves as a vital bridge between the conscious and unconscious, advancing therapeutic progress.

However, beyond the tone and tact of the analyst's language, the therapist's capacity for empathy, holding, compassion, genuine concern, and authentic involvement significantly contributes to understanding the nuanced meanings of transference. These qualities create a safe, attuned environment where such meanings can be explored and integrated.

Conclusion

No single theory can fully capture the complexity of human experience, but many provide valuable frameworks for understanding specific issues from a particular perspective. An analyst who adheres to a single theoretical perspective in interpreting a patient's transference may develop proficiency and a coherent approach. However, this can also lead to oversimplification, repetition, and a lack of adaptability. While such consistency offers the analyst a sense of competence and confidence, it may restrict responsiveness to patients' diverse needs and perspectives. Psychoanalysis, as the study of individual psychology, requires authentic responsiveness to each patient's unique experience. Conversely, an analyst who integrates multiple theoretical orientations must navigate the challenges of mastering various approaches, making continuous choices, and maintaining coherence—risks that may be highlighted if a patient detects inconsistencies in the analytic process.

Given the complexity of the human condition, there is no more effective guide to transference interpretation than the patient's and the analyst's moment-to-moment responses. The analyst who remains attuned to the patient's responses—particularly disagreements—and actively engages with them is better positioned to adapt and respond to the patient's needs. Over-reliance on theoretical frameworks can create an impression of rigidity, potentially obstructing the therapeutic process.

An analyst benefits from incorporating not only professional analytic experiences (personal analysis, supervision, and theory) but also personal, spontaneous experiences, such as memories from childhood, associations with movies, music, or art, or even moments of humor or slips of the tongue. These seemingly peripheral experiences can offer invaluable insights and help foster a sense of immediacy and authenticity in the therapeutic relationship. Such moments can enrich transference interpretation, enabling the analyst to connect with the patient on a deeper level and to create a more dynamic and adaptive therapeutic experience.

Countertransference

Countertransference is a multifaceted concept encompassing the analyst's perceptions, emotions, thoughts, attitudes, and behaviors toward the patient within the analytic context. While all psychoanalytic schools of thought acknowledge countertransference, its definitions vary significantly, reflecting different theoretical perspectives. Broadly, countertransference can be categorized into two approaches: narrow and broad.

The narrow definition of countertransference, rooted in traditional psychoanalysis, views it as the analyst's conscious or unconscious pathological reactions to the patient's transference or personality. These reactions stem from the analyst's unresolved personal conflicts, which may impede the therapeutic process. In this sense, countertransference reflects pathological tendencies within the analyst and signals the need for self-analysis or supervision. Analysts adopting this approach aim to maintain therapeutic neutrality, acting as a "blank screen" for the patient's projections while presuming objectivity in understanding the patient's psyche. This perspective emphasizes eliminating countertransference as a disruptive factor to preserve the analytic process's integrity.

The broad definition of countertransference, prevalent in contemporary psychoanalysis, encompasses all of the analyst's responses to the patient. This includes emotional, cognitive, imaginative, and behavioral reactions, whether stemming from the analyst's unconscious processes or as natural responses to the patient's behavior or situation. The broad approach regards countertransference as an essential tool in the therapeutic process, positioning the analyst as an active participant-observer. It highlights the dynamic interplay between the patient's transference and the analyst's reactions, influenced by the patient's ability to elicit specific responses.

In the broad approach, countertransference serves as a "laboratory" where the analyst uses their responses to infer the patient's inner world, including their self-concept, personality, conflicts, and deficits. Through trial identification, the analyst temporarily and imaginatively steps into the patient's experience, vicariously gaining insights into their psyche. The analyst develops an initial understanding of the patient's transference by synthesizing observations from the patient's free associations, actions, and countertransference reactions. Though these understandings guide therapeutic interventions or interpretations, ongoing therapeutic dialogue treats them as provisional and refined.

While the broad approach offers significant advantages, it also recognizes potential challenges. The "laboratory" can become dysfunctional if the analyst becomes ensnared in pathological countertransference, such as acting out feelings of anger, attraction, idealization, devaluation, or control toward the patient or engaging in boundary violations that jeopardize the therapeutic process. Resolving such issues necessitates introspection, supervision, consultation, or, in some cases, transferring the patient to another analyst to ensure the treatment's integrity.

Patient feedback is a tool for the analyst's self-awareness. Introspection ensures the analyst remains attuned to the therapeutic relationship, prioritizing the patient's needs and focusing on their unique requirements. This collaborative and reflective process strengthens the therapeutic alliance, enabling deeper exploration of the patient's psyche and fostering a treatment approach tailored to their needs.

To manage transference-countertransference dynamics effectively, a therapist should monitor various issues, such as:

- Differences in Perception: Recognize that the patient's view of the therapist's countertransference may differ, requiring clarification and negotiation to maintain trust.
- Therapist's Contributions: Acknowledge how the therapist's countertransference can impact the patient's transference and address any related errors or misunderstandings.
- Psychological Parallels: Identify parallels between the therapist's and patient's responses to uncover unconscious patterns and refine treatment focus.
- Introspection on Predictions and prediction error: Reflect on how the therapist's predictions or assumptions about the patient align with actual behaviors, using surprises to adjust clinical perspectives.
- Admiration and Idealization: Ensure that the therapist does not unconsciously seek admiration from the patient or assign idealized roles, distorting therapeutic dynamics.
- Drowsiness or Boredom: Drowsiness or boredom may signal unresolved countertransference issues, necessitating exploration to understand this reaction and maintain engagement.

- Negative Reactions: Address any anger, disappointment, or devaluation, as these responses can indicate unresolved feelings that may interfere with proper analytic responsiveness.

Resistance

In psychoanalytic treatment, resistance refers to anything in the patient's words or actions that hinders their access to unconscious material. Freud extended this idea to include resistance towards psychoanalysis itself, especially when his discoveries exposed unconscious elements. Resistance reflects the patient's unconscious anxiety about relinquishing familiar psychological compromises and confronting painful self-awareness. It can persist even after becoming consciously recognized and is distinct from general defenses specific to the treatment setting.

Psychoanalytic perspectives recognize resistance as a dynamic tension between the analyst's efforts to help the patient understand their own mind and the patient's unconscious desire to maintain the status quo. Freud emphasized the relationship between transference, where the patient's feelings and attitudes towards the analyst are influenced by past experiences, and resistance, noting that while transference can act as a form of resistance, it is also the most powerful tool for facilitating change. This concept differentiates psychoanalysis from treatments based solely on suggestion or persuasion. Resistance can manifest in various forms, such as mental processes, fantasies, behaviors, or character defenses, all aimed at obstructing the deepening of the analytic process.

Freud characterized id resistance as a repetitive compulsion, a concept associated with the "stickiness" of libido. This phenomenon reflects the id's intrinsic resistance, often manifesting as an unconscious drive to revisit and replay unresolved past conflicts. Id resistances highlight the need for working through in psychoanalysis, as the unconscious tendency to relive these past issues can obstruct change. Even when interpretations offer insight into the origins of a conflict or problem, the individual may resist transformation, remaining trapped in the cycle of repetition. This underscores the importance of addressing these dynamics to facilitate genuine therapeutic progress.

Freud also described several types of *ego resistance*. Early in the analysis, the patient may resist becoming aware of transference wishes and fantasies. As analysis progresses, the ego may resist resolving these transference issues. Another form of ego resistance is *repression*, which involves actively excluding conflicting ideas from consciousness. Additionally, *secondary gain from illness* represents ego resistance, where patients unconsciously maintain their symptoms to avoid change or because of the perceived benefits of being ill.

Freud also discussed *superego resistance*, which is driven by unconscious guilt and manifests as the need for punishment. This can result in the patient refusing to let go of suffering or to benefit from the analysis. The most intense form of superego resistance is seen in the *negative therapeutic reaction*, where productive therapeutic work leads to a paradoxical worsening of the patient's condition.

Relational perspective: Resistance can be understood from a relational perspective, emphasizing intrapsychic or interpersonal dynamics. In Kleinian theory, resistance is viewed from an intrapsychic standpoint, focusing on disturbances in the internalized relationships between self and others. This often manifests through splitting, where the self or others are perceived as part objects, such as the "good breast" and "bad breast," along with projective identification used to manage aggression, anxiety, and conflict. These binary perceptions of people, emotions, or situations as entirely good or bad prevent the integration of opposing elements, thereby hindering personal growth and development.

On an interpersonal level, resistance may manifest as an avoidance of meaningful attachments to the analyst, diminishing the significance of their interactions and blocking transformative change. Conversely, a patient may form an overly intense, indiscriminate attachment to the analyst. Extreme or denial of reactions to separations—whether due to the rhythm of regular weekly analytic sessions, illnesses, or vacations—may also further stall progress.

Self Perspective: From a Self-psychological perspective, resistance-like processes can obstruct therapy by manifesting as disturbances in idealization, grandiosity, twinship, and empathy. A patient may excessively idealize or devalue the therapist, which hinders self-development and stalls therapeutic progress. Similarly, extreme feelings of superiority or inferiority, rooted in grandiosity or poor self-esteem, can impede analytic work. The patient may insist on an exaggerated sense of similarity with the therapist (twinship) or emphasize differences, both of which prevent the formation or understanding of transferences. Additionally, the patient might either uncritically accept the therapist's empathy, overlook apparent errors, or consistently feel misunderstood. These resistance patterns disrupt free association and block the therapeutic process, making it challenging to work through underlying issues.

Intersubjective perspective: From a constructivist intersubjective standpoint, resistance is viewed as a collaborative construct between the patient and the analyst. This perspective emphasizes the active role of both parties in understanding and resolving resistance. It underlines that the therapeutic process is a joint effort, with the patient and the analyst actively contributing to understanding and resolving resistance.

Developmental perspective: Resistance can be interpreted as a developmental phenomenon reflecting a shortfall in mentalization or the capacity to comprehend the mental and emotional states of oneself and others. It is a protective mechanism and indicates delayed development in navigating complex emotions and social signals. From this standpoint, an analyst is guided to recognize that a patient's progress and fixation on specific developmental milestones are shaped by inherent neurobiological factors, attachment, separation, Oedipal conflicts, latency, adolescent relationships, self-concept, and external stressors. The patient's progress in therapy is influenced by these elements, along with their transfer of feelings onto the analyst and their perception of the analyst as a novel figure in their life.

Neurosconscious perspective: From a neuropsychoanalytic perspective, resistance may be linked to an inadequate recognition of the role of prediction in mental processes. According to this view, effective learning comes from recognizing and correcting prediction errors, and resistance can be seen as a failure to integrate or learn from these errors. As resistance is resolved, patients may experience an improvement in the quality of their predictions, particularly in familiar scenarios, as demonstrated by a reduced tendency to be unduly surprised or destabilized by expected events. This reflects a more adaptive mental processing system.

Resistance can manifest in various ways in clinical settings, reflecting a patient's subconscious defense mechanisms against confronting distressing thoughts and emotions. For instance, one common form of resistance is the patient's avoidance of free association or prolonged silence during sessions, signaling an unwillingness to explore complex topics. Communication might become superficial or nonsensical, serving as a way to steer away from meaningful issues. Non-verbal cues, such as tense body language, can also indicate resistance. Behavioral patterns like acting out or disruptive actions can also manifest resistance.

Practical aspects of therapy, such as punctuality, attendance, and payment, may also be affected. Patients may arrive late, miss appointments, or be inconsistent with payments, subtly resisting engagement in the therapeutic process. Some patients may continually focus on discussing third-party issues, diverting attention from their experiences and emotional states. In child therapy, resistance may present as an inability or refusal to engage in therapeutic play, essential for emotional expression and processing in younger patients.

Recognizing these resistance patterns is not just important; it is crucial for clinicians. Understanding and addressing resistance is necessary for advancing therapeutic work or analysis and empowering clinicians with the knowledge and tools to foster emotional growth in their patients.

Defenses

Defense mechanisms safeguard an individual's bio-psycho-social integrity and stability from potential or actual threats. Defense mechanisms are primarily aimed at the management of the demands of internal impulses (instincts) or conflicts relating to associated thoughts, fantasies, or memories of these impulses, as well as intolerably intense affects, super-ego demands, relational impingements, discomfort to the self, surprise stemming from prediction, and unbearable reality. The appearance of signal affects, such as anxiety, guilt, and shame, which are indicative of impending threats to consciousness, activates these defense mechanisms.

The psychoanalytic theory of defenses extensively elaborates on many clinically observable unconscious processes. Unlike neuronal processes, defenses are clinically observable and amenable and offer the possibility of altering the dynamic unconscious.

There are many defenses: repression, regression, reaction-formation, isolation, undoing, projection, introjection, turning against the self, reversal into the opposite, and sublimation. Other defenses include denial in phantasy, idealization, identification with the aggressor, splitting of the object, projective identification, denial of psychic reality, omnipotent control over objects (people), etc. Defenses aid adaptation and keep a person optimally functioning. Inhibitions, symptoms, and anxieties characterize maladaptation and suggest failed defenses. Uninhibited actions and denial of symptoms or anxiety may also mean maladaptive defenses. An internal failed defense or external stress beyond an individual's control produces frustration and calls for additional attention to determine the best possible action to correct the situation.

Surface to depth: Ego psychology prioritizes the examination of conscious defenses and resistances before delving into the deeper unconscious desires, fears, and anxieties. It underscores the necessity of identifying and naming a person's defense mechanisms as a preliminary step. The process begins by acknowledging resistance and identifying the strategies employed for self-protection. Subsequently, the rationale behind these defenses is explored, including related fantasies, wishes, anxieties, and the unconscious desires and impulses they shield. The probe into the unconscious drives and wishes is deferred until the individual's defenses are recognized and their ego strength is adequately established.

Instinctual perspective: Aggression: Aggression can be expressed in both maladaptive and adaptive ways. Maladaptive aggression can manifest in various harmful behaviors, including sadism, where harm is deliberately inflicted upon others, affecting both humans and animals. In some instances, individuals may exhibit sadism as a way to exert control in situations where they otherwise feel passive, identifying with the role of the aggressor and showing a complete absence of empathy for the suffering of the victim. Conversely, masochism involves identification with the victim, where individuals derive gratification from their own pain or humiliation. Conversely, in a healthier psychological state, aggression can manifest as appropriate assertiveness, which involves balancing one's needs and rights while maintaining respect for others. This healthier form of aggression also includes the capacity to understand and empathize with the victim's point of view, allowing for more adaptive and flexible interpersonal interactions.

Sex: Excessive and inappropriate sexualization or inhibition mark unhealthy extremes. In contrast, appropriate sexual wishes, thoughts, fantasies, emotions, and behaviors appropriate to the context and mindfulness of the other's wishes represent normal reciprocal sexuality.

Ego perspective: The ego utilizes defense mechanisms, which are often unconscious, to protect against instinctual drives and different types of anxieties, emotional conditions, difficult circumstances, or expectations from the super-ego. The range of defenses encompasses repression, regression, reaction-formation, isolation, undoing, projection, introjection, turning against oneself, reversal into the opposite, sublimation, denial in phantasy, idealization, and identification with the aggressor.

Relational perspective: Object relations theory subscribes to primitive defenses, including the splitting of the object, projective identification, denial of psychic reality, and omnipotent control over objects.

Self-perspective: The Self-psychological perspective on defense and resistance recognizes that the self must guard not against dangerous desires but against the recurrence of deep psychological harm. This is especially true for childhood traumas that can severely impact self-esteem. A patient's fear that an analyst will not or cannot create a safe environment for a selfobject relationship, or their actual experience of the analyst's lack of empathy for their vulnerabilities, can lead to defensive behaviors, or 'resistance,' in therapy. The analyst's precise grasp of the patient's defensive needs against the activation of selfobject transference, and the joint examination of both the analyst's and patient's roles in any disruptions, are crucial elements of effective therapeutic engagement.

Neurosconscious perspective: The human brain is a complex structure, with the neocortex being a distinctive feature that has undergone significant development. This part of the brain is responsible for higher-order functions such as sensory perception, cognition, and generation of motor commands. The rest of the brain, the subcortical region, contains structures found in other species, indicating a shared evolutionary heritage. Within this subcortical area lies the limbic system, which, although predominantly subcortical, includes some cortical elements. The limbic system is integral to our survival. It acts as a primal guardian by managing the body's response to threats by connecting with the nervous and other bodily systems. It triggers the fight, flight, or freeze reactions by taking control of the autonomic nervous system during times of stress or danger. However, the limbic system does not work alone; the cortex influences it via the central autonomic network, likely affected by signal anxiety. The amygdala, a limbic system component, is crucial in detecting threats. Working in harmony with the hypothalamus, which initiates hormone release, the pituitary gland, which coordinates the hormonal response, and the adrenal glands, which secrete cortisol and adrenaline, the body is primed to react to danger automatically. Defenses consider the interplay between prediction mismatch errors, vigilance, and instinct to expose a person's current challenges.

Psychotic Defenses

These defenses indicate severe dysfunction and impaired reality testing. They manifest through mechanisms like hallucinations, delusions, excessive projection, introjection, and denial.

Borderline Defenses

Common in individuals with borderline traits, these include splitting (viewing things as all good or all bad), primitive idealization and devaluation (alternating between idolizing and devaluing others), acting out or acting in, projective identification, impulsivity, and self-sabotage. These behaviors often disrupt relationships and personal goals.

Anxiety

In psychoanalysis, anxiety is understood as a complex emotional state that arises from internal conflicts, often involving unconscious fears, desires, or instincts. Anxiety can manifest in various forms, reflecting different underlying psychological processes and developmental stages. Here are the main types of anxiety according to psychoanalytic theory:

1. **Signal Anxiety**: This is a normal and adaptive form of anxiety that serves as a warning signal. It alerts the individual to potential danger and helps to prevent overwhelming feelings or traumatic experiences. Signal anxiety arises when unconscious desires or conflicts threaten to enter conscious awareness.

2. **Symptomatic Anxiety**: Anxiety can manifest through specific symptoms, such as panic attacks, general unease, or somatic complaints, where the source of anxiety may be hidden or repressed. This type of anxiety is often a response to unresolved internal conflicts that are expressed indirectly through physical or psychological symptoms.

3. **Phobic Anxiety**: In this form of anxiety, fear becomes attached to a specific object, situation, or symbol. Phobias serve as a defense mechanism, allowing the individual to avoid deeper underlying conflicts by focusing their anxiety on external objects or scenarios.

4. **Denial and Counterphobia**: At the extreme end, denial is a defense mechanism where anxiety is avoided by denying the existence of a threatening situation or feeling. Counterphobia, on the other hand, is the tendency to confront or seek out situations that cause anxiety in an attempt to master or overcome the fear, often without resolving the underlying conflict.

5. **Trauma-related Anxiety**: Trauma can lead to maladaptive responses, such as avoidance, hypervigilance, intrusive thoughts, and hyperarousal. These reactions occur when an individual is unable to cope with traumatic experiences, leading to an inability to integrate the trauma into conscious awareness effectively. This can result in PTSD-like symptoms or a "moribund" response, where the individual becomes emotionally detached or numb.

6. **Eight-Month Anxiety**: Also called **stranger anxiety**, this form of anxiety typically appears around the eighth month of a baby's life. It reflects the child's growing awareness of separateness from their primary caregiver, causing distress when encountering unfamiliar people or situations.

7. **Attachment Anxiety**: This type of anxiety arises from insecure attachment patterns and is characterized by excessive worry about the availability or stability of attachment figures (e.g., caregivers or partners). Anxious attachment styles can lead to clinginess, fear of abandonment, or hypersensitivity to separation.

8. **Separation Anxiety**: A natural developmental phase, separation anxiety involves intense fear or distress related to being separated from a loved one or attachment figure. If unresolved, separation anxiety can persist into adulthood, manifesting as fears of being alone or abandoned.

9. **Castration Anxiety**: This concept originates from Freud's psychosexual theory and refers to the unconscious fear of losing one's sexual power or identity. In males, castration anxiety stems from the fear of losing the penis, whereas in females, it is associated with feelings of inadequacy or envy. Castration anxiety plays a central role in the Oedipus complex and influences psychosexual development.

Each of these types of anxiety reflects different developmental stages, defense mechanisms, or responses to internal or external conflicts. Psychoanalysis seeks to understand and address the unconscious sources of anxiety to resolve these conflicts and restore emotional balance.

Narcissistic Defenses

Characterized by an excessive focus on personal perfection or self-esteem, narcissistic tendencies may include idealization-devaluation, grandiosity, or preoccupation with twinship and the absence of mirroring. Healthy narcissism involves balanced self-esteem and realistic goals.

Neurotic Defenses

These maladaptive strategies, like disorganized regression, repression, displacement, or somatization, can lead to anxiety, inhibitions, and unresolved symptoms.

Healthy Defenses

Constructive mechanisms like creativity, humor, sublimation, altruism, suppression, and adaptive regression allow individuals to manage stress and restore emotional balance. Normal repression, which helps manage distressing thoughts without distorting reality, supports emotional stability and healthy interpersonal functioning.

Clarification

Clarification in therapy involves the therapist providing clear and concise explanations to expand on or elucidate information shared by the client or therapist. It goes beyond simply restating or reflecting feelings and aims to deepen understanding by offering additional context or reorganizing the material.

There are different types of clarifications: (a) Inviting the patient to clarify – the therapist encourages the client to elaborate or offer further context; (b) Tentatively clarifying the patient's communication – the therapist offers their own interpretation or rephrases what the client has said; and (c) Clarifying the therapist's own communication – the therapist ensures their statements are clear and easily understood by the client.

Clarification uncovers associated, background, or hidden meanings, preconscious thoughts, and emotions. It promotes insight and self-awareness, enabling clients to explore their inner world more fully.

In therapy, clarification is vital for dissecting and labeling the components of a patient's symptoms. It also helps in understanding their historical and therapeutic context. It allows for a deeper examination of the elements that influence symptoms, including the emotional exchanges between patient and therapist. This process involves exploring various emotions, drives, desires, intentions, and subconscious imaginings, such as dreams and fears. Clarification also delves into the everyday details of the patient's life and their significance. This collaborative exploration helps both therapist and patient identify observational perspectives and the structure of the therapeutic alliance, including roles, boundaries, and transference issues.

Clarification helps identify triggering events, recognize stress and relational discord sources, and understand the patient's position in specific situations. It examines the patient's defenses or projections, traces the history of symptoms or transference, and precisely identifies key emotions within the therapeutic relationship, such as frustration, anger, or distress. Clarification also addresses the patient's responses to bodily harm, illness, and medical evaluations. It helps them navigate loss, mourning, and the consequences of life choices. It encourages personal growth both within and beyond the therapeutic setting.

The process involves analyzing life and therapy triggers, sequences of events, and various viewpoints. It extends to managing anticipatory, in-session, and post-session anxieties or reactions. Clarification is foundational to therapy because it helps structure the often chaotic and undefined aspects of a patient's inner world. Naming and categorizing are human constructs facilitating order, communication, and exploration.

Clarification encompasses concepts of identity, time, place, and value, exploring the dynamics of closeness and distance, the flow of past, present, and future events, action patterns, continuity and disruption, movement and stillness, internal and external viewpoints, and the weight of specific moments. Our lives are shaped by the nuances of singular versus plural experiences, solitude versus connection, and intricately entwined meanings. An analyst must also clarify to the patient that they are free to disagree with the analyst and pursue their thinking and actions. However, the analyst also must explain that when safety is involved, and the patient is acting dangerously, the analyst may act unilaterally, set limits on the patient, and, if necessary, include parents or third parties.

Interpretation

Interpretations are not just the analyst's work but a collaborative effort between the analyst and the patient in analysis or therapy. They aim to connect different therapeutic elements, bringing a more precise understanding that is believed to aid insight, change, and healing. This collaborative nature of interpretations underscores the integral role of therapists in the therapeutic process, making them feel included and valued. Interpretations can transform the therapeutic process, offering new perspectives and understandings. While interpretations often come after clarifications, they can sometimes happen simultaneously. Interpretations can vary; patients and their therapists might see an event similarly or differently. Exploring these discrepancies can be part of the interpretative work. If interpretations address the emotional dynamics or content related to the therapist-patient relationship, they are known as transference interpretations. Conversely, when a patient makes sense of a therapeutic action or occurrence, it's called a patient interpretation.

Interpretations serve to address the 'why' behind treatment processes. They provide credible explanations for the origins and persistence of symptoms and therapy progression. Specifically, transference interpretations offer insights by connecting the patient's experiences with the therapist's influence, creating a shared understanding. Conversely, extra-transference interpretations do not involve the therapist directly. Interpretation involves crafting a precise, well-timed, and sensitively delivered understanding of previously ambiguous aspects of therapy. By linking symptoms, behaviors, and the dynamics of the patient-therapist relationship, interpretations strive to bring unconscious thoughts to the forefront of conscious awareness, integrating unexplored personality traits into the collaborative exploration of the therapeutic journey.

Interpretations play a crucial role in fostering insight in therapy. They can lead to beneficial changes, enhancing insight, improving relationships, and promoting a deeper understanding of oneself and one's autonomy. They also help clarify the significance of perceived psychological threats and assist in differentiating between what is perceived and what is real. Furthermore, interpretations can shed light on the challenges of acknowledging the dynamic elements of participant observation for both the patient and therapist, affirming the legitimacy of each party's perspective and the complexities involved in attributing meanings. Interpretations must be followed by assessing their impact to ensure they are effective and that interpretative errors are addressed.

1. Purpose of Interpretations: Interpretations aim to connect and explain aspects of therapy, providing clarity and potential healing. They often follow clarifications but can also co-occur.

2. Agreement and Disagreement: It is possible, and often likely, for a patient and analyst to have differing understandings of interpretations, making it essential to revisit these interpretations as part of the ongoing analysis. This stress revisiting interpretations can reassure therapists about the continuing analysis and the effectiveness of their work. The analyst's responsibility is to address any critiques or misunderstandings regarding their interpretations and adjust or readjust them collaboratively with the patient. Reexamining these interpretations helps clarify discrepancies and recognizes that a patient may superficially agree with the therapist's expectations. This interpretative process fosters a deeper and more accurate understanding, ensuring the therapeutic work remains meaningful and effective for the patient.

3. Types of Interpretations: Analytic work may involve many interpretations.

- **Transference Interpretations:** These interpretations focus on how the patient's feelings and reactions towards the therapist and the therapeutic situation influence their symptoms and treatment. Transference is a critical concept in therapy. It refers to the patient's unconscious redirection of feelings from one person to another, often to the therapist. For example, a patient may develop feelings for the therapist that reflect their feelings towards a significant person in their past. Understanding and interpreting transference can provide valuable insights into the patient's emotional dynamics and the therapeutic relationship.

- **Extra Transference Interpretations:** Link symptoms or events to experiences outside the therapist-patient relationship.
- **Genetic Interpretations:** Connect symptoms or events to past experiences with significant figures (e.g., parents, partners).
- **Interpretations of Unconscious Motivation:** The motivations behind our current symptoms, thoughts, emotions, dreams, transferences, and behaviors can be deeply rooted in various psychological frameworks. These include the unconscious drive, which operates beyond our awareness, influencing our actions and reactions. Relational aspects consider the impact of interpersonal relationships on our psyche. The concept of the Self encompasses our identity and sense of personal agency. Intersubjective elements involve the shared understanding and mutual influence between people. Lastly, neurosconscious-based motivations refer to the biological and brain processes that underpin our mental and emotional states.
- **Patient Interpretations:** When the patient independently makes sense of therapeutic processes or events.

4. Function of Interpretations:

- **Explaining Symptoms:** Offer reasons for the presence or continuation of symptoms.
- **Facilitate Insight:** Help patients understand their unconscious processes and dynamics.
- **Address Resistance:** Provide explanations for resistance to change or transference.

- **Impart insights concerning associated meaning:** The goal of interpretation is to convey insights into meanings connected to our perceptions, thoughts, dreams, feelings, and actions. These insights explore the relationship between our innate instincts, personal conflicts, compromises, and relationships. They also consider the combined efforts of the patient and the analyst to contribute to a deeper understanding and anticipation of behaviors and foster a learning environment. This collaborative process is essential in unraveling the complexities of the Self and enhancing the therapeutic journey.

5. Characteristics of Effective Interpretations:

- **Timing, Dosage, and Order:** Must be well-timed, proportionate, and logically presented.
- **Tactfulness:** This should be delivered sensitively to avoid criticism and ensure the patient is ready for the explanation.
- **Evaluation:** Must be assessed for its effectiveness and impact on the patient.
- **Negotiation:** An interpretation by the analyst sets off a significant quest for understanding and acknowledges the analyst's expertise, valuable insights, and fallibility. However, these insights must also resonate with the patient. Therefore, it is essential to blend the perspectives of both the analyst and the patient through the interpretive process. This integration is achieved by negotiating the ultimate significance of interpretation. The result of this process is the elucidation of mutual meanings, encompassing areas of consensus, points of contention, and topics that necessitate additional examination.

6. Interpretation of Transference Events: This includes responses to events like separations, vacations, or terminations and how these influence the therapeutic process.

7. Clarification of Interpretations: After an interpretation, it is crucial to clarify how the patient understands interpretations, including the degree of agreement or disagreement. This clarification process is not just a formality but a responsibility that therapists must take seriously to ensure their patients' and the analyst's understanding is clear and accurate.

8. Role of Therapist and Patient: The therapist and the patient play a crucial role in providing interpretations. Self-interpretation by the patient, which involves understanding meanings without direct input from the therapist, is an essential aspect of the therapeutic process.

9. Day Residue: Interpreting how daily experiences relate to transference issues.

Overall, interpretations in therapy seek to make unconscious elements conscious, facilitate therapeutic change, and enhance understanding of the patient's symptoms and dynamics.

Developmental stages

Psychological development refers to the continuous growth and transformation in cognitive, emotional, intellectual, and social domains from infancy through late adulthood. This process unfolds through various stages, each with specific achievements and challenges. Understanding psychological development is essential for identifying normal growth patterns and recognizing areas where professional guidance may be beneficial.

Psychoanalytic theories outline key developmental stages reflecting changes in a child's self-awareness, relationships, and cognitive functions. Freud's psychosexual stages emphasize bodily pleasure and psychological growth, progressing from the oral stage (0-1 year), where gratification is centered around oral activities, to the anal stage (1-3 years), which focuses on control through toilet training. The phallic stage (3-6 years) involves some preliminary genital gender awareness within the framework of the Oedipus complex, followed by latency (6-puberty), where social development takes precedence, and finally, the behavioral genital stage (puberty onward), marking sexual maturation and capacity for physical and emotional intimate relationships.

Erikson's psychosocial stages include Infancy (0-1 year): Trust vs. Mistrust; Early Childhood (1-3 years): Autonomy vs. Shame and Doubt; Preschool (3-6 years): Initiative vs. Guilt; School Age (6-12 years): Industry vs. Inferiority; Adolescence (12-18 years): Identity vs. Role Confusion; Young Adulthood (18-40 years): Intimacy vs. Isolation; Middle Adulthood (40-65 years): Generativity vs. Stagnation; and Maturity (65+ years): Ego Integrity vs. Despair

Mahler's separation-individuation process explores attachment and identity development, starting with normal autism (0-2 months) and symbiosis (2-5 months), where infants feel fused with caregivers. Differentiation (5-10 months) initiates self-awareness, while rapprochement (16-24 months) reflects a balance between autonomy and dependence, and object constancy (2-3 years) solidifies secure attachment.

Klein's developmental positions focus on early defense mechanisms, starting with the paranoid-schizoid position, where infants split experiences into "good" and "bad" objects. As development progresses, the depressive position (4-6 months onward) helps children integrate these views, fostering relational capacities, resilience, and personality maturation.

Early neurological development begins with subcortical brain regions, which govern essential survival functions and instincts, before integrating more complex cortical areas that support higher-order thinking and behavior regulation. In infancy, automatic behaviors critical for life—such as breathing, feeding, and reflex responses—are controlled by subcortical structures like the brainstem and parts of the limbic system.

As the child grows, cortical regions, particularly the prefrontal cortex, play a more central role, enabling higher-order functions like planning, reasoning, and self-regulation. With its intricate network of neurons, the prefrontal cortex is the seat of these complex cognitive processes. Myelination is a critical process where myelin, a protective fatty layer, coats nerve fibers, speeding up neural communication across brain regions. This begins after birth, as infants' nervous systems start largely unmyelinated, explaining their reliance on reflexive actions. Rapid myelination after birth continues through childhood and adolescence and extends into adulthood, supporting increasingly advanced cognitive and behavioral abilities by enhancing the efficiency and coordination of neural processes as the brain matures.

The brain's development from subcortical to cortical functioning represents a progression from automatic, reflexive responses to increasingly complex behaviors that can operate unconsciously, preconsciously, or consciously where neurological inhibition or facilitation is accomplished. This sequential maturation enables the brain to move from instinctual actions to sophisticated, flexible behaviors that integrate various brain areas. Enhancing neural connections, the myelination process facilitates this shift by supporting faster, more coordinated interactions between subcortical structures (like the brainstem, mid and hindbrain, and limbic system) and cortical regions, enabling whole-brain advanced cognitive, emotional, and behavioral regulation.

Repair and containment of deficits

Deficits

Deficits refer to inadequacies or gaps in psychological functioning that may arise from biological vulnerabilities, misattuned caregiving, or caregivers' inability to facilitate the development of a child's cohesive self.

Biological vulnerabilities can include a range of conditions, such as neurodevelopmental disorders, schizophrenia spectrum disorders, psychotic disorders, bipolar disorders, depressive disorders, anxiety disorders, trauma- and stressor-related disorders, disruptive disorders, impulse-control and conduct disorders, and neurocognitive disorders.

Misattuned caregiving occurs when the child and caregiver are not a good fit. This can lead to difficulties in emotional regulation and managing safety-danger, attachment, bonding, and the separation-individuation processes. In severe cases, such misalignment can result in child abuse or neglect. In these situations, children may employ defenses such as splitting and projective identification to cope with their distress. Here, the difficulty and accompanying conflicts may be termed interpersonal.

When caregivers fail to provide necessary empathy, appropriate mirroring, or idealizing and alter ego experiences, the child may struggle to maintain a coherent sense of self. This can hinder the development of stable self-esteem, self-soothing abilities, and the capacity for empathy, humor, wisdom, transience, and creativity. Consequently, the child may become susceptible to a fragmented sense of self and an obsession with perfection.

In psychoanalysis, deficit models—such as those found in object relations theory and Self-psychology—aim to address and repair these developmental gaps. Therapy focuses on relational or self-repair, with the therapist providing the emotional support that was lacking during early development. These deficits often manifest in treatment through transferences (where a patient redirects feelings for a significant person onto the therapist) and resistances (the unconscious defense mechanisms that obstruct the therapeutic process), allowing unconscious or preconscious material to surface. The therapeutic process works toward identifying, repairing, and rebuilding relational weaknesses and core psychological structures of the self.

In contrast to deficits, conflicts refer to internal struggles among various intrapsychic agencies, particularly between the id, ego, and superego and constructs of the self and others. These internal tensions are often unconscious and arise from conflicting tendencies, all within a person. For example, conflict may arise between an Id impulse and a superego prohibition. Some conflicts are intra-ego conflicts and may be called choice conflicts. Neurotic symptoms, inhibitions, and anxieties arise from such unresolved conflicts.

Psychoanalysis conflict models focus on resolving them by enhancing the patient's self-awareness, providing insight into unconscious motivations, and facilitating compromise formation through conscious and rational decision-making. The therapist plays a central role primarily through transference interpretations and helping the patient resolve these internal conflicts through insight, ultimately leading to greater psychic integration and symptom relief.

Change

The goal of analysis extends beyond merely alleviating symptoms or addressing immediate concerns. It seeks to facilitate deep-seated changes in the fundamental elements of one's character. This process involves gaining insight into the subconscious elements that influence one's thoughts, feelings, fantasies, and behaviors, shaping self-awareness, relational interactions, personal objectives, teamwork, and managing expectations and risks. Ultimately, it represents a path to significant self-discovery and growth. This transformative process involves continuous learning from past mistakes, enhancing the ability to anticipate future outcomes, and fostering a nuanced understanding of one's and others' roles in shaping and observing human interactions. It equips patients to move towards their goals, gaining insight and control over the underlying causes of their distress. Successful therapy enables individuals to take proactive steps in preventing or mitigating future psychological difficulties while maximizing their strengths and opportunities. Change in this context is complex and varies depending on the observer's perspective.

1. **Increased Insight**: Over the course of sessions, the patient gained a deeper understanding of themselves and their underlying issues. Insights emerged like puzzle pieces, forming a clearer picture of their inner world.

2. **Improved Relationships**: The patient's relationships transformed as therapy unfolded. They learned to navigate interpersonal dynamics more skillfully, fostering deeper connections with others.

3. **Increased Empathy**: The patient's empathy expanded. They not only understood their own emotions but also recognized the

therapist's empathic limits. It was like seeing the world through a wider lens.

4. **Feeling Understood**: The patient cherished moments when the therapist provided empathic explanations. Feeling understood validated their experiences and encouraged further exploration.

5. **Affect Containment**: Managing emotions became a strength. The patient learned to express feelings without retaliating toward peers or significant others.

6. **Negotiated Change**: Rather than imposing changes, we collaboratively negotiated them. The patient actively participated in their healing process, making choices aligned with their values.

7. **Reduced Splitting**: The tendency to view situations as purely good or bad decreased. Through clarification and addressing resistance, the patient found a middle ground.

8. **Meaningful Treatment Experience**: Therapy felt meaningful—a compass guiding them toward a more coherent and purposeful life.

9. **New Cognitions**: Insights sparked new ways of thinking. The patient considered options and choices with fresh perspectives.

10. **Reordered Memories**: Memories rearranged themselves, providing richer meaning. Past experiences wove into the present tapestry.

11. **Enhanced Self-Structuring**: The patient's self-concept, relational patterns, and cognitive structures improved. It was like renovating their mental architecture.

12. **Dynamic Connections**: They articulated and understood the intricate web of dynamic connections—within themselves and with others. Communication flowed more freely.

13. **Authentic Descriptions**: The patient crafted genuine, coherent narratives—about personal history, development, symptoms, goals, and the therapeutic journey.
14. **Reciprocal Model of Mind**: Their understanding of themselves and others evolved. Reciprocity replaced rigid views.
15. **Informed Decision-Making**: Armed with insights, the patient made decisions consciously, respecting others' independence.
16. **Reduced Developmental Lags**: Addressing delays in personal growth allowed the patient to catch up. They felt accomplished and successful in their therapeutic journey.

Meaning

In psychoanalysis, "meaning" bridges the analyst's theoretical constructs and the patient's subjective experience. Concepts such as the unconscious, id, ego, superego, Oedipus complex, self, and relational dynamics offer a structural basis for understanding the patient's inner conflicts, psychological states, and behaviors. However, these theories gain therapeutic value only when they resonate with the patient's unique reality. Insights become particularly potent when they reflect the patient's lived experiences, often finding greater meaning through the collaborative therapeutic relationship.

This emphasis on meaning as a co-created aspect of the analytic process highlights that, while an analyst may apply theoretical perspectives to interpret events, the actual therapeutic value emerges when these interpretations are grounded in the patient's personal experience. In this collaborative process, meaning evolves as a relational product, allowing patients to reinterpret the analyst's insights through the lens of their own life history. This dynamic interaction fosters an environment conducive to self-awareness and psychological growth, as patients weave analytic insights into their self-understanding, fostering integration and change.

Furthermore, meanings in psychoanalysis are often layered, containing conscious and unconscious dimensions shaped by instinctual drives, relational needs, and self-perceptions. The significance of these meanings intensifies when tied to specific details of the patient's life, the analytic relationship embedded with emotional relevance. Each patient brings a unique perspective, sometimes aligning with and sometimes diverging from the analyst's interpretations. By exploring these differences, the analyst can gain insight into evolving relational dynamics within the transference, thereby clarifying both perspectives' conscious, preconscious, and unconscious elements. This process establishes boundaries in the therapeutic relationship, deepening the shared understanding of the patient's inner world.

The meaning of any event in the analysis is layered, incorporating verbal exchanges and the analyst's tone, demeanor, and relational stance. These subtleties affect how the patient perceives and interprets the analyst's responses, creating a more nuanced understanding of their own psyche. By constructing meaning in this interactive space, patients access self-awareness, transforming how they see their past, their relationships, and themselves. This approach fosters emotional resilience and integration, empowering patients to heal from past conflicts and achieve inner growth. Ultimately, meaning serves as a pathway for deeper psychological development, enriching both the analytic process and the patient's journey toward self-cohesion and relational harmony.

Termination

Evaluating Treatment Success: Key Indicators of Patient Improvement: In psychoanalytic therapy, treatment success is measured by objective improvements in the patient's functioning and subjective experiences of progress and satisfaction. Key factors that reflect successful outcomes include:

1. Improvement in Functioning: The patient shows clear advancements in daily life, such as enhanced productivity at work, better relationship management, and improved self-care routines.
2. Progress Towards Goals: The patient steadily moves closer to personal and therapeutic goals, such as emotional well-being, career development, or personal growth.
3. Therapeutic Satisfaction: The patient expresses satisfaction with the therapeutic process, valuing the safe and supportive space provided to explore and address their emotions and challenges.
4. Enhanced Capacity for Love, Work, and Creativity: The patient becomes more open and capable of engaging deeply in love relationships, creativity, and work, experiencing joy and fulfillment.
5. Better Regulation of Affect: Emotional regulation improves significantly, allowing the patient to experience emotions without being overwhelmed or shutting down.
6. Increased Signal Anxiety and better management of danger: The patient becomes more aware of anxiety as a helpful signal rather than a crippling experience, using it to gain insight into inner conflicts. Through planning and better precautions, there is better management of dangers.

7. Working Through Trauma: The patient bravely confronts and processes traumatic memories, engaging in mourning and coming to terms with loss.

8. Avoidance of Unnecessary Risks: Impulsivity decreases, and decision-making becomes more thoughtful, leading to healthier life choices.

9. Depth of Relationships: Relationships deepen as the patient becomes more attuned to their own needs and the needs of others, fostering meaningful connections.

10. Empathic Responsiveness: The patient's empathy grows, improving their capacity to listen and respond to others with genuine understanding and care.

11. Symbolic Play and Behavior: The patient is more capable of symbolic expression through art, play, or dreams, which becomes an essential tool for regulating the patient's inner world and emotional state.

12. Affect Containment: The patient learns to contain and manage intense emotions, preventing emotional overwhelm or acting out.

13. Reciprocity and Expressiveness: Communication improves, with the patient becoming more open, expressive, and able to engage in reciprocal interactions with others.

14. Empathic Perspective: Through a reciprocal and feedback-oriented model of the mind of the other, the patient better understands others' experiences, leading to improved relationships and social interactions.

15. Correction of Developmental Lags: The patient works through developmental delays or gaps, leading to optimal personal growth.

16. Meaningful Experience: The patient finds meaning in therapy and life, recognizing patterns and the significance of their experiences, transference, and narrative.

17. Acceptance of Ambiguity: Life's uncertainties no longer cause the patient distress. They develop an ability to tolerate ambiguity, loss, and the unknown.

18. Sense of Agency: The patient's sense of autonomy and personal agency strengthens, enabling them to make decisions and take actions aligned with their values and goals.

19. Attention and Joint Attention: The patient's focus improves, especially in joint attention, leading to better joint work and communication.

20. Recognition and Acceptance of Others' Perspectives: The patient becomes more open to differing viewpoints and recognizes that diversity enriches relationships.

21. Clarification of Differences: The patient embraces differences and approaches disagreements with curiosity rather than defensiveness, fostering more authentic communication.

22. Informed Decision-Making: Decision-making improves, with the patient weighing both short- and long-term consequences more carefully, leading to more balanced choices.

23. Each of these factors contributes to a comprehensive understanding of the patient's progress in therapy, highlighting both external improvements and internal growth. This framework allows the therapist and the patient to track tangible changes and deepen self-awareness and emotional resilience.

Summary

This appendix outlines psychoanalytic concepts and their practical applications in clinical settings, focusing on critical constructs of contemporary psychoanalysis. It emphasizes a holistic view of mental health, recognizing that psychological, social, and physical factors contribute to illnesses. The document highlights that health goes beyond the absence of disease, emphasizing overall well-being. Symptoms reflect underlying psychological, relational, and biological factors involving both conscious and unconscious elements. Therapy involves individual and interpersonal dynamics, focusing on mutually shaped interactions between the patient and therapist. Ant treatment is premised on professional and ethical conduct by the analyst.

Key aspects include understanding transference, the patient's active role in therapy, and addressing both symptoms and deeper personality structures to promote growth. The treatment framework and its external factors, such as institutional and supervisory contexts, also impact therapy. The document stresses the educational aspect of therapy and the importance of collaboration with other professionals when necessary.

Therapeutic change is facilitated through insight, empathy, and creating a safe environment. The book fosters resilience, addresses trauma, and clarifies patient choices. It also discusses the significance of active listening and working through processes to promote understanding and personal development. Other important concepts include the therapist's responsibility for patient safety, the acknowledgment of the patient's strengths, and the therapist's influence on the therapeutic process.

Additionally, this appendix attempted to outline key psychoanalytic concepts, including unconscious processes, transference, resistance, defense mechanisms, and the role of clarification and interpretation in therapy. It also addresses the importance of empathy, the containment of deficits, and how these elements contribute to therapeutic change. By enhancing self-awareness, improving relational dynamics, and fostering personal growth, these ideas—rooted in various schools of psychoanalytic thought—support a comprehensive framework for understanding and facilitating psychological healing.

About the Author

BHASKAR SRIPADA, M.D., is a Board-Certified Adult and Child and adolescent Analyst who has practiced psychoanalysis in Chicago since 1980. A faculty member at the Chicago Institute for Psychoanalysis since 1995, Dr. Sripada teaches, supervises, and has published widely in the field.

He is the developer of Essential Psychoanalysis, a contemporary model that reaffirms Freud's core principles—unconscious processes, transference, and resistance—interpreting them through the lens of modern psychoanalytic insights and discoveries. Essential Psychoanalysis draws flexibly from various traditions, including instinct theory, ego psychology, object relations, self psychology, intersubjectivity, and new developments in neuropsychoanalysis. Offering a pluralistic and integrative framework, it values the perspectives of both patient and analyst. While Essential Psychoanalysis recognizes the importance of theoretical coherence for the analyst, it maintains that the true measure of analytic work lies in the impact the analyst has on the patient, helping the patient understand their suffering, facilitating change where possible, and fostering richer, more meaningful experiences of love and work.

In his book, *When Suicide Beckons*, Dr. Sripada brings his model to life by providing an account of the analytic process. He presents a unique first-person narrative that alternates between the voices of patient and analyst, revealing his own evolving responses and memories. His forthcoming book, *Psychoanalytic Supervision*, extends this approach to the supervisory process. In both works, he emphasizes experience-near, first-person communication over abstract theorizing, focusing on lived experience and the personal connection between analyst and patient.